# Frommer's®

## PORTABLE
# Charleston

### 3rd Edition

## by Darwin Porter & Danforth Prince

**Here's what critics say about Frommer's:**

"Amazingly easy to use. Very portable, very complete."

—*Booklist*

"Detailed, accurate, and easy-to-read information for all price ranges."

—*Glamour Magazine*

Wiley Publishing, Inc.

Published by:

**WILEY PUBLISHING, INC.**

111 River St.
Hoboken, NJ 07030-5774

ISBN: 978-0-470-10053-0

Editor: Billy Fox
Production Editor: Katie Robinson
Cartographer: Anton Crane
Photo Editor: Richard Fox
Anniversary Logo Design: Richard Pacifico
Production by Wiley Indianapolis Composition Services

For information on our other products and services or to obtain technical
support, please contact our Customer Care Department within the U.S. at
800/762-2974, outside the U.S. at 317/572-3993 or fax 317/572-4002.

Wiley also publishes its books in a variety of electronic formats. Some con-
tent that appears in print may not be available in electronic formats.

Manufactured in the United States of America

5   4   3   2   1

# Contents

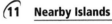

# List of Maps

## ABOUT THE AUTHORS

As a team of veteran travel writers, **Darwin Porter** and **Danforth Prince** have produced numerous titles for Frommer's, including best-selling guides to Italy, France, the Caribbean, England, and Germany. Porter, a former bureau chief of *The Miami Herald,* is also a Hollywood biographer. His most recent releases are *Brando Unzipped* and *Jacko: His Rise and Fall.* Prince was formerly employed by the Paris bureau of the *New York Times* and today is the president of Blood Moon Productions and other media-related firms.

## AN INVITATION TO THE READER

In researching this book, we discovered many wonderful places—hotels, restaurants, shops, and more. We're sure you'll find others. Please tell us about them, so we can share the information with your fellow travelers in upcoming editions. If you were disappointed with a recommendation, we'd love to know that, too. Please write to:

*Frommer's Portable Charleston,* 3rd Edition
Wiley Publishing, Inc. • 111 River St. • Hoboken, NJ 07030-5774

## AN ADDITIONAL NOTE

Please be advised that travel information is subject to change at any time—and this is especially true of prices. We therefore suggest that you write or call ahead for confirmation when making your travel plans. The authors, editors, and publisher cannot be held responsible for the experiences of readers while traveling. Your safety is important to us, however, so we encourage you to stay alert and be aware of your surroundings. Keep a close eye on cameras, purses, and wallets, all favorite targets of thieves and pickpockets.

## FROMMER'S STAR RATINGS, ICONS & ABBREVIATIONS

Every hotel, restaurant, and attraction listing in this guide has been ranked for quality, value, service, amenities, and special features using a **star-rating system.** In country, state, and regional guides, we also rate towns and regions to help you narrow down your choices and budget your time accordingly. Hotels and restaurants are rated on a scale of zero (recommended) to three stars (exceptional). Attractions, shopping, nightlife, towns, and regions are rated according to the following scale: zero stars (recommended), one star (highly recommended), two stars (very highly recommended), and three stars (must-see).

In addition to the star-rating system, we also use **seven feature icons** that point you to the great deals, in-the-know advice, and unique experiences that separate travelers from tourists. Throughout the book, look for:

| | |
|---|---|
| *Finds* | Special finds—those places only insiders know about |
| *Fun Fact* | Fun facts—details that make travelers more informed and their trips more fun |
| *Kids* | Best bets for kids and advice for the whole family |
| *Moments* | Special moments—those experiences that memories are made of |
| *Overrated* | Places or experiences not worth your time or money |
| *Tips* | Insider tips—great ways to save time and money |
| *Value* | Great values—where to get the best deals |

The following **abbreviations** are used for credit cards:

| | | | | | |
|---|---|---|---|---|---|
| AE | American Express | DISC | Discover | V | Visa |
| DC | Diners Club | MC | MasterCard | | |

## FROMMERS.COM

Now that you have this guidebook to help you plan a great trip, visit our website at **www.frommers.com** for additional travel information on more than 3,500 destinations. We update features regularly to give you instant access to the most current trip-planning information available. At Frommers. com, you'll find scoops on the best airfares, lodging rates, and car rental bargains. You can even book your travel online through our reliable travel booking partners. Other popular features include:

- Online updates of our most popular guidebooks
- Vacation sweepstakes and contest giveaways
- Newsletters highlighting the hottest travel trends
- Online travel message boards with featured travel discussions

# The Charleston Experience

In the closing pages of *Gone With the Wind,* Rhett tells Scarlett that he's going back home to Charleston, where he can find "the calm dignity life can have when it's lived by gentle folks, the genial grace of days that are gone. When I lived those days, I didn't realize the slow charm of them." In spite of all the changes and upheavals over the years, Rhett's endorsement of Charleston still holds true.

If the Old South lives throughout South Carolina's Low Country, it positively thrives in Charleston. All our romantic notions of antebellum days—stately homes, courtly manners, gracious hospitality, and above all, gentle dignity—are facts of everyday life in this old city, in spite of a few scoundrels here and there, including an impressive roster of pirates, patriots, and presidents.

Located on the peninsula between the Cooper and Ashley rivers in southeastern South Carolina, Charleston is the oldest and second-largest city in the state. Notwithstanding a history dotted with earthquakes, hurricanes, fires, and Yankee bombardments, Charleston remains one of the best-preserved cities in America's Old South. It boasts 73 pre–Revolutionary War buildings, 136 from the late 18th century, and more than 600 built before the 1840s. With its cobblestone streets and horse-drawn carriages, Charleston is a place of visual images and sensory pleasures. Charleston's Old City Market is bustling with craftspeople jammed under the covered breezeways. Sweetgrass basket weavers hum spirituals; horse-drawn carriages clop down the street; and thousands of tourists eat, drink, and shop their way along. Jasmine and wisteria scent the air; the aroma of she-crab soup (a local favorite) wafts from sidewalk cafes; and antebellum architecture graces the historic cityscape. "No wonder they are so full of themselves," said an envious visitor from Columbia, which may be the state capital but doesn't have Charleston style.

In its annual reader survey, *Condé Nast Traveler* magazine names Charleston the number-five city to visit in America. Visitors are drawn here from all over the world. Each spring the city hosts the

**Spoleto Festival U.S.A.,** one of the most prestigious performing-arts events in the country, even the world.

Does this city have a modern side? Yes, but it's well hidden. Chic shops abound, as do a few supermodern hotels, but Charleston has no skyscrapers. You don't come to Charleston for anything cutting edge, though. You come to glimpse an earlier, almost-forgotten era.

Many local families still own and live in the homes that their planter ancestors built. Charlestonians manage to maintain a way of life that in many respects has little to do with wealth. The simplest encounter with Charleston natives seems to be invested with a social air, as though the visitor were a valued guest. Yet there are those who detect a certain snobbishness in Charleston—and truth be told, you'd have to stay here a hundred years to be considered an insider.

A minimum 3-day stay is required if you are to discover Charleston by day and night. Try to include a trip over the Cooper River Bridge to the string of islands that have rebounded from the massive destruction of Hurricane Hugo.

## 1 Frommer's Favorite Charleston Experiences

- **Playing Scarlett & Rhett at Boone Hall:** Over in Mount Pleasant, you can pretend that you're one of the romantic figures in Margaret Mitchell's *Gone With the Wind* by paying a visit to this 738-acre estate, a cotton plantation settled by Maj. John Boone in 1681. Its gorgeous Avenue of Oaks was used for background shots in *Gone With the Wind* and the miniseries *North and South.* See chapter 8.

- **Going Back to Colonial Days:** At Charles Towne Landing, you get the best insight into how colonists lived 300 years ago when they established the first English settlement in South Carolina. Even the animals the settlers encountered, from bears to bison, roam about. Enjoy 80 acres of gardens by walking along the marsh or biking past lagoons that reflect blossoming camellias and azaleas. See chapter 8.

- **Taking in the View from the Battery:** The Battery, as locals call White Point Gardens, offers the best perspective of the historic district. The gardens lie at the end of the peninsula, opening onto Cooper River and the harbor, where Fort Sumter sits. For the best walk, head along the sea wall on East Battery Street and Murray Boulevard. Later you can relax in the landscaped park, beneath wonderful live oaks. See chapter 8.

- **Tasting She-Crab Soup:** She-crab soup is to the local Charlestonian what clam chowder is to a New Englander. This rich delicacy has many permutations, but in most kitchens it is fashioned from butter, milk, heavy cream, sherry, salt, cayenne pepper, and, of course, crabmeat picked free of shells and cartilage. The secret ingredient: crab roe. See chapter 7.

- **Shopping Along King Street:** In 1854, painter Charles Fraser wrote of King Street and its "dazzling display of goods emulating a Turkish bazaar." The street's decline began with the Civil War and continued through subsequent natural disasters and 20th-century suburban sprawl. Today, King Street has bounced back. While it may never have the dazzle of a Turkish bazaar, it now ranks as one of the most attractive shopping promenades in the South. See chapter 9.

- **Exploring Fort Sumter:** Few events have had such a far-reaching impact on American history as the first shot of the Civil War fired here on April 12, 1861. Remembering what happened on that awful day and how it would rend the fabric of the nation gives great import to a tour of this fortress, its gun emplacements and artifacts on shining display. You can almost hear the bombardment as Yankee ships fired on the fort, whose Confederate troops valiantly resisted until the final day of surrender 4 years after that fateful shot. See chapter 8.

- **A Night in a B&B:** Few cities in the South recapture that antebellum feeling as much as a stay in a restored bed-and-breakfast lodging in Charleston. The Old English theme prevails, with stucco-finished walls, muslin curtains, draped rice beds, exposed beams, an occasional tapestry, and crystal chandeliers. Listen for the clank of an iron gate in front of a columned house as the scent of jasmine fills the air. See chapter 6.

- **Strolling Through the City as a Garden:** The entire district of Charleston seems to be one lush garden—not just the public plantings, such as the oleanders that line the Battery, but the nooks and crannies of private courtyards, where even the smallest patch of earth is likely to be filled with lush plantings. Wherever you stroll you can peer through wrought-iron gates into private edens planted with everything from wisteria to Confederate jasmine, tea olives to ginger lilies. Pink-blossomed crape myrtles line the streets, and camellias and magnolias sweeten the air.

- **A Horse and Carriage:** Nothing in Charleston quite captures the languid life of the Low Country more than a horse-drawn-carriage ride through the semitropical landscape. Most times of the year, the streets of Charleston are heavenly scented, perhaps from the blossoms of tea olives, jasmine, or wisteria. As the horse pulls you along, you'll feel you're back in the antebellum South as you slowly clip-clop past sun-dappled verandas and open-air markets selling fruits, vegetables, and straw baskets. See "Organized Tours," in chapter 8.

## 2 Best Hotel Bets

See chapter 6, "Where to Stay," for complete reviews of all these accommodations.

- **Best Classical Hotel:** The city's premier hostelry, **Charleston Place Hotel,** 205 Meeting St. (© **800/611-5545** or 843/722-4900; www.charlestonplacehotel.com), rises like a postmodern French château in the historic district. Visiting dignitaries and celebs like Mel Gibson bunk here. Acres of Italian marble, plush bedrooms, and a deluxe restaurant await you. See p. 45.
- **Best and Most Prestigious Inn:** One of the signers of the Declaration of Independence built the **John Rutledge House Inn,** 116 Broad St. (© **866/720-2609** or 843/723-7999; www.charminginns.com), which has been restored to its former Federalist grandeur. All the modern comforts have been added to the gracious, antiques-filled bedrooms. See p. 46.
- **Best and Grandest B&B:** Hailed by many as one of the top B&Bs in the South, the **Philip Porcher House,** 19 Archdale St. (© **843/722-1801**), is an impressively restored 1770 Georgian house at the core of the historic district. Once the home of a French Huguenot planter, the property was converted into this plush hotel in 1997. Period antiques and evocative art and objects from yesterday are graciously used in this nostalgic, inviting setting. See p. 46.
- **Best Small Luxury Hotel:** For those who like their inns on the small scale but as luxurious as any first-class competitor, there's the **Planters Inn,** 112 N. Market St. (© **800/845-7082** or 843/722-2345; www.plantersinn.com). This beautiful little hotel next to the Old City Market was opulently renovated in 1994, transforming it into an enclave of colonial charm, filled with 18th-century antiques and good reproductions. One of Charleston's best restaurants and bars is on-site. See p. 48.

- **Best Survivor of the Gilded Age:** A landmark Charleston hotel, **Wentworth Mansion,** 149 Wentworth St. (© **888/ 466-1886** or 843/853-1886; www.wentworthmansion.com), is an 1886 Second Empire building filled with the kind of luxurious architectural details that America's robber barons used to decorate their lavish estates: hand-carved marble fireplaces, Tiffany stained-glass windows, and elaborate wood and plasterwork. Built by a rich cotton merchant, the mansion has been successfully converted into one of South Carolina's grandest hotel addresses. See p. 50.

- **Best Boutique Hotel:** The **French Quarter Inn at Market Square,** 166 Church St. (© **866/812-1900** or 843/722-1900; www.fqicharleston.com), has a facade that evokes an 18th-century town house in Paris. Although it's modernized, the hotel blends in beautifully with the surrounding neighborhood, as if it's always been there. You stay in dignified, luxurious comfort here, enjoying nostalgic reminders of the architecture of yesterday, such as high ceilings, monumental staircases, and wrought-iron fixtures. See p. 55.

- **Best Harbor View:** No inn in Charleston is more aptly named than **HarbourView Inn,** 2 Vendue Range (© **888/853-8439** or 843/853-8439; www.harbourviewcharleston.com), a four-story inn in the heart of Charleston, across from Waterfront Park. From the hotel windows you can look out at one of the best city seascapes in South Carolina, a historic setting where the first round in the Civil War was fired. The traditions of the Old South are heeded here, and the sea-grass rugs and rattan chairs are of the sort Charleston sea captains used to bring back from their voyages. See p. 56.

- **Best Conversion from Existing Buildings:** No one will mistake **Maison Du Pré,** 317 E. Bay St. (© **800/844-4667** or 843/723-8691; www.maisondupre.com), for a dull roadside Days Inn. Five historic structures—three of them here since 1803, with two moved into position from their original perches—have been combined by the Mulholland family into a harmonious compound of free-standing 19th-century houses. This is one of Charleston's best examples of recycling existing buildings. The result is a hotel of charm and grace arranged around two landscaped courtyards. See p. 57.

- **Best Historic Hotel:** Constructed in grandeur and steeped in the history of Charleston, the **Mills House Hotel,** 115 Meeting

St. (© **800/874-9600** or 843/577-2400; www.millshouse. com), is a deluxe address. Its guest roster has ranged from Robert E. Lee to Elizabeth Taylor. Many of the original furnishings remain from 1853, when it was built for the then-astronomical price of $200,000. Although much altered over the years, it still has antebellum charm. See p. 59.

- **Best Moderately Priced Hotel:** Constructed as a private house—probably for slaves—**The Elliott House Inn,** 78 Queen St. (© **800/729-1855** or 843/723-1855; www.elliott houseinn.com), has been converted into one of Charleston's most charming inns. Even though none of the hotels in the historic district are particularly cheap, this one offers good value in its comfortable, carefully maintained bedrooms. Rooms are arranged off tiers of balconies opening onto a verdant courtyard, and each comes with a four-poster bed. See p. 62.

- **Best for Value:** If you want antebellum charm, but at an affordable price, check into **The Rutledge Victorian Guest House,** 114 Rutledge Ave. (© **888/722-7553** or 843/722-7551; www. charlestonvictorian.com), an Italianate building from the 19th century that is one of the city's better inns. In keeping with its name, its rooms are furnished with Victorian antiques along with an intriguing assortment of beds ranging from Italian "rope beds" to the famous rice beds of South Carolina. To go really economical, ask for one of the units without a private bathroom, the most reasonably priced in the historic district. See p. 63.

- **Best Modern Hotel:** For the best of contemporary luxury living, head to **The Inn at Middleton Place,** 4290 Ashley River Rd. (© **800/543-4774** or 843/556-0500; www.theinnat middletonplace.com), a newly created and striking modern luxury hotel now receiving guests on the grounds of the historic 18th-century Middleton Plantation, one of the area's major sightseeing attractions. It was the creation of Charles Duell, one of the descendants of Middleton's original owners, who deliberately wanted to escape "ersatz colonial." See p. 66.

## 3 Best Dining Bets

See chapter 7, "Where to Dine," for complete reviews of all these restaurants.

- **Best French Restaurant:** With top-notch cuisine, formal service, and an upmarket clientele, **Robert's of Charleston,** 182 E.

Bay St. (© **843/577-7565**), stands up there with some of the most outstanding restaurants of Paris. The seasonally adjusted menu is the showcase for the culinary talents of chef and owner Robert Dickson, who has brought a new dimension to French-inspired cooking in Charleston. See p. 70.

- **Best Low Country Cuisine:** Hip and stylish, **Anson,** 12 Anson St. (© **843/577-0551**), is filled with Low Country charm. The way it handles the recipes and foodstuffs of coastal South Carolina is reason enough to visit. Time-tested recipes are often given imaginative modern twists, as exemplified by the lobster, corn, and black-bean quesadillas or the cashew-crusted grouper in champagne sauce. See p. 72.

- **Best Historic Restaurant:** Of course, George Washington no longer dines at **McCrady's,** 2 Unity Alley (© **843/577-0025**), on his visits to Charleston, but this citadel of upmarket American/French cuisine is still going strong. *Esquire* magazine recently heralded it as one of the best restaurants in America, even though it's set in a historic tavern of exposed beams and wide-plank floors. Even the most basic dish is magical here—take potato soup, for example. Here it's creamy and enlivened with chive oil, truffles, and leek foam. See p. 74.

- **Best for Sunday Brunch:** In the historic Mills House Hotel, taking Sunday brunch at the **Barbados Room Restaurant,** 115 Meeting St. (© **843/577-2400**), is a Charleston tradition. In an antebellum setting, you can enjoy some of the best Low Country brunch specialties in the city. Shrimp and grits are traditional, but who can resist Chef Gibson's jumbo crab cakes? See p. 75.

- **Best for Seafood:** Most restaurants in Charleston serve seafood dishes, more or less, but for authentic Low Country fish dishes we always head for **Hank's,** 10 Hayne St. (© **843/723-3474**), a converted turn-of-the-20th-century warehouse overlooking Old City Market. The she-crab soup, that invariable Charleston appetizer, is prepared to sheer perfection here. See p. 78.

- **Best for Barbecue:** For Tennessee-style barbecue, the kind Elvis loved, head for the aptly named **Sticky Fingers,** 235 Meeting St. (© **843/853-7427**), where the barbecue is hickory smoked and the sauce is zesty. Ribs are prepared in the traditional slow-smoking process for extra flavor. The hickory-smoked chicken isn't bad either. See p. 84.

- **The Best Restaurant in South Carolina:** In the town of Summerville, outside Charleston, some of the most discerning palates in the South have ruled that the elegant **Dining Room at Woodlands,** 125 Parsons Rd. (© **800/774-9999**), is the finest in the state. Readers of *Condé Nast Traveler* magazine, in fact, have rated it one of the top restaurants in North America for several years in a row. Low Country cuisine is prepared here to near perfection. See p. 89.

- **Best for Romantic Dining:** In the carriage house of Wentworth Mansion, **Circa 1886 Restaurant,** 149 Wentworth St. (© **843/853-7828**), is the city's most elegant setting for a romantic dinner for two. That it also serves some of the city's best Low Country and French cuisine comes as an added bonus. To get you in the right romantic mood, take in the water views from the restaurant's cupola. See p. 69.

- **Best Chef in Charleston:** Hitting town from the Wild Boar in Nashville, Chef Bob Waggoner wowed local foodies when he took charge at the **Charleston Grill** in the Charleston Place Hotel, 224 King St. (© **843/577-4522**). His French cuisine, with Low Country influences, draws raves, and his is the only restaurant in Charleston that boasts the much-coveted Mobil Four-Star rating. See p. 72.

- **Best for Steak:** Since the '90s, **High Cotton,** 199 E. Bay St. (© **843/724-3815**), has won a clientele devoted to its steaks. Using the finest cut of meats, the results are tender, juicy, and succulent steaks. To go the full Southern route, ask for a steak with bourbon sauce. See p. 74.

- **Best for Oysters:** Long known for its oysters, **A. W. Shucks,** 70 State St. (© **843/723-1151**), settles the demands of city dwellers who really know their bivalves. Oysters, perhaps the best in the South, are prepared here in various delightful ways, including, of course, chilled and served on the half shell after they are carefully shucked. See p. 74.

- **Best for Kids:** A short walk from the Old City Market, **Bocci's,** 158 Church St. (© **843/720-2121**), has one of the best family dining rooms in Charleston, known for its good-value Italian cuisine. Kids love to dig into the full-flavored pastas. There's a special menu for children. See p. 76.

# 2

# The History of Charleston

The rich history of Charleston has led to countless Gothic romances, the last major one being *Scarlett,* the faintly praised sequel to *Gone With the Wind.* Although a relatively small state—40th in size among the 50 states—South Carolina has had an enormous impact on the nation, none more significant than the firing on Fort Sumter in Charleston Harbor that launched the American Civil War. Where did this rich, gamy tale begin?

## 1 Charleston Past

### COLONIAL DAYS

It is estimated that some 18,000 Native Americans were living in what is now the state of South Carolina when the first European invaders arrived in the 16th century. The Spanish, sailing from what is now the Dominican Republic and entering South Carolina waters through St. Helena Sound (between Beaufort and Edisto Island), landed ashore on August 18, 1520. The next year, two more Spanish galleons arrived at Winyah Bay (north of Charleston), the site of present-day Georgetown. Indian settlers ran out to greet them—a big mistake. The choicest specimens were taken back to the Dominican Republic as slaves.

The first Spanish settlement in South Carolina came when

### Dateline

- **1520** The Spanish arrive from the Caribbean.
- **1562** French Huguenots first settle in the Charleston area.
- **1670** First permanent settlement by the English; plantation economy launched.
- **1740s** Massive slave importations to work plantations.
- **1776** Charleston becomes major battleground of the American Revolution.
- **1780** British troops under Cornwallis occupy Charleston.
- **1793** Eli Whitney's cotton gin revolutionizes local economy.
- **1860** South Carolina secedes from the Union.
- **1861** Firing on Fort Sumter in Charleston Harbor marks beginning of Civil War.
- **1863** Charleston bombarded by Union ships.

Lucas Vásquez de Ayllón of Toledo, a Spanish don, sailed into the South Carolina waters with an estimated 500 settlers. They had come to found San Miguel, a community that pre-dated the English settlement at Jamestown, Virginia, by exactly 81 years.

Attacks by hostile Indians, widespread disease, and a particularly bad winter forced the settlers to abandon their colony. Only 150 men and women remained to be evacuated.

In 1562, fleeing religious persecution from the French Catholics, Huguenot settlers sailed into Port Royal Sound (between Hilton Head and the town of Beaufort). Under their leader, Jean Ribaut, they came ashore at Parris Island, today the site of a U.S. Marine Corps station.

Their little settlement was to last only 4 years. In 1566, the conquistador Pedro Menéndez de Avilés routed the Huguenots. Under his command, Fort San Felipe was constructed.

By 1586, with Sir Francis Drake and his British warriors raiding St. Augustine in Florida, the Spanish settlers withdrew.

The British came as settlers in the 1670s. In London, King Charles II awarded the territory of "Carolina," stretching from Virginia to Spanish Florida, to eight so-called "Lord Proprietors."

- **1865** Sherman invades South Carolina as South loses war.
- **1870s** Reconstruction era marks long decline of Charleston's once-golden economy.
- **1918** Some 70,000 men from South Carolina join U.S. military during World War I.
- **1941** Military training centers established in South Carolina, as 173,642 people join in World War II effort.
- **1960** Civil rights demonstrations launched.
- **1961** Desegregation extended to public transportation.
- **1975** James Edwards becomes first Republican governor in a century.
- **1980s** Massive return of blacks from Northern cities to their homeland in South Carolina.
- **1989** Category 5 Hurricane Hugo causes mass destruction to the barrier islands around Charleston.
- **2002** Strom Thurmond, Dixiecrat poster boy and U.S. senator from South Carolina for 47 years, resigns at the age of 100.
- **2003** The so-called "Granddaddy of South Carolina"—Strom Thurmond—dies, as scandal erupts.
- **2005** New Copper River Bridge links Charleston to Mount Pleasant.

## THE RULE OF THE LORD PROPRIETORS

From the British-held colony of Barbados in the southern West Indies, the lord proprietors recruited sugar-cane and tobacco planters. The first shipload came in 1670, arriving at Albemarle Point on the Ashley River.

Throughout the 1670s these planters crossed the river to found Charles Towne, which in time became Charleston.

In the 18th century the plantations launched by these settlers from Barbados spread throughout the Sea Islands and the Low Country (generally defined as the coastal region between Charleston and Savannah). Settlers were constantly harassed by American Indians, especially the Cherokees, Westoes, and Yemassees, and they also endured attacks from pirates, notably Blackbeard. Even the Spanish raided ships sailing north from Florida. In spite of all the hardships, Charles Towne became the richest colony in America, a prize highly valued by the throne in London.

The importation of slaves to work the land continued at such a rapid rate that nearly 25,000 slaves (figures vary) were said to be living in and around Charleston in the 1740s—outnumbering the white population three to one. Most of the slaves were shipped over from Sierra Leone and Senegal.

Slaves were used for the most monumental of tasks, such as clearing swamps and constructing dikes. In great demand by hungry markets, rice became the crop of choice for American colonists. Rice production increased annually, and plantation owners grew rich with British pounds. Indeed, the merchants, shippers, and plantation owners in and around Charleston were the richest people in 18th-century America, when direct trade with England was six times in Charleston what it was in the other colonies. Ships arriving from London brought fashionable goods and exotic spices to the port of Charles Towne. While slaves toiled in the rice fields, Charleston's landed gentry celebrated with balls, races, concerts, and festivities.

## THE REVOLUTIONARY WAR

Change was in the air in the latter part of the 18th century. Word of the Battle of Bunker Hill in Massachusetts reached the colony in South Carolina. Less than a month later, on July 12, 1775, local rebels seized Fort Charlotte in McCormick County. This was the first English military installation to be captured in the oncoming Revolutionary War.

To the minds of many, South Carolina is more strongly associated with the Civil War than the Revolutionary War. But the state was actually a major battleground of the American Revolution. A total of 137 battles were fought on South Carolina soil.

So severe was hatred against Tory Loyalists that they were rounded up, tarred, feathered, and then paraded through the streets of Charleston.

The Revolutionary War hero of South Carolina was Francis Marion, a descendant of the Huguenots. Born in a settlement near Georgetown in 1732, he was brought up in the swamps and thickets of the state's backcountry. What Marion learned about guerilla warfare fighting the Cherokees in the Up Country, he used to his state's advantage against the British, who in time nicknamed him the "Swamp Fox." He made periodic raids on British installations, and then disappeared with his men into the swamps, where he could not be routed.

With the help of log fortifications (such as Fort Moultrie, which can be visited today), the rebels delayed the advance of British troops into Charleston until 1780. Lord Cornwallis, who'd established himself as the ruler of Charleston, planned to join forces with Up Country colonials still loyal to the crown and advance against the forces of George Washington in Virginia.

But when Up Country colonials learned that English forces had massacred rebels of the Continental Army as they were surrendering at Lancaster, the Up Country colonials become so incensed that they at long last joined the Low Country rebellion.

Up Country rebels defeated the Cornwallis forces at the Battle of Kings Mountain, marking a turning point in the war. After that, the British surrender at Yorktown became inevitable.

## ANTEBELLUM DAYS

A major blow to the prestige of Charleston came in 1786 when the capital of South Carolina was moved from that city to the more centrally located Columbia, a sort of border country between the always-jealous people of the Low Country and their traditional rival, the Up Country. In 1788, South Carolina would ratify the U.S. Constitution, becoming the eighth state to join the newly emerging Union.

Charleston was profoundly affected by the invention of Eli Whitney's cotton gin in 1793. In time, rice barons turned to raising cotton, and Sea Island cotton became highly valued for its long, silky fibers. By the mid-1830s South Carolina's cotton crop was nearing 70 million pounds, accounting for more than half of America's

## Impressions

*To describe our growing up in the lowcountry of South Carolina, I would have to take you to the marsh on a spring day, flush the great blue heron from its silent occupation, scatter marsh hens as we sink to our knees in the mud, open you an oyster with a pocketknife and feed it to you from the shell and say, "There. That taste. That's the taste of my childhood." I would say, "Breathe deeply," and you would breathe and remember that smell for the rest of your life, the bold, fecund aroma of the tidal marsh, exquisite and sensual, the smell of the South in heat, a smell like new milk, semen, and spilled wine, all perfumed with seawater.*

—Novelist Pat Conroy, *The Prince of Tides*

exports to Europe. Cotton would remain king in and around South Carolina right up to the advent of the Civil War.

Charleston's bankers and shippers constructed canals to export slaves outward from their arrival point at the city's port, and to bring cotton from the interior of South Carolina quickly to the harbor of Charleston where ships were waiting to take it abroad.

"The Best Friend of Charleston," as the new South Carolina Canal & Railroad Company was called, opened up newer and faster markets, as rail lines in the 1840s were extended as far as the Up Country.

Challenges from Georgia and Alabama finally brought havoc to the cotton planters, who had greatly overexpanded. Nonetheless, politics in the antebellum South were still dominated by South Carolina, with Charleston wielding the greatest influence.

The emerging spokesperson for South Carolina's interests was the towering figure of John C. Calhoun, who'd married a Low Country plantation heiress. Resigning as the vice president to Andrew Jackson in 1832, he devoted all his considerable intellect and power to preserving both the cotton industry and slavery. Elected to the U.S. Senate, he fought against federal export taxes on cotton.

Threats to secede were issued by South Carolina from 1832 until the actual outbreak of the Civil War. Charleston financiers and Low Country planters, more than any other force in the South, took the dangerous steps to divide the nation, especially in the wake of the election of Abraham Lincoln, who swept into the presidency without a single electoral vote south of the Mason-Dixon Line.

## Recommended Books: History of a Southern City

Many writers have tried to capture the legend and lore of Charleston. *Mary's World,* by Richard N. Cote, is notable in that it was based on more than 2,500 pages of unpublished letters, diaries, and journals written by a Southern aristocrat named Mary Pringle. This is a moving chronicle of the life her family led in antebellum Charleston, during the Civil War, and in the Reconstruction era.

For a quick overview of the city, the best guide is *A Short History of Charleston,* by Robert Rosen, going from the founding of Charles Towne to Hurricane Hugo's destruction in 1989. It's all here: from the rice plantations in the Low Country to Charleston's roles in the Revolutionary War and again in the Civil War.

*Charleston! Charleston! History of a Southern City,* by Walter J. Fraser, goes from 1670 to the present day—and what a saga it is. From the bars to the bedrooms of the bordellos, this is an insider guide to the city. You go into prisons and schools, churches and orphanages, meeting black and white, rich and poor. From economic booms to devastating busts, this book takes you on a roller coaster ride of history.

## THE CIVIL WAR

That dreadful day, one of the most important in the history of America, came on April 12, 1861, as South Carolina troops began their bombardment of Fort Sumter under Union control. The Union troops held out for 34 hours of shelling before surrendering their citadel. By May 11, President Abraham Lincoln in Washington had declared war against the Confederate States of America.

Although the port of Charleston came under heavy bombardment by Union forces, especially in 1863, South Carolina was hardly a major battleground during the Civil War, certainly not in the way it was during the American Revolution. The state's major battle—not among the great Civil War conflicts—was the Battle of Rivers Bridge in February 1865, just two months before Robert E. Lee surrendered at Appomattox.

The port of Charleston did play a major role in blockade running during the war, however. Amazingly, only 7 months after the firing on Fort Sumter, Union forces occupied Hilton Head, Beaufort, and St. Helena Island on the doorstep of Charleston, and remained in control there throughout the war.

Even by 1863, Union forces had begun land redistribution, awarding parcels of Sea Island and various hunks of plantations to freed slaves. Some 40,000 freedmen took over nearly half a million acres of plantation lands. It was to be only a temporary grant, however. By 1866, President Andrew Johnson had given most of the land back to the former white landowners, the landed gentry.

At the end of the war, victors from the North occupied Charleston, filling the city with "carpetbaggers," the name derisively given to carpetbag-carrying Yankees who flooded the South during Reconstruction hoping to make a quick buck. The golden age of antebellum life was over, and South Carolina remains to this day one of the poorest states in America.

## 2 Modern Times

Charleston remained under Union forces until 1877. The abolition of slavery and the end of the plantation era brought economic stagnation that would not be relieved until the coming of World War II.

It wasn't that king cotton wasn't being produced. It was, and in greater bulk than it had been during its antebellum heyday. It was *too* plentiful, as it would turn out. Planters grew more and more cotton, causing the price to fall lower and lower.

Rice and cotton met bitter ends: A fierce hurricane in 1911 destroyed rice production, and the pesky boll weevil finished off the Sea Island cotton industry around 1922.

One positive result of the ongoing poverty of post–Civil War Charleston was that few could afford to revamp their homes in the latest Victorian style. "Too poor to paint; too proud to whitewash," went the rallying cry. The result is a city whose collection of antebellum architecture is unsurpassed.

Many communities in South Carolina became cotton-mill towns, with low wages granted to the all-white mill workers. Smallpox became the curse of the mill towns. Charleston and South Carolina sank deeper and deeper into depression long before the actual Depression was set in motion in the wake of the Wall Street crash of 1929.

---

*Fun Fact*  **A Nationwide Craze**

In the 1920s the musical *Running Wild* introduced the Charleston, which quickly became a nationwide craze. Silent movies, such as *Our Dancing Daughters* with Joan Crawford, were particularly fond of depicting the dance. Even the stuffy Duke of Windsor took Charleston lessons.

---

On the eve of the United States entry into World War I, the state had little more than a dozen public schools. Locals, especially mill owners, opposed sending the children to schools, wanting them to work in factories instead. Farmers kept their children on the family spread, toiling in the sun.

At the outbreak of World War I, some 70,000 men from South Carolina, many of them from Charleston, joined the military; during World War II, more than double that number of men (and women) signed up for military duty.

But few suffered more than the state's black populace, who had little chance of making a living in the South. During the first 4 decades of the 20th century, black Southerners began a vast migration to Washington, New York, Cleveland, Detroit, and Chicago, among other cities. On the eve of the Japanese attack on Pearl Harbor, more white people than black were living in Charleston and South Carolina at large. This had not been true since the dawn of the 18th century.

Much of the history of modern South Carolina has been marred by ugly racial conflicts. Civil rights demonstrations began in 1960, followed by desegregation in 1961. Often the front lines in the battle for racial fairness stretched bitterly across schoolyards, college campuses, and public-transportation facilities. By 1970, the first blacks elected to the legislature since the dawn of the 20th century were voted into office.

Feeling betrayed by their long-cherished Democratic Party, right-wing conservatives in 1975 elected James Edwards, the first Republican governor in more than a century.

South Carolina legislators disgraced themselves and their state in the 1980s and early '90s, especially during the 1989 sting "Operation Lost Trust." Among others, 17 members of the state legislature were arrested for selling their votes for money.

The death of the oldest living senator, Strom Thurmond, in 2003 was followed immediately by headlines. Although Thurmond had stood for "segregation today, segregation tomorrow, segregation forever," it was revealed that he was the father of a child born out of wedlock and conceived in an illicit affair with a black woman.

The latest trends show a reversal of the great emigration pattern in the early decades of the 20th century that saw some 6.5 million blacks uproot themselves and head north. Urban decay and increasing violence in many Northern cities have led to a reverse emigration pattern. At the post millennium, figures showed a return by thousands of blacks to the South and burgeoning growth in their population figures.

At long last in 2005 the Arthur Ravenel, Jr., Bridge (or the New Copper River Bridge) linked downtown Charleston with its satellite of Mount Pleasant. With a main span of 1,546 feet, it is the longest cable-stayed bridge that carries vessels other than public transport in the Western Hemisphere.

# 3

# Art & Architecture

The epitome of Southern graciousness, the plantation culture of Charleston and its surrounding Low Country spans 2 centuries that saw everything from a glorious antebellum past (for the landed gentry, not the slaves) to depression, decay, and the passing of a way of life.

The most remarkable buildings were constructed between 1686 and 1878 (yes, 13 years after the Civil War, during Reconstruction) along the South Carolina coastal plain centered at Charleston.

Many of these once-elegant structures still stand today to enchant us, although they are in varying states of preservation, some no more than ruins. Only the camera has captured some of these stately Low Country manses for posterity. From churches to gardens, chapels to memorable homes, plantation houses to graceful frame structures, Charleston has it all.

## 1 The Architecture of Charleston 101

### THE GOLDEN AGE

All you need to do is walk down Broad Street in the center of Charleston to see three dozen ornately decorated and historic structures on the block between East Bay and Church streets. Much of what has been saved was because of an ordinance passed in 1931 that preserved whole sectors of town—and not just individual buildings. Although some other American cities now do this, Charleston was the first city in the world to adopt such a preservation law.

To many visitors today, the so-called historic core lies **south of Broad Street.** This sector is certainly one of the great districts of architecture in the Deep South. But the landed gentry in the heyday of the plantation era also built many superb homes and mansions in other sections of the city, such as **Harleston Village** and **Radcliffeborough.** Harleston Village lies west of the historic district. Directly north of Harleston is the neighborhood of Radcliffeborough, beginning north of Calhoun Street. Some of the grandest Victorian manses stand around **Colonial Lake.** These neighborhoods deserve at least an hour of your time to walk around. Lacy iron gates, 19th-century ornaments, towering old trees, and private gardens make it worthwhile, even if you're not particularly interested in architecture.

The Georgian Palladian style reigned supreme in historic Charleston, lasting over the centuries, and surely there are more Tara-like columns in Charleston today than in a small Greek city in classical days. One of the finest Georgian mansions in America stands at **64 S. Battery St.,** dating from 1772 when it was built by William Gibbes, a successful ship owner and planter. He modeled it after English designs but was also inspired by Palladio. The house is not pure Georgian, however, as Adamesque features, such as wrought-iron railings, were added later.

The columned single house prevailed for 250 years—perhaps there are some 3,000 such houses standing in Charleston today. Its most defining feature was its single-room width, and it was also set at right angles to the street. One of the most evocative examples of a Charleston single house is the **Col. Robert Brewton House** at 71 Church St. The domestic structure of the single house is one of Charleston's greatest contributions to city architecture in America. Almost from the day the first settlement of Charles Towne was launched, locals showed a surprising, almost feverish, interest in the shape of their domestic dwellings.

Some were more lavish than others, of course, but even less expensive dwellings were adorned with wrought-iron balconies or two-columned porches. Even today, some of the city's grander manses, churches, and banks evoke the entrance to Greek temples.

Although much great architecture is gone, what remains is impressive: nearly 75 buildings from the colonial period, approximately 135 from the 18th century, and more than 600 built during the antebellum heyday before the coming of the Civil War.

## COLONIAL TO ADAMESQUE

In the beginning, roughly from 1690 to 1740, there was the colonial style, with such defining features as clapboard wooden siding, low foundations, and steeply pitched roofs. The **John Lining House,** at 106 Broad St., is the most evocative building of that period. Coexisting for a certain time with colonial architecture was Georgian, a style that flourished between 1700 and 1800. Its defining features were box chimneys, hipped roofs, flattened columns, and raised basements. Nowhere is this style better exemplified than in the **Miles Brewton House** at 27 King St.

As colonial and Georgian faded, another style of architecture appeared, especially during a 3-decade span beginning in 1790. Although it was called Federalist architecture in the North, most Charlestonians referred to the structures of this era as "Adamesque" or "the Adam period," a reference to what those brothers from Scotland, James and Robert Adam, were creating in the British Isles. The heyday of the Adam influence was in the mid-1700s. The best example of Federalist/Adamesque architecture in Charleston is the **Nathaniel Russell House** at 51 Meeting St., which is open to the public (see chapter 8).

Constructed around the same time as the Nathaniel Russell House, the **James Moultrie House,** at 20 Montagu St., is an Adamesque treasure of delicate proportions. Although it was built by a planter, Daniel Cobia, it became more famous as the address of the Moultrie family in 1834. Dr. Moultrie, related to the Revolutionary War hero Gen. William Moultrie, was one of South Carolina's early physicians, founding its first medical school.

A magnificent Adamesque mansion, built around 1802, was constructed at 60 Montagu St. The restored **Gaillard-Bennett House,** constructed by a rice planter, Theodore Gaillard, is famous for its fluted columns with so-called "Tower-of-the-Winds" capitals, along with an elliptically shaped window in its portico gable and a modillion cornice, with other Palladian architectural motifs. In 1870, 5 years after the end of the Civil War, Robert E. Lee was a guest of the Bennett family, who then owned the manse, and he spoke to admiring well-wishers from the second-floor balcony.

Another stellar example of the Adamesque style is the **Jonathan Lucas House,** built around 1808, at 286 Calhoun St. Several generations of rice barons lived here, establishing rice milling as a big industry in the southeastern United States.

---

## Impressions

*Outwardly discreet, the landscape masks extremes of beauty and terror. Hidden in the loveliest places are narratives of horror: Some of the region's most beautiful gardens were created by forced labor. Its peaceful cypress swamps, now refuges for alligators, egrets, and herons, were likewise built by slaves as freshwater impoundments for the cultivation of rice, which Africans were brought here to grow.*

—John Beardsley, *Art and Landscape in Charleston and the Low Country*

---

## GREEK REVIVAL VS. GOTHIC REVIVAL

The Regency style came and went quickly in Charleston, filling in a transitional period between Adamesque and the Greek Revival style. The most evocative example of Regency is the **Edmondston-Alston House,** at 21 E. Battery St., erected by Charles Edmondston in 1825. The purity of the original style was later altered by Charles Alston, a rice planter who added Greek Revival details. From its precincts, General Beauregard watched the attack on Fort Sumter in 1861, and Robert E. Lee once took refuge here when a fire threatened the Mills House Hotel where he was lodged. This historic home is open to the public (see chapter 8).

The Greek Revival period, which flourished roughly from 1820 to 1875 (a full 10 years after the Civil War), had an enormous impact on the cityscape of Charleston. Its defining features were, of course, heavy columns and capitals (often Doric), along with a hipped or gabled roof and a wide band of trim. One of the most solid examples of this form of bold architecture is the **Beth Elohim Reform Temple,** at 90 Hasell St., the oldest synagogue in continuous use in the United States, first organized in 1749.

However, the most spectacular example of the Greek Revival style is at **172 Tradd St.,** built in 1836 by Alexander Hext Chisolm, who made his fortune in rice. The lavish capitals are copies of those designed in Athens in 335 B.C. The architect is thought to be Charles F. Reichardt of New York.

At the turn of the 19th century, Gabriel Manigault, a French Huguenot, was the biggest name in the architecture of Charleston. His greatest buildings at the time have been torn down, and those that remain have been only loosely attributed to him. One such structure is today's **City Hall,** at the corner of Broad Street at its junction with Meeting Street. Constructed in 1801, City Hall is a stellar example of the Adamesque-Palladian style of architecture. It was originally a bank building before becoming City Hall in 1818.

One of the few buildings that can be directly traced to the architectural drawing board of Manigault is the house at **350 Meeting St.** that the architect designed for his brother, Joseph, in 1803. Many critics hail it as one of the most impressive Adamesque homes in America. Manigault's father, also known as Gabriel Manigault, was in his day not only the richest man in Charleston but also one of the wealthiest in the country. The **Joseph Manigault House** is one of the few historic homes in Charleston open to the public. See chapter 8.

> ( *Fun Fact*   **The Gullah Tongue Makes It to Broadway**
>
> In the 1920s while he was living in Charleston, DuBose Heyward wrote *Porgy,* which in time became a Broadway play. Later, it became even more famous as a folk opera created by George Gershwin and retitled *Porgy and Bess.* Living for a time in Charleston, Gershwin incorporated sounds and rhythms he'd seen in black churches around the Low Country. Heyward was inspired by the city's rich heritage, even though the glorious mansions of old had fallen into disrepair and Charlestonians were going through hard times—"too poor to paint, too proud to whitewash." Heyward used not only the byways of Charleston but also his setting for the Gullah language for his dialogues.

Another national landmark attributed to Manigault is at **18 Bull St.,** an Adamesque manse constructed at the turn of the 19th century by William Blacklock, a wine merchant. At its lowest point this mansion became a cheap boardinghouse and barely escaped bulldozers in 1958.

Robert Mills, who designed the Washington Monument, filled in when Manigault resettled in Philadelphia. But Mills was never as well received, although he left the monumental **First Baptist Church** (1819–22) on lower Church Street and the five-columned **Fireproof Building** (1822–26) at Chambers and Meeting streets.

When an 1838 fire destroyed a large part of antebellum Charleston, many districts were reconstructed in the Greek Revival style. Doric columns were particularly fashionable, along with rectangular shapes inspired by Greek temples, such as those found in Sicily.

A monumental "pillar" to Greek Revival is the columned **Centenary Methodist Church,** at 60 Wentworth St., an 1842 structure by Edward Brickell White. This is one of the grandest examples of a Greek Doric temple in America.

Along came Andrew Jackson Downing, the mid-19th-century arbiter of America's taste in architecture, who ridiculed Charleston's obsession with Greek Revival. The way was paved for the emergence of E. B. White, who brought in the Gothic Revival design, which

## Recommended Books

The best and most helpful practical guide—virtually a street-by-street survey—is *Complete Charleston, A Guide to the Architecture, History, and Gardens of Charleston,* by Margaret H. Moore, with photographs by Truman Moore. Sold all over Charleston, the book divides Charleston into 11 neighborhoods and takes you on a tour of each, a voyage of discovery of the city's world-class architecture and lush secret gardens.

*Art and Landscape in Charleston and the Low Country,* by John Beardsley, was published as part of the 21st season of the Spoleto U.S.A. Festival. The color photographs of Charleston and the Low Country alone are reason enough to purchase this guide. Its chief focus is on contemporary art in the Low Country, landscape history, and garden design with many architectural perspectives.

prevailed from 1850 to 1885 and was characterized by pointed arches and buttressed stone tracery. The best example of Gothic Revival is the **French Protestant (Huguenot) Church,** at 136 Church St.

## AFTER THE CIVIL WAR

Also dominating the 1850s, the decade before the Civil War, were the architects F. D. Lee and Edward C. Jones. Together and separately they began to change the cityscape of Charleston, creating, for example, the Moorish-style fish market, their most exotic invention—alas, now gone. They pioneered the use of cast iron, which became a dominant feature in city architecture and can still be seen at its most prolific on the western side of Meeting Street, stretching from Hasell to Market streets.

One of the most talented of all Charleston architects, Jones designed the **Trinity Methodist Church,** on Meeting Street, in 1850. This impressive edifice has a pedimented Palladian portico of Corinthian columns. But in just 3 years he shifted his style to Italianate, which remained popular until the dawn of the 20th century. The architecture was defined by verandas, low-pitched roofs, and balustrades. An evocative example of the style is the **Col. John Ashe House,** at 26 S. Battery St., which was designed by Jones.

In 1853, Jones designed his first commercial building in the Italianate Renaissance Revival style at **1 Broad St.** Evocative of a corner building in London, it housed a bank. At one time this building was owned by George A. Trenholm, a cotton broker and blockade runner, one of several 19th-century power brokers in Charleston who were said to have inspired Margaret Mitchell's character of Rhett Butler in *Gone With the Wind.*

Still one of the city's most magnificent landmarks, the columned building at **200 E. Bay St.** is the most stellar example of the Italian Renaissance Revival style, built over a period of 26 years, from 1853 to 1879. This U.S. Custom House was the creation of Ammin Burnham, a Boston architect who'd created a similar building in his home city. Burnham was largely instrumental in launching the tradition of designing federal buildings, such as post offices, in a classical style. The Roman Corinthian portico of this splendid temple is much photographed by visitors.

About 20 years before Charleston got sucked up in the Civil War, all purism in architectural style vanished. Most architects and builders were more interested in a dramatic facade. This period saw the bastardization of a lot of Charleston's landscape. Architects reached out internationally for inspiration—perhaps to the Moors, to Persia, to the Norman style of church, or even Gothic Venice, if they were fanciful.

The best example of this bastardized, though architecturally beautiful, style is at **67 Rutledge Ave.,** the circa-1851 home that Col. James H. Taylor ordered built "in the style of a Persian villa," with Moorish arches as ornamentation. This was a famous address in its heyday, entertaining the likes of such distinguished guests as the 19th-century politician, tastemaker, and orator, Daniel Webster.

And then came the Civil War, when all building ceased except for fortifications. Much great architecture was destroyed during Union bombardments, especially in 1863.

After the war, the Victorian style arrived in Charleston and would prevail from 1870 until the coming of World War I. This style did not predominate as much as it did in other American cities because many Charlestonians, wiped out economically from the effects of the Civil War, did not have money to build. Nonetheless, you'll see some fine Victorian manses in Charleston today, notably the **Sottile House,** with its wide verandas opening onto Green Street on the College of Charleston campus.

When Victorian architects did design buildings in Charleston, they often created "fantasies," as exemplified by the manse that stands at **40 Montagu St.** Built by food merchant Bernard Wohlers in 1891, the house was restored in 1963. Its unique style combines Charles Eastlake with Queen Anne motifs. This startling house seems underappreciated in a city that prizes its colonial and antebellum homes more than Victorian grandeur.

Not all Charlestonians during the latter Victorian Age were building in the Victorian style. Albert W. Todd, for example, an architect and state senator, constructed one of Charleston's most magnificent private residences at **40 Rutledge Ave.** in the Colonial Revival style at the turn of the 20th century. With its verandas and splendid columned portico, this house is worth a detour.

**Rainbow Row** (79–107 E. Bay St.) is one of the most celebrated blocks in the city. It got its name in the 1930s when the entire block was rejuvenated and then painted in colors used by the colonials. The architecture is mainly of the so-called British style, in that there was a store on the ground floor with the living accommodations on the floors above. Rainbow Row is the longest such Georgian block of buildings in America, and it inspired DuBose Heyward's "Catfish Row" in *Porgy and Bess.*

Although it's an arguable point, a Florida professor, Sigmund Heinz, once stated: "For all practical purposes, the Civil War brought an end to the grandeur of Charleston architecture. As for the 20th century, the kindest thing is not to mention it."

## 2 The Art of Charleston 101

As might be expected, Charleston is far more distinguished by its architecture than by its art. But it's had some peaks and valleys over the years, and today boasts a creative core of artists whose works are displayed at the Spoleto Festival U.S.A. and in museums in the city—and often showcased in traveling exhibitions around the state.

In the colonial period, the art decorating the antebellum homes of England—most often landscapes or portraits of dogs and horses—was imported from London and brought over by British ships sailing into Charleston Harbor. When families grew rich from rice and indigo, portrait painters, many of them itinerant, did

**Impressions**
*Come quickly, have found heaven.*
—Artist Alfred Hutty, in a wire to his wife
upon discovering Charleston

idealized portraits of the founding father of a dynasty and his wife (always made out to be far more beautiful than she was), or else the whole brood gathered for an idealized family portrait.

Out of this lackluster mess, one artist rose to distinguish himself.

## CHARLESTON'S RENAISSANCE MAN

Born in South Carolina of Scottish descent, Charles Fraser became the best-known artist in Charleston for his miniature portraits, many of which you can see in the **Gibbes Museum of Art** (see chapter 8). Although he was also a distinguished landscape painter, he is mainly known for his miniatures today.

When the Marquis de Lafayette came to Charleston in 1825, he sat for a portrait by Fraser. In turn the artist gave the marquis one of his miniatures as a gift. Lafayette later wrote that the portrait was a "very high specimen of the state of arts in America."

Fraser received his artistic training at the age of 13 when he studied with Thomas Coram. He was educated at the Classical Academy, which in time became the College of Charleston. For 11 years he was a lawyer before giving up his practice in 1818 to devote himself to art full time.

As a miniaturist, he became quickly known in Charleston, and he captured the essence of many of the city's most distinguished citizens. His color was relatively flat, but his compositions were filled with linear detail, and he was known for his delicate, lyrically stylized art.

Fraser had many other talents as well, not only as an attorney. He distinguished himself as a civil leader, and he was also a designer, having provided the plans for the steeple on St. John's Lutheran Church at 10 Archdale St. In 1854 he wrote a valuable history of the city, *Reminiscences of Charleston*. Charlestonians hailed Fraser as "a faithful citizen, a pillar, and an ornament."

## THE CHARLESTON RENAISSANCE

The long, dreary years of the Reconstruction era, when much of Charleston was mired in poverty, did not encourage the growth of great art. In the early 20th century, however, the "Charleston Renaissance" was born. This cultural movement spanned the decades between 1915 and 1940 on the eve of the U.S. entry into World War II. Fostered by artists, musicians, architects, and poets, the Renaissance rescued Charleston from the physical devastations of the Civil War and later from the deep mire of the Depression.

**Laura Bragg,** the director of the Charleston Museum from 1920 to 1931, presided over a salon at her home at 38 Chambers St. In time this parlor became as famous in the South as the salon of Gertrude Stein and her longtime companion, Alice B. Toklas, became in Paris. Much of the Southern literary world, including the novelist and playwright Carson McCullers from Georgia, dropped by.

**Elizabeth O'Neill Verner** (1883–1979) has emerged as the towering figure of the Charleston Renaissance artists. As she once put it, "I had two hobbies, art and love of Charleston. I combined them into one profession." Charleston-born and -bred, she studied art in Philadelphia from 1901 to 1903 before returning to Charleston. When she found herself unexpectedly widowed, she turned to art to earn a living to support herself and her two small children.

Verner specialized in beautiful etchings and drawings of Charleston scenes, as exemplified by her *Avenue at the Oaks.* She chose such subjects as churches, beautiful homes, columns, porticos, and wrought-iron gates. But her forte was in depicting scenes of the vendors in the city market, none more evocative than her pastel on silk *Seated Flower Seller Smoking Pipe.*

She was instrumental in reviving an interest in art in Charleston during the 1920s and 1930s. As she aged, she switched to pastels and worked almost until the time of her death at the age of 96.

Another major artist of the period was **Alice Ravenel Huger Smith** (1876–1958), a Charleston native who was intrigued by the Low Country landscape, with its acres of marshes, cypress swamps, palmettos, rice fields, egrets, herons, and lonely beaches. Her sketches were filled with imagery. After 1924 she worked mainly in watercolor, which she found best for depicting the hazy mist of the Low Country. One of her most evocative works was the 1919 *Mossy Tree.* Her interest in Japanese-style prints led to the creation of the Charleston Etchers' Club.

Another native of South Carolina, **Anna Heyward Taylor** (1879–1956) found her inspiration in Charleston, which she considered a city of "color and charm." Her paintings, in private collections and major galleries today, are steeped in the misty aura of the Low Country. Our favorite among her works is the 1930 rendition of *Fenwick Hall* in which she captured the rot, despair, and decay of this laconic plantation before its renovation.

Another notable artist is Michigan-born **Alfred Hutty** (1877–1954), who began a lifelong love affair with Charleston when he was sent here to establish an art school for the Carolina Art Association. His greatest fame came as an etcher, although he was an accomplished painter as well. His works today are displayed in such institutions as the British Museum in London and the Metropolitan Museum in New York. Our favorite of his works, *White Azaleas-Magnolia Gardens,* done in 1925, captures the luxuriant vegetation of the Low Country that was evocative of the Ashley River plantations.

# 4

# Planning Your Trip to Charleston & Hilton Head

In the pages that follow, we've compiled everything you need to know to handle the practical details on planning your trip: airlines, a calendar of events, visitor information, and more.

## 1 Visitor Information

Before you leave home, write or call ahead for specific information on sports and sightseeing. Contact the **South Carolina Division of Tourism,** 1205 Pendleton St. (P.O. Box 71), Columbia, SC 29202 (© **866/224-9339;** fax 803/734-0138; www.discoversouth carolina.com) or the **Charleston Area Convention and Visitors Bureau (CACVB),** 423 King St. (© **843/853-8000;** www. charlestoncvb.com). The CACVB has five area visitor centers. The main location at 375 Meeting St. is open Monday to Friday from 8:30am to 5pm.

When you enter South Carolina, look for one of the 10 **travel information centers** located on virtually every major highway near the border with neighboring states. Information sources for specific destinations in the state are listed in the South Carolina chapters that follow. A particularly useful resource for travel information is the Citysearch website for Charleston (**www.charleston.citysearch. com**), which provides the latest events, entertainment, and restaurant and bar reviews.

## 2 When to Go

### CLIMATE

Although Charleston can be quite hot and steamy in summer (to say the least), temperatures are never extreme the rest of the year, as shown in the average highs and lows noted in the accompanying charts.

**Charleston Average Temperatures & Rainfall**

|            | Jan | Feb | Mar | Apr | May | June | July | Aug | Sept | Oct | Nov | Dec |
|------------|-----|-----|-----|-----|-----|------|------|-----|------|-----|-----|-----|
| High (°F)  | 59  | 61  | 68  | 76  | 83  | 87   | 89   | 89  | 85   | 77  | 69  | 61  |
| High (°C)  | 15  | 16  | 20  | 24  | 28  | 31   | 32   | 32  | 29   | 25  | 21  | 16  |
| Low (°F)   | 40  | 41  | 48  | 56  | 64  | 70   | 74   | 74  | 69   | 49  | 49  | 42  |
| Low (°C)   | 4   | 5   | 9   | 13  | 18  | 21   | 23   | 23  | 21   | 9   | 9   | 6   |
| Rain (in.) | 3.5 | 3.3 | 4.3 | 2.7 | 4.0 | 6.4  | 6.8  | 7.2 | 4.7  | 2.9 | 2.5 | 3.2 |

# LOW COUNTRY CALENDAR OF EVENTS

## January

**Low Country Oyster Festival,** Charleston. Steamed buckets of oysters greet visitors at Boone Hall Plantation. Enjoy live music, oyster-shucking contests, children's events, and various other activities. Contact the Greater Charleston Restaurant Association at © **843/577-4030.** End of January.

## February

**Southeastern Wildlife Exposition,** Charleston. More than 150 of the finest artists and more than 500 exhibitors participate at 13 locations in the downtown area. Enjoy carvings, sculpture, paintings, live-animal exhibits, food, and much more. Call © **843/723-1748** or go to www.sewe.com for details. Mid-February.

## March

**Festival of Houses and Gardens,** Charleston. For nearly 50 years, people have been enjoying some of Charleston's most historic neighborhoods and private gardens on this tour. Contact the Historic Charleston Foundation, P.O. Box 1120, Charleston, SC 29402. Call © **843/722-3405** or go to www.historiccharleston.org for details. Mid-March to mid-April.

**Cooper River Bridge Run,** Charleston. Sponsored by the Medical University of South Carolina, this run and walk starts in Mount Pleasant, goes over the Cooper River Bridge, and ends in the center of Charleston. The run is one of the best organized and best conducted 10K races in the world. Beginning in 2006, the participants ran over the new Artheur Ravenel, Jr., Bridge, which is 2.5 miles long and 200 feet high. For information, call © **843/792-0345** (www.bridgerun.com). Late March.

**Flowertown Festival,** Summerville. More than 180 booths of arts and crafts, a road race, a "Youth Fest," and lots of entertainment are set in this historic city surrounded by brilliant azalea and dogwood blossoms. Contact the YMCA at © **843/871-9622** or go to www.flowertownfestival.com to learn more. Late March to early April.

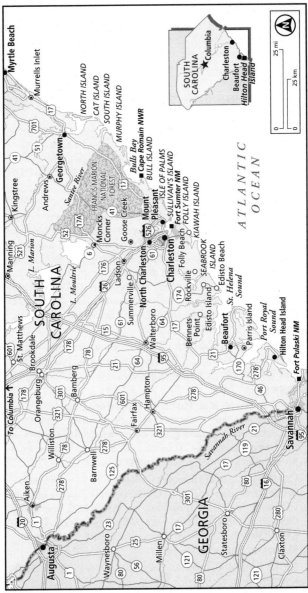

## April

**Family Circle Cup,** Charleston. Moved from Hilton Head to a modern tennis center in Charleston, the Family Circle Cup WTA tournament is one of the oldest on the women's pro tour. For information, call ℂ **843/856-7900** or go to www.familycirclecup.com. Early April.

**Verizon Heritage,** Hilton Head. This $5.3-million tournament brings an outstanding field of PGA tour professionals to the Low Country each year. The weeklong tournament is held at Harbour Town Golf Links in Sea Pines Plantation. Contact Classic Sports, Inc., 71 Lighthouse Rd., Suite 414, Hilton Head, SC 29928 (ℂ **800/234-1107** or 843/671-2448; www.verizonheritage.com). Mid-April.

## May

**Spoleto Festival U.S.A.,** Charleston. This is the premier cultural event in the tri-state area. This famous international festival—the American counterpart of the equally celebrated one in Spoleto, Italy—showcases world-renowned performers in drama, dance, music, and art in various venues throughout the city. For details and this year's schedule, contact Spoleto Festival U.S.A., P.O. Box 157, Charleston, SC 29402. For more information, call ℂ **843/722-2764** or go to www.spoletousa.org. Late May through early June.

## June

**Edisto Riverfest,** Walterboro. The main attractions at this festival are guided trips down the blackwater Edisto River. Call ℂ **843/734-0156** or go to www.edistoriver.org for details. Mid-June.

## September

**Scottish Games and Highland Gathering,** Charleston. This gathering of Scottish clans features medieval games, bagpipe performances, Scottish dancing, and other traditional activities. Call the Scottish Society of Charleston at ℂ **843/224-7867** or go to www.charlestonscots.org. Mid-September.

**Candlelight Tour of Homes & Gardens,** Charleston. Sponsored by the Preservation Society of Charleston, this annual event provides an intimate look at many of the area's historic homes, gardens, and churches. For more information, call ℂ **843/722-4630** or go to www.preservationsociety.org. Late September to late October.

**MOJA Festival,** Charleston. Celebrating the rich African-American heritage in the Charleston area, this festival features lectures, art exhibits, stage performances, historical tours, concerts, and much more. Contact the Charleston Office of Cultural Affairs at ⓒ **843/724-7305** or go to www.mojafestival.com. Late September to early October.

### October

**A Taste of Charleston,** Charleston. Held in 2004 at Boone Hall Plantation, this annual event offers an afternoon of food, fun, entertainment, and more. A selection of Charleston-area restaurants offers their specialties in bite-size portions, so you can sample them all. For more information, call ⓒ **843/577-4030** or go to www.charlestoncvb.com. Early October.

**Fall Festival of Houses,** Beaufort. Frank Lloyd Wright's Aldbrass Plantation is only one of the beautiful homes on this tour. The public is invited to get a rare view of this coastal city's most stately residences during a 3-day tour. For more information, call ⓒ **843/379-3331** or go to www.historic-beaufort.org. Late October.

### November and December

**Christmas in Charleston,** Charleston. This month-long celebration features home and church tours, Christmas-tree lightings, craft shows, artistry, and a peek at how Old Charleston once celebrated the holiday season. For more information on how to participate or to visit, call ⓒ **800/774-0006** or go to www.christmasincharleston. com. Early November to late December.

## 3 Money

It's getting easier all the time to access your bank account while you're on the road. You won't have any problem finding ATMs all over the state connected to the major national networks. For specific locations of **Cirrus** machines, call ⓒ **800/424-7787** or go to www.mastercard.com; for the **PLUS** network, dial ⓒ **800/843-7587** or go to www.visa.com.

If you run out of funds on the road, you can have a friend or relative advance you some money through **MoneyGram;** www. moneygram.com. This service allows you to transfer funds from one person to another in less than 10 minutes from thousands of locations.

## 4 The Active Vacation Planner

**BEACHES**    The South Carolina coast, both north and south of Charleston, is the true gem of the state, and many of the best beaches in the South—even the country—are an easy commute from Charleston. Along more than 280 miles of seashore are white-sand

| What Things Cost in Charleston | US$ |
| --- | --- |
| Taxi from Charleston airport to city center | 20.00–25.00 |
| Bus fare (exact change) | 1.25 |
| Double room at the Planters Inn (expensive) | 275.00 |
| Double room at 1837 Bed & Breakfast (moderate) | 175.00 |
| Double room at Best Western King Charles Inn (inexpensive) | 89.00 |
| Lunch for one at Magnolias (moderate) | 17.00–25.00 |
| Lunch for one at A.W. Shucks (inexpensive) | 14.00 |
| Dinner for one, without wine, at Charleston Grill (expensive) | 45.00 |
| Dinner for one, without wine, at Magnolias (moderate) | 28.00 |
| Dinner for one, without wine, at Hyman's Seafood Co. Restaurant (inexpensive) | 18.00 |
| Bottle of beer | 3.00 |
| Coca-Cola | 1.00 |
| Cup of coffee | 1.50 |
| Admission to the Charleston Museum | 10.00 |
| Movie ticket | 7.50 |
| Ticket to a Charleston Symphony concert | 25.00 |

beaches shaded by palms, stretching from the Grand Strand to the mouth of the Savannah River. If you're looking for seclusion, head for Edisto Beach. For a luxury-resort experience, you can't beat Hilton Head. For a combination of both, check out Kiawah Island.

**BIKING**   The aptly named Low Country has basically flat terrain, which makes for some of the country's best biking areas. The hard-packed sand of the beaches is particularly good for bike riding. Resorts such as Hilton Head have extensive paved bike trails, and many rental outfits operate just off the beaches.

**CAMPING**   Many of South Carolina's lakes have lakefront campsites. Reservations aren't necessary, but you are strongly advised to make reservations for such big weekends as Memorial Day or Labor Day. Campsites are also available in South Carolina's 34 state parks, many of which lie within easy reach of Charleston.

For more information, contact the **South Carolina Department of Parks, Recreation, and Tourism,** 1205 Pendleton St., Columbia, SC 29201 (© **866/224-9339** or 803/734-0156; www.southcarolina parks.com).

**FISHING & HUNTING**   Fishing is abundant in South Carolina, especially along coastal Carolina north and south of Charleston. On the coast, fish for amberjack, barracuda, shark, king mackerel, and other species. In South Carolina's many lakes and streams, fish for trout, bass, and blue and channel catfish. No license is required for saltwater fishing, but a freshwater license is needed. Hunting on public lands is illegal, but many hunting clubs allow you to join temporarily if you provide references. For information, write the **South Carolina Department of Natural Resources,** P.O. Box 167, Columbia, SC 29202 (© **803/734-3883;** www.dnr.state.sc.us).

**GOLF**   Some of the best golf in the country is available in South Carolina, at courses like the one at fabled Harbour Town in Hilton Head. Contact the **South Carolina Department of Parks, Recreation, and Tourism,** 1205 Pendleton St., Columbia, SC 29201, or call © **866/224-9339** or 803/734-0156; www.southcarolina parks.com. Ask for the "South Carolina Golf Guide."

**THE LAKES**   South Carolina's rivers feed lakes all over the state, offering plentiful opportunities for boating, fishing, and camping. With 450 miles of shoreline, the lakes are a magnet for commercial development. While lakeside resort communities are booming, 70% of the lakeshore is slated to remain in a natural state. Many operators and marinas rent boats and watercraft. For information about staying lakeside, contact the **South Carolina Department of Parks, Recreation, and Tourism,** 1205 Pendleton St., Columbia, SC 29201, or call © **866/224-9339** (www.southcarolinaparks.com).

**STATE PARKS**   Camping, fishing, boating, and extensive hiking are available in South Carolina's many state parks, including those in and around Charleston (in particular Francis Marion National Forest). Cabin accommodations are rented all year in 14 of the 34 parks. All cabins are heated, air-conditioned, and fully equipped with cooking utensils, tableware, and linens. Rates range from $60 to $144 per night or $288 to $959 per week. Cabins can accommodate anywhere from 4 to 12 people. Advance reservations are necessary for summer. For full details, contact **South Carolina State Parks,** 1205 Pendleton St., Columbia, SC 29201 (© **866/224-9339;** www.southcarolinaparks.com).

## 5 Specialized Travel Resources

The Charleston telephone directory contains a special section of community service numbers. It's quite comprehensive and includes services for most of these groups.

**TRAVELERS WITH DISABILITIES**    South Carolina has numerous agencies that assist people with disabilities. For specific information, call the **South Carolina Disability Resources** (© 843/795-3951; www.sciway.net). Two other agencies that may prove to be helpful are the **South Carolina Protection & Advocacy System for the Handicapped** (© 803/782-0639), and the **Commission for the Blind** (© 803/898-8800; www.sccb.state.sc.us). For transportation within South Carolina individuals with disabilities can contact **Wheelchair Getaways, Inc.** (© 866/288-8118 or 864/271-3127; www.wheelchairgetaways.com).

**GAY & LESBIAN TRAVELERS**    The most important gay center in the state is the **South Carolina Pride Center,** 1108 Woodrow St., Columbia, SC 29205 (© 803/771-7713; www.scglpm.org). It's open on Wednesday and Sunday from 1 to 6pm, on Friday from 7 to 11pm, and on Saturday from 1 to 8pm. On the premises are archives, a "gay pride" shop, an inventory of films, and a meeting space.

**SENIOR TRAVEL**    Seniors may want to contact the **Retired Senior Volunteer Program** (© 803/252-7734; www.senior resourcesinc.org). When you're sightseeing or attending entertainment events, always inquire about discounts for seniors; they're plentiful.

**FOR FAMILIES**    A great vacation idea is to rent a cabin in one of South Carolina's state parks, including reserves around Charleston. For rates, see "State Parks," above. For details on advance reservations and on accommodations at the 14 other state parks, contact **South Carolina State Parks,** 1205 Pendleton St., Columbia, SC 29201 (© 803/734-0156; www.southcarolinaparks.com).

## 6 Getting There

**BY PLANE**    **American Airlines** and **American Eagle** (© 800/ 433-7300; www.aa.com), **Continental Airlines** (© 800/523-3273; www.continental.com), **Delta Air Lines** and **Delta Connection** (© 800/221-1212; www.delta.com), **United Airlines** and **United Express** (© 800/241-6522; www.united.com), and **US Airways**

(© 800/428-4322; www.usairways.com) are the major airlines serving South Carolina. **Myrtle Beach** has scheduled air service via Continental, Delta, US Airways, AirTran (© 800/247-8726; www.airtran.com), and Spirit (© 800/772-7117; www.spiritair.com). You can fly into **Charleston** on Continental, Delta, United and United Express, and US Airways. If you're traveling to **Hilton Head,** you have the option of flying US Airways directly to the island or flying into the Savannah (Georgia) International Airport via Continental or Delta, then driving or taking a limousine to Hilton Head, which is 1 hour away.

**BY CAR**    Interstate 95 enters South Carolina from the north near Dillon and runs straight through the state to Hardeeville on the Georgia border. The major east-west artery is I-26, running from Charleston northwest through Columbia and on up to Hendersonville, North Carolina. U.S. 17 runs along the coast, and I-85 crosses the northwestern region of the state.

South Carolina furnishes excellent travel information to motorists, and there are well-equipped, efficiently staffed visitor centers at the state border on most major highways. If you have a cellular phone in your car and need help, dial © *47 (HP) for Highway Patrol Assistance.

**BY TRAIN**    South Carolina is on the **Amtrak** (© **800/USA-RAIL;** www.amtrak.com) New York–Miami and New York–Tampa runs, serving Charleston, among other South Carolina cities. Amtrak also has tour packages that include hotel, breakfast, and historic-site tours in Charleston at bargain rates. Be sure to ask about the money-saving "All Aboard America" regional fares or any other current fare specials. Amtrak also offers attractively priced rail/drive packages in the Carolinas.

**BY BUS**    Greyhound (© **800/231-2222;** www.greyhound.com) has good direct service to major cities such as Charleston from out of state, with connections to almost any destination. With a 21-day advance purchase, you can get a discounted "Go Anywhere" fare (some day-of-the-week restrictions apply). Call for information and schedules, or contact the Greyhound depot in your area.

## 7 Getting Around

**BY PLANE**    **Delta Air Lines** and **US Airways** (see "Getting There," above) both have flights within South Carolina, although connections are sometimes awkward.

**BY CAR**   South Carolina has a network of exceptionally good roads. Even when you leave the major highways for the state-maintained roadways, driving is easy on well-maintained roads. **AAA** services are available through the Carolina Motor Club in Charleston at © **864/421-9510.**

In South Carolina, vehicles must use headlights when windshield wipers are in use as a result of inclement weather. Remember that drivers and front-seat passengers must wear seat belts.

---

## *FAST FACTS:* South Carolina

*Area Code*   It's **843** for Charleston and the South Carolina coast.

*Emergencies*   Dial © **911** for police, ambulance, paramedics, and the fire department. You can also dial © **0** (zero, *not* the letter *O*) and ask the operator to connect you to emergency services. Travelers Aid can also be helpful; check local telephone directories.

*Fishing*   A **fishing hot line** (© **800/ASK-FISH**) gives you an up-to-date fishing report on South Carolina's major lakes, as well as information on fishing regulations. For more information, contact **South Carolina Deptartment of Natural Resources,** P.O. Box 167, Columbia, SC 29202 (© **803/734-3886;** www.dnr.state.sc.us).

*Liquor Laws*   The minimum drinking age is 21. Some restaurants are licensed to serve only beer and wine, but a great many offer those plus liquor in mini-bottles, which can be added to cocktail mixers. Beer and wine are sold in grocery stores 7 days a week, but all package liquor is offered through local government-controlled stores, commonly called "ABC" (Alcoholic Beverage Control Commission) stores, which are closed on Sundays.

*Newspapers & Magazines*   The major paper in the Low Country is the *Charleston Post and Courier* (www.charleston.net).

*Police*   In an emergency, call © **911** (no coin required in pay phones).

*Taxes*   South Carolina has a 5% sales tax and the city of Charleston adds a 2% accommodations tax (room or occupancy tax) to your hotel bill. Charleston County's sales tax, however, is 5.5%.

*Time Zone*   South Carolina is in the Eastern Standard Time zone and goes on daylight saving time in summer.

*Weather*   Phone © **803/822-8135** for an update.

# 5

# Getting to Know Charleston

South Carolina's grandest and most intriguing city—in fact, one of the most spectacular cities to visit in America—is really a series of communities and islands centered around a historic core. First-time visitors will quickly get the hang of it, and locals are quick to make them feel at home.

This chapter provides a brief orientation to Charleston and a preview of its most important neighborhoods. It also tells you the best ways of getting around and concludes with some fast facts covering everything from hot lines to what to do if you get a toothache.

## 1 Orientation

### ARRIVING

**BY PLANE**   See "Getting There," in chapter 4. **Charleston International Airport** is in North Charleston on I-26, about 12 miles west of the city. Taxi fare into the city runs about $25, and the airport **shuttle service** (© **843/767-1100**) has a $10 fare. All major car-rental facilities, including Hertz and Avis, are available at the airport. If you're driving, follow the airport-access road to I-26 into the heart of Charleston.

**BY CAR**   The main north-south coastal route, U.S. 17, passes through Charleston; I-26 runs northwest to southeast, ending in Charleston. Charleston is 120 miles southeast of Columbia via I-26 and 98 miles south of Myrtle Beach via U.S. 17.

**BY TRAIN**   Amtrak (© **800/USA-RAIL;** www.amtrak.com) trains arrive at 4565 Gaynor Ave., North Charleston.

### VISITOR INFORMATION

**Charleston Area Convention and Visitors Bureau (CACVB),** 375 Meeting St., Charleston, SC 29402 (© **843/853-8000;** www.charlestoncvb.com), just across from the Charleston Museum, provides maps, brochures, and access to South Carolina Automated Ticketing. The helpful staff can also assist you in finding accommodations. Numerous tours depart hourly from the Visitors Bureau, and restroom facilities, as well as parking, are available. Be sure to allow time to view the 24-minute multi-image presentation *Forever Charleston* and pick up a copy of the visitor's guide. The center is open daily from 8:30am to 5:30pm (closing at 5pm Nov–Feb; closed Christmas Day, New Year's Day, and Thanksgiving Day).

## CITY LAYOUT

Charleston's streets are laid out in an easy-to-follow grid pattern. The main north–south thoroughfares are King, Meeting, and East Bay streets. Tradd, Broad, Queen, and Calhoun streets cross the city from east to west. South of Broad Street, East Bay becomes East Battery.

Unlike most cities, Charleston offers a most helpful map, and it's distributed free. *The Map Guide—Charleston* includes the streets of the historic district as well as surrounding areas, and offers tips on shopping, tours, and what to see and do. Maps are available at the **Visitor Reception & Transportation Center,** 375 Meeting St., at John Street (© **843/853-8000**).

# THE NEIGHBORHOODS IN BRIEF

**The Historic District**    In 1860, according to one Charlestonian, "South Carolina seceded from the Union, Charleston seceded from South Carolina, and south of Broad Street seceded from Charleston." The city preserves its early years at its southernmost point: the conjunction of the Cooper and Ashley rivers. The White Point Gardens, right in the elbow of the two rivers, provide a sort of gateway into this area, where virtually every home is of historic or architectural interest. Between Broad Street and Murray Boulevard (which runs along the south waterfront), you'll find such sightseeing highlights as St. Michael's Episcopal Church, the Edmondston-Alston House, the Heyward-Washington House, Catfish Row, and the Nathaniel Russell House.

**Downtown**    Extending north from Broad Street to Marion Square at the intersection of Calhoun and Meeting streets, this area encloses noteworthy points of interest, good shopping, and a gaggle of historic churches. Just a few of its highlights are the Old City Market, the Dock Street Theatre, Market Hall, the Old Powder Magazine, Congregation Beth Elohim, the French Huguenot Church, St. John's Church, and the Unitarian church.

**Above Marion Square**    The visitor center is located on Meeting Street north of Calhoun. The Charleston Museum is just across the street, and the Aiken-Rhett House, Joseph Manigault House, and

Old Citadel are within easy walking distance in the area bounded by Calhoun Street to the south and Mary Street to the north.

**North Charleston** Charleston International Airport is at the point where I-26 and I-526 intersect. This makes North Charleston a Low Country transportation hub. Primarily a residential and industrial community, it lacks the charms of the historic district. It's also the home of the North Charleston Coliseum, the largest indoor entertainment venue in South Carolina.

**Mount Pleasant** East of the Cooper River, just minutes from the heart of the historic district, this community is worth a detour and it's now linked by a bridge. It encloses a historic district along the riverfront known as the Old Village, which is on the National Register's list of buildings. Its major attraction is Patriots Point, the world's largest naval and maritime museum; it's also the home of the aircraft carrier USS *Yorktown*.

**Outlying Areas** Within easy reach of the city are Boone Hall Plantation, Fort Moultrie, and the public beaches at Sullivan's Island and the Isle of Palms. Head west across the Ashley River Bridge to pay tribute to Charleston's birth at Charles Towne Landing, and visit such highlights as Drayton Hall, Magnolia Plantation, and Middleton Place.

## 2 Getting Around

**BY BUS** City bus fares are $1.25, and service is available daily from 5:35am to 10pm (until 1am to North Charleston). Between 9am and 3:30pm and after 6pm, seniors pay 60¢. The fare for persons with disabilities (all day) is 30¢. Exact change is required. For route and schedule information, call © **843/724-7420.**

**BY TROLLEY** The **Downtown Area Shuttle (DASH)** is the quickest way to get around the main downtown area daily. The fare is $1.25, and you'll need exact change. A day pass costs $4. For hours and routes, call © **843/724-7420.**

**BY TAXI** Leading taxi companies are **Yellow Cab** (© **843/577-6565**) and **Safety Cab** (© **843/722-4066**). Each company has its own fare structure. Within the city, however, fares seldom exceed $3 or $4. You must call for a taxi; there are no pickups on the street.

**BY CAR** If you're staying in the city proper, park your car and save it for day trips to outlying areas. You'll find **parking facilities** scattered about the city, with some of the most convenient at Hutson Street and Calhoun Street, both of which are near Marion

Square; on King Street between Queen and Broad; and on George Street between King and Meeting. If you can't find space on the street to park, the two most centrally located **garages** are on Wentworth Street (② **843/724-7383**) and at Concord and Cumberland (② **843/724-7387**). Charges are $8 all day.

Leading car-rental companies are **Avis** (② **800/331-1212** or 843/767-7030), **Budget** (② **800/527-0700,** 843/767-7051 at the airport, 843/760-1410 in North Charleston, or 843/577-5195 downtown), and **Hertz** (② **800/654-3131** or 843/767-4554).

---

## *FAST FACTS:* Charleston

*American Express* The local American Express office is at 10 Carriage Lane (② **843/556-9051**), open Monday to Friday from 9am to 5pm.

*Camera Repair* The best option is **Focal Point,** 4 Apollo Rd. (② **843/571-3886**), open Monday to Thursday from 9am to 1pm and 2 to 5pm, and on Friday from 9am to noon.

*Car Rentals* See "Getting Around," above.

*Climate* See "When to Go," in chapter 4.

*Dentist* Consult **Palmetto Dental Clinics,** 34 Morris St. (② **843/ 577-9444**).

*Doctor* For a physician referral or 24-hour emergency-room treatment, contact **Charleston Memorial Hospital,** 326 Calhoun St. (② **843/792-2300**); or **Roper Hospital,** 316 Calhoun St. (② **843/724-2000**). Contact **Doctor's Care** (② **843/556-5585**) for the names of walk-in clinics.

*Emergencies* In an emergency, dial ② **911.** If the situation isn't life threatening, call ② **843/577-7070** for the fire department or ② **843/577-7077** for the police.

*Eyeglass Repair* Try **Jackson Davenport Vision,** 379 King St. (② **843/722-4416**), open Monday to Friday 9am to 3pm and Saturday 9am to 5pm.

*Hospitals* Local hospitals operating 24-hour emergency rooms include **AMI East Cooper Community Hospital,** 1200 Johnnie Dodds Blvd., Mount Pleasant (② **843/881-0100**); **Charleston Memorial Hospital,** 326 Calhoun St. (② **843/792-2300**); and **Medical University of South Carolina,** 171 Ashley Ave. (② **843/ 792-1414**). For medical emergencies, call ② **911.**

*Hot Lines* Crisis counseling is available at ② **843/744-HELP.**

**Newspapers & Magazines** The *Post and Courier* is the local daily.

**Pharmacies** Try **CVS**, 1603 Hwy. 17 N. (© **843/971-0764**), open Monday to Saturday from 8am to 10pm and on Sunday from 10am to 8pm.

**Post Office** The main post office is at 83 Broad St. (© **843/ 577-0688**), open Monday to Friday from 9am to 5pm.

**Restrooms** These are available throughout the downtown area, including at Broad and Meeting streets, at Queen and Church streets, on Market Street between Meeting and Church streets, and at other clearly marked strategic points in the historic and downtown districts.

**Safety** Downtown Charleston is well lighted and patrolled throughout the night to ensure public safety. People can generally walk about downtown at night without fear of violence.

**Taxes** South Carolina has a 5% sales tax. Charleston tacks a 2% accommodations tax (room or occupancy) onto your hotel bill and 2% onto dining.

**Weather** Call © **843/744-3207** for an update.

# 6

# Where to Stay

Charleston has many of the best historic inns in America, even surpassing those of Savannah. Hotels and motels are priced in direct ratio to their proximity to the 789-acre historic district; if prices in the center are too high for your budget, find a place west of the Ashley River, and drive into town for sightseeing. In the last decade, the restoration of inns and hotels in Charleston has been phenomenal, although it's slowing somewhat. Charleston ranks among the top cities of America for hotels of charm and character.

Bed-and-breakfast accommodations range from historic homes to carriage houses to simple cottages, and they're located in virtually every section of the city. For details and reservations, contact **Historic Charleston Bed and Breakfast,** 57 Broad St., Charleston, SC 29401 (© **800/743-3583** or 843/722-6606; www.historiccharleston bedandbreakfast.com; open Mon–Fri 9am–5pm).

During the Spring Festival of Houses and the Spoleto Festival, rates go up, and owners charge pretty much what the market will bear. Advance reservations are essential at those times.

In a city that has rooms of so many shapes and sizes in the same historic building, classifying hotels by price is difficult. Price often depends on the room itself. Some expensive hotels may in fact have many moderately priced rooms. Moderately priced hotels, on the other hand, may have special rooms that are quite expensive. When booking a hotel, ask about package plans—deals are most often granted to those who are staying 3 nights or more.

The downside regarding all these inns of charm and grace is that they are among the most expensive in the South. Staying at an inn or B&B in the historic district is one of the reasons to go to Charleston and can do more to evoke the elegance of the city than almost anything else. Innkeepers and B&B owners know this all too well and charge accordingly, especially in the summer season.

> **⟨Tips⟩  Charleston's Fluctuating Room Rates**
>
> Charleston's hotel and B&B rates are sort of like the weather in South Carolina—if you wait 5 minutes, it will change. Most establishments rate their room prices based on high and low seasons, as well as the type of room you're staying in. High season is from April to October. In addition, the rates also may vary if you stay during the week or if you stay over a weekend. You will find that the cheapest rates are generally on weekdays during low season, which is usually in January, February, and, sometimes, late August.

## 1 Making Reservations

You may make your reservations by telephone, mail, fax, and the Internet. You can usually cancel a room reservation 1 week ahead of time and get a full refund. A few places will return your money on cancellations up to 3 days before the reservation date; others won't return any of your deposit, even if you can cancel far in advance. It's best to clarify this issue when you make your reservation. And always ask for a reservation confirmation number.

If you simply can't afford a stay in one of the finer inns in the historic district, you can confine your consumption of Charleston to dining and sightseeing in the old city. For many people, that's a satisfying compromise. During the day, soak in the glamour of the city, and at night retire to one of the less-expensive choices in the historic district or one of the many clean, comfortable—and, yes, utterly dull—chain motels on the outskirts. See the most representative samples with names, phone numbers, and rates under our "Inexpensive" and "Moderate" categories, below.

## 2 Charleston's Top Hotels

### VERY EXPENSIVE

**Charleston Place Hotel** 𝒻𝒻𝒻    Charleston's premier hostelry, an Orient Express Property, is an eight-story landmark in the historic district that looks like a postmodern French château. It's big-time, uptown, glossy, and urban—at least, a former visitor, Prince Charles, thought so. Governors and prime ministers from around the world, as well as members of Fortune 500 companies, even visiting celebs such as Mel Gibson, prefer to stay here instead of one of the more intimate B&Bs. Guest rooms are among the most spacious and handsomely furnished in town—stately, modern, and maintained in state-of-the-art condition. This hotel represents the New South at its most confident, a stylish giant in a district of B&Bs and small converted inns. Acres of Italian marble grace the place, leading to plush guest rooms with decor inspired by colonial Carolina. The deluxe restaurant, **Charleston Grill,** is recommended in chapter 7. A cafe provides a more casual option.

205 Meeting St., Charleston, SC 29401. (C) **800/611-5545** or 843/722-4900. Fax 843/724-7215. www.charlestonplacehotel.com. 440 units. $259–$539 double; $679–$1,900 suite. Seasonal packages available. AE, DC, DISC, MC, V. Parking $10–$15. **Amenities:** 2 restaurants; bar; indoor/outdoor pool; 2 tennis courts; fitness center; spa; sauna; 24-hr. room service; nonsmoking rooms; rooms for those w/limited mobility. *In room:* A/C, TV, dataport, minibar, kitchenette (in some), hair dryer, iron, safe.

**John Rutledge House Inn** 𝕬𝕬𝕬    Many of the meetings that culminated in the emergence of the United States as a nation were conducted in this fine 18th-century house, now one of the most prestigious inns in Charleston. The inn towers over its major rivals, such as the Planters Inn and the Ansonborough Inn, which are also excellent choices. The original builder, John Rutledge, was one of the signers of the Declaration of Independence; he later served as chief justice of the U.S. Supreme Court. The inn was built in 1763, with a third story added in the 1850s. Impeccably restored to its Federalist grandeur, it's enhanced with discreetly concealed electronic conveniences.

116 Broad St., Charleston, SC 29401. (C) **866/720-2609** or 843/723-7999. Fax 843/720-2615. www.charminginns.com. 19 units. Apr–Oct $290–$350 double, $395 suite; Nov–Mar $225–$350 double, $349–$395 suite. Rates include continental breakfast. AE, DC, DISC, MC, V. Free parking. **Amenities:** Continental breakfast, tea, and afternoon sherry served in upstairs sitting room; access to nearby health club; massage; babysitting; laundry service; dry cleaning; concierge. *In room:* A/C, TV, dataport, wi-fi, fridge, hair dryer, iron.

**Philip Porcher House** 𝕬𝕬    Hailed by *Travel & Leisure* as one of the top B&Bs in the South, this beautifully restored 1770 Georgian home stands in the heart of the historic district. Built by a French Huguenot planter, Philip Porcher, the house was renovated in 1997. Handsome Georgian Revival oak paneling was installed from the demolished executive offices of the Pennsylvania Railroad in Pittsburgh. The one rental unit in the house, an apartment on the ground floor, consists of five rooms, and is rented to only one party (with two bedrooms, the apartment can accommodate up to four

# Greater Charleston Accommodations, Dining & Attractions

SOUTH CAROLINA
★Columbia
Charleston

402

0        3 mi
0        3 km

N

78  ①
26  17  176
O Summerville
78

NORTH CHARLESTON

②
③

41

642
78

52
78

Charleston
Air Force
Airport ✈

61
④

Rivers Ave.

Cooper River

Daniel
Island

8

⑤
Ashley River Rd.

Charleston
International
Airport
⑦
26
526
⑥

526

⑨

Wando River

41  17

⑩

I.O.P Connector

MT. ⑪
PLEASANT

61

7

78

The Citadel ■

17

⑫

⑬

703

Isle of
Palms

30

Sullivans
Island

⑭

17

162

Main Rd.

Maybank Hwy.

171
Folly Rd.

⑮
⑯

James
Island

ATLANTIC
OCEAN

Wadmalaw
Island
700

Folly
Beach

Kiawah Island

**ACCOMMODATIONS**
Charleston Harbor Resort & Marina **13**
The Inn at Middleton Place **5**
La Quinta Charleston **4**
North Charleston Inn **4**
Quality Suites **4**
Woodlands Resort & Inn **1**

**DINING**
California Dreaming **15**
The Dining Room at Woodlands **1**
Gullah Cuisine Lowcountry
  Restaurant **11**
J. Bistro **13**
Locklears **13**
The Red Drum **12**
See Wee **8**
Sienna **9**

**ATTRACTIONS**
Boone Hall Plantation **10**
Charles Pinckney National Historic Site **13**
Charles Towne Landing **7**
Cypress Gardens **2**
Drayton Hall **6**
Fort Moultrie **14**
Fort Sumter Natl. Monument **16**
Francis Marion National Forest **3**
Magnolia Plantation **6**
Middleton Place **5**
Old St. Andrew's Parish Church **6**
Palmetto Islands County Park **13**

guests, ideal for families). It's attractively furnished with period antiques and 18th-century engravings; good books and music create a cozy environment. A comfortable sitting room has a working fire-place. One twin-bedded bedroom has a fireplace. One bathroom has an elegant glass shower and double sinks. A screened gallery opens onto a wonderful secret walled garden.

19 Archdale St., Charleston, SC 29401. ✆ **843/722-1801**. www.bbonline.com/sc/porcher. 1 unit. 2-bedroom apt $250 for 2, $400 for 4. Rates include continental breakfast. No credit cards. Free parking. No children under 12. **Amenities:** Non-smoking rooms. *In room:* A/C, kitchenette, hair dryer.

**Planters Inn** 🏩🏩🏩   For many years, this distinguished brick-sided inn next to the City Market was left to languish. In the 1990s, a multi-million-dollar renovation transformed the place into a cozy but taste-ful and opulent enclave of Colonial charm, turning it into one of the finest small luxury hotels of the South. The inn has a lobby filled with reproductions of 18th-century furniture and engravings, a staff clad in silk vests, and a parking area with exactly the right amount of spaces for the number of rooms in the hotel. The spacious guest rooms have hardwood floors, marble bathrooms, and 18th-century decor (the work of award-winning decorators). The suites are appeal-ing, outfitted very much like rooms in an upscale private home. Afternoon tea is served in the lobby, and a well-recommended restau-rant, the **Peninsula Grill,** is described in chapter 7.

112 N. Market St., Charleston, SC 29401. ✆ **800/845-7082** or 843/722-2345. Fax 843/577-2125. www.plantersinn.com. 62 units. $175–$475 double; $425–$750 suite. AE, DC, DISC, MC, V. Parking $16. **Amenities:** Restaurant; lounge; limited room service; laundry service; dry cleaning; nonsmoking rooms; rooms for those w/limited mobility. *In room:* A/C, TV, dataport, hair dryer, iron, safe.

**Two Meeting Street Inn** 🏩   Set in an enviable position near the Battery, this house was built in 1892 as a wedding gift from a pros-perous father to his daughter. Inside, the proportions are as lavish and gracious as the Gilded Age could provide. Stained-glass win-dows, mementos, and paintings were either part of the original deco-rations or collected by the present owners, the Spell family. Most guest rooms contain bathrooms with tub/shower combinations, four-poster beds, ceiling fans, and (in some cases) access to a net-work of balconies. A continental breakfast with home-baked breads and pastries is available.

2 Meeting St., Charleston, SC 29401. ✆ **843/723-7322**. www.twomeetingstreet.com. 9 units. $219–$435 double. Rates include continental breakfast and afternoon tea. No credit cards. No children under 12. **Amenities:** Breakfast room; lounge; nonsmoking rooms. *In room:* A/C, TV, hair dryer, iron, safe.

# Historic Charleston Accommodations

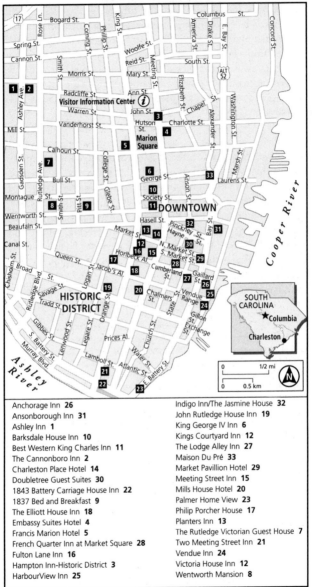

Anchorage Inn **26**
Ansonborough Inn **31**
Ashley Inn **1**
Barksdale House Inn **10**
Best Western King Charles Inn **11**
The Cannonboro Inn **2**
Charleston Place Hotel **14**
Doubletree Guest Suites **30**
1843 Battery Carriage House Inn **22**
1837 Bed and Breakfast **9**
The Elliott House Inn **18**
Embassy Suites Hotel **4**
Francis Marion Hotel **5**
French Quarter Inn at Market Square **28**
Fulton Lane Inn **16**
Hampton Inn-Historic District **3**
HarbourView Inn **25**

Indigo Inn/The Jasmine House **32**
John Rutledge House Inn **19**
King George IV Inn **6**
Kings Courtyard Inn **12**
The Lodge Alley Inn **27**
Maison Du Pré **33**
Market Pavillion Hotel **29**
Meeting Street Inn **15**
Mills House Hotel **20**
Palmer Home View **23**
Philip Porcher House **17**
Planters Inn **13**
The Rutledge Victorian Guest House **7**
Two Meeting Street Inn **21**
Vendue Inn **24**
Victoria House Inn **12**
Wentworth Mansion **8**

**Wentworth Mansion** ✿✿✿    An example of America's Gilded Age, this 1886 Second Empire Inn touts such amenities as hand-carved marble fireplaces, Tiffany stained-glass windows, and detailed wood and plasterwork. If it is grand accommodations that you seek, you've found them. When a cotton merchant built the property, it cost $200,000, an astronomical sum in the 1800s. In the mid-1990s a team of local entrepreneurs spent millions renovating it into the smooth and seamless inn you see today. Prior to its reopening in 1998, it had been a run-down office building. The guest rooms and suites are large enough to have sitting areas. All units have a king-size bed and a well-kept bathroom with a shower and whirlpool tub, and most have working gas fireplaces. The mansion rooms and suites also come with a sleeper sofa for extra guests, who are charged an additional $50 per night.

A full European breakfast is served in the inn's sun room each morning, and guests are invited to relax each evening in the lounge for cordials or spend some quiet time reading in the library. The inn's **Circa 1886 Restaurant,** one of the grandest in Charleston, is recommended even if you're not a guest of the Wentworth (see chapter 7).

149 Wentworth St., Charleston, SC 29401. ✆ **888/466-1886** or 843/853-1886. Fax 843/720-5290. www.wentworthmansion.com. 21 units. $325–$435 double; $415–$705 suite. Rates include breakfast buffet and afternoon tea and cordials. AE, DC, DISC, MC, V. Free parking. **Amenities:** Restaurant; bar; limited room service; babysitting; laundry service; dry cleaning; nonsmoking rooms; rooms for those w/limited mobility. *In room:* A/C, TV, dataport, minibar (soft drinks only), hair dryer, iron, safe.

## EXPENSIVE TO MODERATE

The following hotels don't fit into easy-to-classify categories. Room rates vary wildly, depending on the time of year you book and your choice of accommodations. In certain low seasons, for example, some of the following hotels, such as Best Western King Charles Inn or Cannonboro Inn, might be considered inexpensive.

**Anchorage Inn** ✿✿    Other than a heraldic shield out front, few ornaments mark this bulky structure, which was built in the 1840s as a cotton warehouse. The inn boasts the only decorative theme of its type in Charleston: a mock-Tudor interior with lots of dark paneling; references to Olde England; canopied beds with matching tapestries; pastoral or nautical engravings; leaded casement windows; and, in some places, half-timbering. Because bulky buildings are adjacent to the hotel on both sides, the architects designed all but a few rooms with views overlooking the lobby. (Light is indirectly filtered inside through the lobby's overhead skylights—a plus during Charleston's hot summers.) Each room's shape is different from that of its neighbors, and the expensive ones have bona-fide windows overlooking the street outside. The inn serves a continental breakfast and an afternoon tea (complete with sherry, wine and cheese, and fruit and crackers).

26 Vendue Range, Charleston, SC 29401. © **800/421-2952** or 843/723-8300. Fax 843/723-9543. www.anchoragencharleston.com. 19 units. $99–$199 double; $189–$289 suite. Rates include continental breakfast and afternoon tea. AE, MC, V. Parking $10. **Amenities:** Breakfast room; babysitting; laundry service; dry cleaning; nonsmoking rooms. In room: A/C, TV, dataport, hair dryer, iron.

**Ansonborough Inn** *Kids*    This is one of the oddest hotels in the historic district. Most visitors really like the unusual configuration of rooms, many of which are spacious enough to house families. Set close to the waterfront, the massive building, once a 1900 warehouse, has a lobby that features exposed timbers and a soaring atrium filled with plants. Despite the building's height, it only has three floors, which allows guest rooms to have ceilings of 14 to 16 feet and, in many cases, sleeping lofts. Guest rooms are outfitted with copies of 18th-century furniture and accessories, and the bathrooms contain tubs and shower stalls.

Breakfast is the only meal served, but many fine dining rooms are located nearby.

21 Hasell St., Charleston, SC 29401. © **800/522-2073** or 843/723-1655. Fax 843/577-6888. www.ansonboroughinn.com. 37 units. Mar–Nov $159–$270 suite; low season $99–$235 suite. Rates include continental breakfast. Children 11 and under stay free in parent's room. AE, DISC, MC, V. Parking $10. **Amenities:** Breakfast room; lounge; babysitting; nonsmoking rooms; rooms for those w/limited mobility. In room: A/C, TV, dataport, fridge, hair dryer, iron, safe.

**Ashley Inn**    Partly because of its pink clapboards and the steep staircases that visitors must climb to reach the public areas, this imposing bed-and-breakfast inn might remind you of an antique house in Bermuda. Built in 1832 on a plot of land that sold at the time for a mere $419, it has a more appealing decor than the Cannonboro Inn (below), which belongs to the same owners. Breakfast and afternoon tea are served on a wide veranda overlooking a brick-paved driveway whose centerpiece is a formal fountain/goldfish pond evocative of Old Charleston. The public rooms, with their high ceilings and deep colors, are appealing. If you have lots of luggage, know in advance that negotiating this inn's steep and frequent stairs might pose something of a problem.

201 Ashley Ave., Charleston, SC 29403. ℂ **800/581-6658** or 843/723-1848. Fax 843/579-9080. www.charleston-sc-inns.com. 8 units. $120–$195 double; $170–$250 suite; $195–$285 carriage house. Rates include full breakfast and after-noon tea. AE, DISC, MC, V. Free off-street parking. No children under 10. **Amenities:** Breakfast room; nonsmoking rooms. *In room:* A/C, TV, kitchenette (in carriage house), no phone.

## Barksdale House Inn ✿

This is a neat, tidy, and well-proportioned Italianate building near the Old City Market, constructed as an inn in 1778 but altered and enlarged by the Victorians. Behind the inn, guests enjoy a flagstone-covered terrace where a fountain splashes. Bedrooms contain four-poster beds, working fireplaces, and bathrooms equipped with tub/shower combinations with about half a dozen of those containing whirlpool tubs. Throughout, the furnishings, wallpaper, and fabrics evoke the late 19th century. Sherry and tea are served on the back porch in the evening.

27 George St., Charleston, SC 29401. ℂ **888/577-4980** or 843/577-4800. Fax 843/853-0482. www.barksdalehouse.com. 14 units. Summer $149–$205 double; low season $99–$169. Rates include continental breakfast. MC, V. Free parking. No children under 7. Closed Dec 23–27. **Amenities:** Breakfast room; lounge; non-smoking rooms. *In room:* A/C, TV, wi-fi.

## Best Western King Charles Inn *Kids*

One block from the historic district's market area, this three-story hotel has rooms that are better than you might expect from a motel and are likely to be discounted off season. Some rooms have balconies, but the views are limited. Although short on style, the hotel is a good value and convenient to most everything. An all-you-can-eat buffet breakfast is served in a Colonial-inspired restaurant, and the hotel has a small pool and a helpful staff.

237 Meeting St. (between Wentworth and Hazel sts.), Charleston, SC 29401. ℂ **800/528-1234** or 843/723-7451. Fax 843/723-2041. www.kingcharlesinn.com. 93 units. $115–$140 double. Children 18 and under stay free in parent's room. AE, DC, DISC, MC, V. Free parking. **Amenities:** Restaurant; lounge; outdoor pool; limited room service; laundry service; dry cleaning; nonsmoking rooms; rooms for those w/limited mobility. *In room:* A/C, TV, dataport, wi-fi, coffeemaker, hair dryer, iron.

## The Cannonboro Inn

This buff-and-beige 1853 house was once the private home of a rice planter. The decor isn't as carefully coordinated or as relentlessly upscale as those of many of its competitors; throughout, it has a sense of folksy informality. Although there's virtually no land around this building, a wide veranda on the side creates a "sit-and-talk-a-while" mood. Each unit contains a canopy bed; formal, old-fashioned furniture; and a cramped, somewhat dated bathroom with shower.

184 Ashley Ave., Charleston, SC 29403. ⓒ **800/235-8039** or 843/723-8572. Fax 843/723-8007. www.charleston-sc-inns.com. 6 units. $110–$250 double. Rates include full breakfast and afternoon tea and sherry. AE, DISC, MC, V. Free parking. No children under 10. **Amenities:** Breakfast room; lounge; free bicycles; nonsmoking rooms. *In room:* A/C, TV, kitchenette.

**Doubletree Guest Suites** *(Kids*   A somber five-story 1991 building adjacent to the historic City Market, the Doubletree offers family-friendly suites instead of rooms, each outfitted with a wet bar, refrigerator, and microwave oven. The accommodations tend to receive heavy use, thanks to their appeal to families, tour groups, and business travelers. Breakfast is the only meal served.

181 Church St., Charleston, SC 29401. ⓒ **877/408-8733** or 843/577-2644. Fax 843/577-2697. www.charlestondoubletree.com. 212 units. $109–$339 1-bedroom suite; $180–$590 2-bedroom suite. AE, DC, DISC, MC, V. Parking $16. **Amenities:** Breakfast room; fitness center; babysitting; laundry service; dry cleaning; nonsmoking rooms; rooms for those w/limited mobility. *In room:* A/C, TV, dataport, microwave, wet bar, fridge, coffeemaker, hair dryer, iron, free cribs.

**1843 Battery Carriage House Inn** *☞*   In one of the largest antebellum neighborhoods of Charleston, this inn offers guest rooms in a carriage house behind the main building. In other words, the owners save the top living accommodations for themselves but have restored the bedrooms out back to a high standard. Recent renovations added four-poster beds and a Colonial frill to the not-overly-large bedrooms. All units contain well-managed bathrooms with mostly tub/shower combinations. Don't stay here if you want an inn with lots of public space; that, you don't get. But you can enjoy the location, which is a short walk off the Battery—a seafront peninsula where you can easily imagine a flotilla of Yankee ships enforcing the Civil War blockades.

Unfortunately, if you call, you're likely to get only a recorded message until the owners are able to call you back. Despite the inaccessibility of the main house and the difficulty of reaching a staff member, this place provides comfortable and convenient lodging in a desirable neighborhood.

Breakfast, during nice weather, is served in a carefully landscaped brick courtyard. Evening wine is also served to guests.

20 S. Battery, Charleston, SC 29401. ⓒ **800/775-5575** or 843/727-3100. Fax 843/727-3130. www.batterycarriagehouse.com. 11 units. $99–$299 double. Rates include continental breakfast served in courtyard or room. AE, DISC, MC, V. Free parking. No children under 12. **Amenities:** Lounge; nonsmoking rooms. *In room:* A/C, TV, dataport.

**1837 Bed & Breakfast** Built in 1837 by Nicholas Cobia, a cotton planter, this place was restored and decorated by two artists. It's called a "single house" because it's only a single room wide, which makes for some interesting room arrangements. Our favorite room is no. 2 in the Carriage House, which has authentic designs, exposed-brick walls, warm decor, a beamed ceiling, and three windows. All the rooms have refrigerators and separate entrances because of the layout, and all contain well-kept bathrooms and canopied poster rice beds. On one of the verandas, you can sit under whirling ceiling fans and enjoy your breakfast (sausage pie or eggs Benedict, and homemade breads) or afternoon tea. The parlor room has cypress wainscoting and a black-marble fireplace; the breakfast room is really part of the kitchen.

126 Wentworth St., Charleston, SC 29401. © **877/723-1837** or 843/723-7166. Fax 843/722-7179. www.1837bb.com. 9 units. $79–$175 double. Rates include full breakfast and afternoon tea. AE, DISC, MC, V. Free off-street parking. No children under 7. **Amenities:** Breakfast room; lounge; all nonsmoking rooms. *In room:* A/C, TV, fridge, coffeemaker, hair dryer, iron.

**Embassy Suites Hotel** ⟁ One of Charleston's most interesting historic renovations is this mock-feudal pink stucco fortress rising imperiously above a street corner in the historic district. Bristling with the architectural details you'd have expected in a medieval castle, it originated in 1758 as a fort guarding the then-British-controlled city of Charleston. The form the building has today was in place by around 1826, when it was an arsenal storing gunpowder and weapons. In 1842, it was designated as the headquarters of the Citadel Military College, where military cadets performed maneuvers every day in what is now nearby Marion Park, before the college moved to a riverfront location about 3 miles away in 1922. Listed on the National Register of Historic Places, the building was radically reconfigured in 1995 by adding a glass, greenhouse-style roof and a hardwood floor above and below the once-open dirt-bottomed central courtyard.

Today, richly appointed in a style inspired by the English colonial plantation houses of the West Indies, the courtyard is a reception area and lobby whose artifacts, antique photographs, and displays of military memorabilia are fascinating to anyone with a military background. Even if you're not staying here, consider dropping in for a look at the lobby's roster of antique sepia-toned photographs and the display cases of military and archaeological remnants dug out of the site during the building's renovations in 1995. Elevators zoom up the side of the atrium to the building's accommodations, each of which is a two-room suite with a wet bar, simple cooking facilities, and a bathroom with tub/shower combination. The only drawback to the accommodations is their smallish, fortresslike windows, none of which can be changed because of the building's protection as a historic and architectural landmark. But considering the history of the site and the wealth of insight it offers into South Carolina's past, no one really seems to care.

337 Meeting St., Charleston, SC 29403. © 800/362-2779 or 843/723-6900. Fax 843/723-6938. www.embassysuites.com. 153 units. $159–$249 double. AE, DC, DISC, MC, V. Parking $10 per day in city lot behind hotel, or valet parking $16 per day. **Amenities:** Restaurant; bar; outdoor pool; fitness center; room service; laundry service; dry cleaning. *In room:* A/C, TV, wet bar, fridge, coffeemaker, hair dryer, iron, microwave.

**Francis Marion Hotel** ☆   A $14-million award-winning restoration has returned this historic hotel to its original elegance. Although the 12-story structure breaks from the standard Charleston decorative motif and has rooms furnished in traditional European style, it is not devoid of Charleston charm. Guest rooms feature a king-size, queen-size, or double bed, and the renovated bathrooms contain tub/shower combinations with brass fixtures. The hotel's restaurant, **Swamp Fox Restaurant & Bar,** serves breakfast, lunch, and dinner, and features classic Southern cuisine.

387 King St., Charleston, SC 29403. © 877/756-2121 or 843/722-0600. Fax 843/853-2186. www.francismarioncharleston.com. 227 units. $99–$250 double; $270–$300 suite. Children 11 and under stay free in parent's room. AE, DC, DISC, MC, V. Parking $10–$15. **Amenities:** Restaurant; bar; fitness center; limited room service; babysitting; laundry service; dry cleaning; nonsmoking rooms; rooms for those w/limited mobility. *In room:* A/C, TV, dataport, wi-fi, minibar, coffeemaker, hair dryer, iron.

**French Quarter Inn at Market Square** ☆☆ *Finds*   When the designers of this boutique hotel positioned it in the midst of historic Charleston, they made sure that the architecture blended in gracefully with the surrounding buildings. The result is a brick exterior that evokes the 18th-century private town houses of Paris, and an interior with monumental staircases, elaborate wrought iron, public areas with high ceilings and handcrafted touches, and comfortable and extremely elegant furnishings. Bedrooms are relatively large, with quietly dignified furnishings. Some have fireplaces, and each has a marble- or tile-trimmed bathroom, some with whirlpool and all with tub/shower combinations. The staff works hard to give the hotel the personal feel of a private bed-and-breakfast, offering champagne and pastries at check-in, afternoon wine and cheese, and elaborate bedding that's a lot more upscale than that used by many of its competitors. The hotel has a restaurant on-site, and at least 40 independently operated restaurants are within a short walk.

166 Church St., Charleston, SC 29401. © **866/812-1900** or 843/722-1900. www.fqicharleston.com. 50 units. Rates $209–$299 double. Rates include continental breakfast. AE, DC, DISC, MC, V. Valet parking $10 per day. **Amenities:** Restaurant; bar; gift shop; room service; babysitting; laundry; dry cleaning; all nonsmoking rooms. *In room:* A/C, TV, hair dryer, iron.

### HarbourView Inn 𝒦

Spruced up and looking better than ever, this four-story inn lies in the heart of Charleston, across from the landmark Waterfront Park. From its windows you can see some of the best seascapes in the city. Known for its Old South hospitality and attentive service, this is one of the best and most comfortable inns in the historic zone. Guest rooms have an understated elegance, with plush four-poster beds, wicker chests, sea-grass rugs, and rattan chairs—decor very much in the style of an old-time Charleston sea captain's town house. Expect pampering here, from morning (when a continental breakfast is delivered to your door) to night (when turndown service comes with "sweet dream good night candy" on your pillow). The beautifully maintained private bathrooms come with both tub and shower. The most elegant unit is the penthouse with its whirlpool bathroom, working fireplace, and private balcony.

2 Vendue Range, Charleston, SC 29401. © **888/853-8439** or 843/853-8439. Fax 843/853-4034. www.harbourviewcharleston.com. 52 units. Sun–Thurs $169–$249 double, Fri–Sat $199–$289 double; Sun–Thurs $239–$309 penthouse, Fri–Sat $269–$349 penthouse. Rates include continental breakfast. AE, DC, DISC, MC, V. Parking $6. **Amenities:** Business services; limited room service; babysitting; laundry service; dry cleaning; nonsmoking rooms; rooms for those w/limited mobility. *In room:* A/C, TV, dataport, hair dryer, iron.

### Indigo Inn/The Jasmine House 𝒦

These two hotels are set across the street from each other, with the same owners and the same reception area in the Indigo Inn. Built as an indigo warehouse in the mid-19th century, and gutted and radically reconstructed, the Indigo Inn (the larger of the two) offers rooms with 18th-century decor and comfortable furnishings. Rooms in the Jasmine House, an 1843 Greek Revival mansion whose exterior is painted buttercup yellow, are much more individualized. Each unit in the Jasmine House has a ceiling of about 14 feet, its own color scheme and theme, crown moldings, bathrooms with shower and whirlpool tubs, and floral-patterned upholsteries. Both inns serve breakfast on-site for their respective guests. Children are welcome at the Indigo Inn, but not at the Jasmine House.

1 Maiden Lane, Charleston, SC 29401. © 800/845-7639 or 843/577-5900. Fax 843/577-0378. www.indigoinn.com; www.jasminehouseinn.com. 40 units (Indigo Inn), 10 units (Jasmine House). $109–$255 double in the Indigo Inn; $135–$305 double in the Jasmine House. Rates include continental breakfast. 10% discounts available in midwinter. AE, DC, DISC, MC, V. Parking $6. **Amenities:** Breakfast room; lounge; Jacuzzi; babysitting; nonsmoking rooms; rooms for those w/limited mobility. *In room:* A/C, TV, hair dryer, gas fireplace (in some).

**The Lodge Alley Inn** ⍟    This sprawling historic property extends from its entrance on the busiest commercial street of the Old Town to a quiet brick-floored courtyard in back. It was once a trio of 19th-century warehouses. Today, it evokes a miniature village in Louisiana, with a central square, a fountain, and landscaped shrubs basking in the sunlight. Units include rather standard hotel rooms, suites, and duplex arrangements with sleeping lofts. Throughout, the decor is American country, with pine floors and lots of Colonial accents. Some rooms have fireplaces, and most retain the massive timbers and brick walls of the original warehouses. The staff is usually polite and helpful, but because the hotel hosts many small conventions, they may be preoccupied with the demands of whatever group happens to be checking in or out. A full or continental breakfast is available each morning.

195 E. Bay St., Charleston, SC 29401. © 888/482-9965 or 843/722-1611. Fax 843/577-7497. www.bluegreenrentals.com. 87 units. $169 double; $187–$225 suite. Children 12 and under stay free in parent's room. AE, DISC, MC, V. Parking $10. **Amenities:** Limited room service; laundry service; dry cleaning; nonsmoking rooms; rooms for those w/limited mobility. *In room:* A/C, TV, dataport, minibar, kitchenette, coffeemaker, hair dryer, iron.

**Maison Du Pré** ⍟⍟ *Finds*    Don't be fooled by the artful juxtaposition of the five historic buildings that comprise this graceful inn. Whereas three have been on-site since as early as 1803, two were moved into position from their original sites on Calhoun Street, a few blocks away, in the mid-1980s, under the sponsorship of the Mulholland family. The result is a compound of free-standing antique houses, each built between 1803 and 1830, arranged around two carefully landscaped courtyards on two separate long, narrow, side-by-side lots. The history here is rich: The main building was built by a trader and planter of French descent (Benjamin Du Pré) who lived in the building for only a year before pulling up stakes to work a plantation in western South Carolina. In the 1860s, the house functioned as a Confederate hospital.

The Mulhollands took over and lavished time and attention on the site, adding fountains, brick-floored patios, raised flowerbeds, and more. When you register, you'll be given a key to the front door of the building you'll occupy, as well as a key to your individual room. The most lavish of the suites covers the entire top floor of the main building; lesser suites include a duplex affair in one of the carriage houses. Regardless of which room you occupy, it will be a personalized, well-maintained dwelling filled with period furniture, Oriental carpets, antique armoires, and, in some cases, a four-poster Charleston-style rice bed. The tile-covered, marble-accented bathrooms come with tub/shower combinations. A complimentary Low Country tea, served every afternoon, is included in the rate.

317 E. Bay St. (entrance on George St.), Charleston, SC 29401. ☎ **800/844-4667** or 843/723-8691. Fax 843/723-3722. www.maisondupre.com. 15 units. $165–$185 double; $199–$265 suite. Rates include breakfast and afternoon tea. AE, DISC, MC, V. Parking $8 in city lot across the street. **Amenities:** Breakfast lounge. *In room:* A/C, TV.

**Market Pavilion Hotel** ⊛ *Finds*    Its designers worked hard to emulate the kind of turn-of-the-century exterior that you might have expected from a Main Street hotel around 1906, with stucco and granite trim, big windows, and the kind of exterior detailing that fits gracefully into Charleston's historic core. The interior is outfitted with reproduction early-19th-century furniture and lots of flower-patterned fabrics. Bedrooms are small- to medium-size, but their plushness compensates for the slightly cramped dimensions. Bathrooms are sheathed in marble or ceramic tiles, with tub/shower combinations or separate tubs and showers, and European toiletries. Guests are invited to a complimentary tea, wine, and cheese reception every afternoon.

225 E. Bay St., Charleston, SC 29401. ☎ **877/440-2250** or 843/723-0500. www.marketpavilion.com. 66 units. Rates $299–$365 double. AE, MC, V. Valet parking $15. **Amenities:** Restaurant; bar; outdoor pool; gym; room service; babysitting; laundry service; dry cleaning. *In room:* A/C, TV, hair dryer, safe.

**Meeting Street Inn** ⊛    Charming and nostalgic, and graced with the kind of expansive balconies that you'll really want to sit on, this inn as you see it today originated in 1874, when a German-born entrepreneur built a saloon and beer distributorship on the site. Later, somewhat battered from its role as a workday saloon, it became a brewery, an ice factory, a private men's club, an antiques store, and a restaurant, but its fortunes declined until 1989, when Hurricane Hugo bashed out whatever life remained in the business here. After that, the property lay rotting in the streaming sunlight until 1992, when hotel entrepreneur Frances Limehouse poured time and money into rebuilding the place into a gracious and comfortable inn that's less pretentious, and less expensive, than some of its grander competitors.

The expansive balconies extend down the length of a long urban lot flanked with raised flowerbeds, brick walkways, fountains, shrubbery, and a Jacuzzi. All but about six of the accommodations lie in a modern wing that was added to the original 1870s core in the early 1980s, but the styles of design between new and old are so similar that you'd need to look very carefully to see the differences. Rooms contain reproduction antique furnishings, some with four-poster rice beds. Each has a modern bathroom that looks old-fashioned, with a tub/shower combination. The only meal available here is breakfast, a leisurely and relatively formal affair, although complimentary hors d'oeuvres and wine are served every day between 5:30 and 6:30pm. Do not confuse this upper-middle-bracket inn with the more posh, better furnished, more expensive, and more exclusive Two Meeting Street Inn, which is recommended separately in this section and whose waiting list for reservations is much longer.

173 Meeting St., Charleston, SC 29401. © 800/842-8022 or 843/723-1882. Fax 843/577-0851. www.meetingstreetinn.com. 56 units. High season $149–$259 double; low season $99–$159 double. Rates include continental breakfast. AE, DC, DISC, MC, V. Parking $12. **Amenities:** Bar; Jacuzzi; babysitting; laundry service; dry cleaning. In room: A/C, TV, hair dryer, iron, safe.

**Mills House Hotel** 🐟🐟    Few other hotels in Charleston can compete with the deep-rooted sense of grandeur and history that surrounds the Mills House. It was built in 1853 by entrepreneur Otis Mills, for the then-astronomical price of $200,000 (unfurnished), and received Robert E. Lee as an overnight guest during a difficult night early in the Civil War. Guests since then have included Elizabeth Taylor, Paul Newman and Joanne Woodward, and George H. W. Bush and his wife Barbara, prior to his election as U.S. president. In the late 1960s, its interior was gutted and reconfigured, and although the building's original height was retained, the interior was divided into seven floors (more than in the original building), and many of the building's architectural remnants were salvaged and recycled. At least two of the companies that choreograph walking tours of Charleston make it a point to showcase this pink-sided hotel to participants, and at least one of the companies actually begins their city tours in the hotel's lobby.

Today, many of the hotel's original furnishings remain as valued adornments, and an elevator hauls clients upstairs (an improvement from the hotel's early days), past hallways containing at least two or three valuable pieces of furniture. A concierge—a hip local resident who's meticulously trained in the nuances of the building's history—is on hand to answer questions and handle problems. Operated today as one of the gems in the Six Continents Hotel Chain, the hotel offers small- to medium-size rooms (they're definitely not large) tastefully outfitted in antebellum manor-house style. Each has a bathroom with a combination tub/shower.

115 Meeting St., Charleston, SC 29401. ℂ **800/874-9600** or 843/577-2400. Fax 843/722-0623. www.millshouse.com. 214 units. High season $198–$369 double; low season $99–$239 double. AE, DC, DISC, MC, V. Parking $14–$16. **Amenities:** Restaurant; 2 bars; outdoor pool; room service; babysitting; laundry service; dry cleaning. *In room:* A/C, TV, coffeemaker, hair dryer, iron.

**Palmer Home View** 👁👁👁    This is a media favorite, having been consistently voted as one of the most outstanding B&Bs in the country by everybody from the *Travel Channel* to *Travel Leisure* magazine. Now operated by the third generation owner, the house was built in 1848 by John Revenel, whose son designed "The Little Devil," the first semi-submersible vessel and the forerunner to the submarine.

In operation as a B&B since 1977, Palmer Home is beautifully decorated and furnished with antiques dating back 200 years. Guest rooms are midsize to spacious and open onto panoramic views of Charleston Harbor and historic Fort Sumter. Many of the bedrooms contain four-posters. The most elegant—also the most expensive—way to stay here is to rent the on-site carriage house.

5 East Battery, Charleston, SC 29401. ℂ **888/723-1574** or 843/853-1574. Fax 843/723-7983. www.palmerhomebb.com. 4 units. $169–$225 double; $275 suite. AE, MC, V. **Amenities:** Outdoor pool. *In room:* A/C, TV.

**Vendue Inn** 👁    This three-story inn manages to convey some of the personalized touches of a B&B. Its public areas—a series of narrow, labyrinthine spaces—are full of antiques and Colonial accessories that evoke a cluttered, and slightly cramped, inn in Europe. Guest rooms do not necessarily follow the lobby's European model, however, and appear to be the result of decorative experiments by the owners. Room themes may be based on aspects of Florida, rococo Italy, or 18th-century Charleston. Marble floors and table-tops, wooden sleigh beds, and (in some rooms) wrought-iron canopy beds, while eclectically charming, might be inconsistent with your vision of colonial Charleston. Overflow guests are housed in a historic, brick-fronted annex across the cobblestone street. The inn's restaurant is called the **Kitchen House** (for dinner only). The chef here offers a menu of local favorites with unusual twists. The other restaurant, the **Roof Top Terrace,** offers a more informal atmosphere with a panoramic view of the harbor and of the historic district. A complete luncheon and dinner menu of local and American favorites is offered here.

19 Vendue Range, Charleston, SC 29401. (℃ **800/845-7900** or 843/577-7970. Fax 843/577-2913. www.vendueinn.com. 65 units. $159–$209 double; $239–$339 suite. Rates include full Southern breakfast. AE, DC, DISC, MC, V. Parking $14. **Amenities:** 2 restaurants; bar; limited room service; babysitting; laundry service; dry cleaning; nonsmoking rooms; rooms for those w/limited mobility. *In room:* A/C, TV, dataport, wi-fi, kitchenette (in some), hair dryer, iron, safe.

## Victoria House Inn/Fulton Lane Inn/Kings Courtyard Inn 𝒜

*Finds*   These three inns lie immediately adjacent to each other on a street loaded with antiques dealers, and all three are owned and managed by the same organization, Charming Inns, Inc. Each was built in the late 19th century, of brick and clapboards, and each has been radically upgraded and restored into a well-managed cluster of unpretentious and relatively affordable boutique hotels that boast charm, whimsy, and touches of elegance. Largest of the three, with 41 rooms, is the **Kings Courtyard Inn.** Conceived from its beginnings as a hotel, it has the most expansive courtyard of the three, an outdoor Jacuzzi, and a more extroverted social life than either of its two siblings. The **Fulton Lane Inn,** with 27 rooms, originated as an apartment building above a row of shops, and takes pride in a decor that might remind you of an old-fashioned West Indies plantation, with lots of wicker, rattan, and potted palms. The 18-room **Victoria House Inn,** a late-Victorian brick structure built in the then-popular Romanesque Revival style, originated as a YMCA, and is today the smallest and the coziest of the three. Each inn maintains its own separate check-in and breakfast rituals, but you'll quickly realize the degree to which the three share a common staff and management philosophy. The clientele tends to be well-heeled couples eager to experience the fine food and architecture of Charleston, but overall the prices here are lower than at the other two hotels owned by this chain, the Wentworth Mansion and the John Rutledge House. Rooms are outfitted with well-crafted reproductions of 19th-century antiques, sometimes with fireplaces and antique armoires. Each comes with either a well-maintained combination tub/shower, or else just shower. Breakfast at the inns is served in your bedroom, but guests can opt to take theirs on the outdoor courtyard of the Kings Courtyard Inn. Free wine tastings in the courtyard of the Kings Courtyard are offered to guests of all three inns and are served daily from 5 to 6pm.

Kings Courtyard, 198 King St., Charleston, SC 29401. © **866/720-2949** or 843/720-2949; fax 843/720-2608. Fulton Lane Inn, 202 King St. © **866/720-2940** or 843/720-2600; fax 843/720-2940. Victoria Inn, 208 King St. © **866/720-2946** or 843/720-2946. www.charminginns.com. 86 units. High season $205–$255 double; low season $170–$255 double. Rates include fresh pastries delivered to room and afternoon wine and sherry. AE, DC, DISC, MC, V. Parking $10. **Amenities:** Babysitting; laundry service; dry cleaning. *In room:* A/C, TV, fridge.

## MODERATE TO INEXPENSIVE

In the confused price structure of the city of Charleston, you can stay at the following inns at a moderate or even inexpensive cost, depending on the time of year and your choice of rooms.

**The Elliott House Inn**    Historians have researched anecdotes about this place going back to the 1600s, but the core of the charming inn that you see today was built as a private home—probably for slaves—in 1861. You get a warm welcome from a very hip staff, and there's lots of Colonial inspiration in the decor of the comfortable and carefully maintained rooms. But despite all the grace notes and the landscaping (the flower beds are touched up every 2 weeks), the place seems like a raffish, indoor/outdoor motel, which some guests find appealing. The rooms are arranged in a style that you might expect in Key West—off tiers of balconies surrounding a verdant open courtyard. Each room contains a four-poster bed (the one in no. 36 is especially nice) and provides a feeling of living in an upscale cottage. Avoid those rooms with ground-level private outdoor terraces, however; they're cramped and claustrophobic, don't have attractive views, and tend to be plagued by mildew problems. Conversation often becomes free and easy beneath the city's largest wisteria arbor, near a bubbling whirlpool designed for as many as 12 people at a time.

78 Queen St., Charleston, SC 29401. © **800/729-1855** or 843/723-1855. Fax 843/722-1567. www.elliotthouseinn.com. 24 units. $129–$195 double. Rates include continental breakfast. AE, DISC, MC, V. Parking $6. **Amenities:** Breakfast room; lounge; Jacuzzi; free bikes; nonsmoking rooms. *In room:* A/C, TV, dataport, hair dryer.

**Hampton Inn—Historic District**    Few other buildings in Charleston have been trampled over and recycled as frequently as this white-sided, five-floor testimonial to the changing nature of urban real estate. It was originally built in the 1880s as a railway station and warehouse, servicing the trains that used to rumble by along John Street. (If you look carefully, you can still see the faint indentations in the pavement where tracks were buried several decades ago.) An enclosed courtyard inside contains ornamental shrubbery, patios, and an outdoor swimming pool. Very few of the building's original architectural details remain in place today, having been ripped out long ago in favor of a dignified but somewhat bland replication of a late-18th-century Southern manor house. Bedrooms are conservative, comfortable, and not overly large, with flowered upholsteries and fabrics and a faint whiff of nostalgia for the antebellum glory days. Each has either a king-size or two queen-size beds, and in most cases, tub/shower combinations. The only meal served in the hotel is breakfast, although an elegant and rather upscale French restaurant (**39 Rue de Jean,** recommended in chapter 7) lies next door.

345 Meeting St., Charleston, SC 29403. (*C*) 843/723-4000. Fax 843/722-3725. www.hampton-inn.com. 171 units. Sun–Wed $99–$199 double; Thurs–Sat $179–$239 double. Rates include continental breakfast. AE, DC, DISC, MC, V. Parking $12 per day in city parking lot next door to hotel. Children under 18 stay free in parent's room. **Amenities:** Outdoor pool; babysitting; laundry service; dry cleaning. *In room:* A/C, TV, high-speed Internet, minibar, coffeemaker, hair dryer, iron.

**King George IV Inn**    This four-story 1790 Federal-style home in the heart of the historic district serves as an example of the way Charleston used to live. Named the Peter Freneau House, it was formerly the residence of a reporter and co-owner of the *Charleston City Gazette.* All rooms have wide-planked hardwood floors, plaster moldings, fireplaces, and 12-foot ceilings, and are furnished with antiques. Beds are either Victorian or four-poster double or queen-size. Each unit has a well-kept bathroom, most with tub/shower combinations. All guests are allowed access to the three levels of porches on the house. The location is convenient to many downtown Charleston restaurants; tennis is a 5-minute drive, the beach is 15 minutes away, and some 35 golf courses are nearby. The continental breakfast consists of cereals, breads, muffins, pastries, and fruit.

32 George St., Charleston, SC 29401. (*C*) 888/723-1667 or 843/723-9339. Fax 843/723-7749. www.kinggeorgeiv.com. 10 units, 2 with shared bathrooms. $89–$189 double. Rates include continental breakfast. AE, DISC, MC, V. Free parking. **Amenities:** Breakfast room; nonsmoking rooms. *In room:* A/C, TV, dataport.

**The Rutledge Victorian Guest House**    This 19th-century structure is a sibling property of the King George IV Inn (described above). The Italianate building is kept immaculate; rooms, as well as the inn, are furnished with Victorian antiques and have four-poster, rice, mahogany, or Italian rope beds in double, queen, and twin sizes. The location is a short trek from many of Charleston's notable restaurants, and activities such as golf and tennis are just minutes away. Some rooms have working fireplaces, and most have private bathrooms with shower units. In addition, the Rutledge Victorian Guest House has accommodations at another nearby property, **Number Six Ambrose Alley.**

114 Rutledge Ave., Charleston, SC 29401. © **888/722-7553** or 843/722-7551. Fax 843/727-0065. www.charlestonvictorian.com. 10 units, 8 with private bathroom. No children under 12. $99–$170 double without private bathroom; $120–$190 double with private bathroom. Rates include continental breakfast. MC, V. Free parking. **Amenities:** Breakfast room; nonsmoking rooms. *In room:* A/C, TV, dataport (in most), hair dryer, iron.

## INEXPENSIVE

To avoid the high costs of the elegant B&Bs and deluxe inns of historic Charleston, try one of the chain motels such as **Days Inn,** 2998 W. Montague Ave., Charleston, SC 29418 (© **843/747-4101;** fax 843/566-0378), near the International Airport. Doubles range from $50 to $80, with an extra person housed for $6. Children under 12 stay free, and cribs are also free. **Lands Inn,** 2545 Savannah Hwy., Charleston, SC 29414 (© **843/763-8885;** fax 843/556-9536), is another bargain, with doubles costing from $59 to $79, and an extra $10 charged for each additional person. Children under 16 stay free. At **Red Roof Inn,** 7480 Northwoods Blvd., Charleston, SC 29406 (© **843/572-9100;** fax 843/572-0061), doubles cost $50 to $65, and $6 is charged for each additional person. Those 18 and under stay for free.

## NORTH CHARLESTON
### MODERATE

**Quality Suites** *Kids*    The location of this modern member of a national chain, a 25-minute drive north of historic Charleston, isn't particularly convenient for people interested in wandering spontaneously through the streets of the historic zone, but the amount of space and the in-room mini-kitchens in each unit might make up for it. Each suite has at least one bedroom and a separate living room that can double as a bedroom for teenagers or toddlers. The layout—much like that of a clean, contemporary, and comfortable (albeit blandly furnished) apartment with limited cooking facilities—sometimes encourages business travelers to check in for a week or more. It's also a family favorite. The hotel's green lung and social center is its outdoor courtyard, which is accented with rambling

## (Kids) Family-Friendly Hotels

**Ansonborough Inn** (p. 51)   This is a good value for families who want to stay in one of the historic inns, as opposed to a cheap motel on the outskirts. Many of the high-ceilinged rooms in this converted warehouse have sleeping lofts.

**Best Western King Charles Inn** (p. 52)   This is one of the best family values in Charleston. Children 17 and under stay free in their parent's room. The location is only a block from the historic district's market area, and there's a small pool.

**Doubletree Guest Suites** (p. 53)   This is a good choice for families who want extra space and a place to prepare meals. Some suites are bi-level, giving families more privacy. The location is adjacent to the Old City Market.

**La Quinta Charleston** (see below)   The sturdy, well-designed units here are tough enough for the most spirited of kids.

**Quality Suites** (p. 64)   The suite accommodations and mini-kitchens make this a family favorite.

patios and decks, a hot tub, a swimming pool, and landscaped trees and shrubs. The culinary high point of this place is breakfast, when the staff shows its best and most hospitable side. Monday to Saturday, from 5:30 to 8pm, the hotel offers free cocktails, beer, and wine as part of a "manager's cocktail party," where guests might or might not make attempts at dialogue with one another and with the manager, if he or she actually shows up. Honeymoon and Presidential suites have mirrored ceilings, whirlpool tubs, and king-size beds.

5225 N. Arco Lane, North Charleston, SC 29418. © **877/899-2098** or 843/253-4156. Fax 843/253-4707. www.qualitysuitescharleston.com. 168 units. $119–$169 suite. Rates include free cook-to-order breakfast. AE, DC, DISC, MC, V. Free parking. **Amenities:** Restaurant; bar; outdoor pool; exercise room; outdoor Jacuzzi; laundry service; dry cleaning. *In room:* A/C, TV, wi-fi, fridge, coffeemaker, hair dryer, iron, microwave, pullout sleeper sofa.

### INEXPENSIVE

**La Quinta Charleston** (Kids)   This sturdy, well-designed, and childproof member of a nationwide hotel chain has an exterior that's attractively designed like a Spanish hacienda, replete with terra-cotta roof tiles, thick stucco walls, a bell tower, and references to the mission churches of California. It lies in the rather nondescript jumble of North Charleston, near the busy interstate and close to row upon row of shopping malls, chain restaurants, and fast-food joints. Historic Charleston is a clearly signposted 25-minute drive away. Each guest room is midsize and comfortably laid out with upholstered chairs, a writing (or dining) table, and a sense of Tex-Mex whimsy.

2499 La Quinta Lane, Charleston, SC 29420. © 800/531-5900 or 843/797-8181. Fax 843/569-1608. www.laquinta.com. 122 units. $62–$85 double; $92–$98 suite. Rates include continental breakfast. AE, DC, DISC, MC, V. Free parking. Children under 18 stay free in parent's room. **Amenities:** Outdoor pool; nonsmoking rooms; rooms for those w/limited mobility. *In room:* A/C, TV, kitchenette, coffeemaker, hair dryer, iron.

**North Charleston Inn**   This major competitor of the Holiday Inns is hardly in the same class as the historic inns discussed earlier in this chapter, but it's kind to the frugal vacationer. An outpost for the weary interstate driver, the inn is convenient to the airport and major traffic arteries, and provides free transportation to and from the airport. Charleston's downtown mass transit system doesn't serve this area, however, so you'll have to depend on your car. Your buck gets more than you might expect at this well-run chain member. Although you don't get charm, you do get good maintenance and proper service, and a refrigerator and microwave are available upon request. All rooms have well-kept bathrooms with tub/shower combinations. An on-site restaurant serves three meals a day, and other choices (including a Red Lobster) are within walking distance. The hotel also offers a lounge that features nightly entertainment ranging from country music to karaoke and even comedy specialties.

2934 W. Montague Ave., North Charleston, SC 29418. © 877/464-2700 or 843/744-8281. Fax 843/744-6230. www.northcharlestoninn.com. 155 units. Mar–Oct $99 double; off season $49–$59 double. $10 each additional person. AE, DC, DISC, MC, V. Free parking. 8 miles NW of Charleston off Interstate 26. **Amenities:** Breakfast room; lounge; outdoor pool; laundry service; dry cleaning. *In room:* A/C, TV, hair dryer.

## NORTHWEST CHARLESTON
### EXPENSIVE

**The Inn at Middleton Place** ★★ *(Finds)*   It's a long way from Tara and Rhett Butler, but if your lodging preferences south of the Mason-Dixon line run toward strikingly modern luxury hotels, this is the place for you. The inn is a direct counterpoint to the adjoining Middleton Place (p. 104), an 18th-century plantation that's a sightseeing attraction. Charles Duell, a descendant of Middleton's original owners, wanted a departure from ersatz Colonial and deliberately commissioned architects to create an inn devoid of "Scarlett and her antebellum charm." That said, the inn, with its live oaks and setting on the bluffs of the Ashley River, still has Southern grace and a warm and inviting interior. The guest rooms are filled with handcrafted furniture, wood-burning fireplaces, and cypress paneling; bathrooms have oversize tubs and private showers. You can patronize the inn's restaurant if you're not a guest, enjoying classic plantation fare ranging from pan-fried quail to crawfish cakes. Ever had pecan-encrusted duck breast?

4290 Ashley River Rd., Charleston, SC 29414. © **800/543-4774** or 843/556-0500. Fax 843/556-5673. www.theinnatmiddletonplace.com. 53 units. $149–$260 double; $350–$450 suite. Rates include full breakfast. AE, DISC, MC, V. Free parking. **Amenities:** Restaurant; lounge; outdoor pool; kayaking rentals; bike rentals; horseback riding; babysitting; laundry service; dry cleaning; admission to Plantation. *In room:* A/C, TV, dataport, wi-fi, coffeemaker, hair dryer, iron.

## 3 Other Area Accommodations

### MOUNT PLEASANT

#### EXPENSIVE

**Charleston Harbor Resort & Marina** ⟨✦⟩   Until the mid-1990s, the low-lying land on which this hotel stands was flat and marshy—an undeveloped headland jutting into Charleston Harbor, to the east of the city's historic core. Today, in a site that's immediately adjacent to the USS *Yorktown* museum, it glitters as a sprawling but well-designed compound of hotel and resort facilities that to many clients is a destination in its own right, and unlike anything else in Charleston. Heavily booked by corporate conventions, but with lots of individual clients as well, it services the hotel and dining needs of boat owners who moor their sometimes-spectacular craft in the hotel's 455-slip deepwater marina. Sunbathers can stretch out on a sandy beach that the resort developers built by dumping massive amounts of sand onto the harbor's once-muddy bottom. The hotel's 18-hole golf course (under separate management) is just a 5-minute drive away, and deep-sea fishing is available. Your experience here might be as much about relaxation as it is about exposure to historic Charleston—many guests spend their days getting serious beach and outdoor pool time. But if you do decide to stamp through the city's historic neighborhoods, a complimentary water shuttle departs at intervals of between 60 and 120 minutes throughout the day and evening, depending on the time of day and the day of the week. Bedrooms are spacious and flooded with sunlight from big windows. All contain tub/shower combinations, and most have a private balcony.

20 Patriots Point, Mount Pleasant, SC 29464. (C) **888/856-0028** or 843/856-0028. Fax 843/856-8333. www.charlestonharborresort.com. 131 units. High season $189–$309 double; low season $119–$239 double; $319–$795 suite (year-round). AE, DC, DISC, MC, V. Free parking. **Amenities:** Restaurant; bar; outdoor pool; nearby golf courses; gym; children's programs; room service; laundry service; dry cleaning. *In room:* A/C, TV, coffeemaker, hair dryer, iron.

## SUMMERVILLE
### VERY EXPENSIVE

**Woodlands Resort & Inn** ✹✹✹    This three-story 1906 Greek Revival home is one of the grandest places to stay in all of South Carolina, or even America. Standing on 42 private acres, it is surrounded by moss-draped live oaks and magnolia trees, a stellar cliché of elegant Old South living. The stage is set when you arrive and are presented with fresh flowers and chilled champagne. In the afternoon you can enjoy complimentary tea, antebellum style. Sit out on the front veranda in a rocking chair and admire the Greek columns and the grounds beyond. It's definitely a luxury retreat, with prices to match.

Each individually decorated bedroom has been impeccably restored in an English-country-house style, with comfortable, beautiful furnishings and deluxe bathrooms with tub and shower. Each guest room has its own personality, the creation of David Eskell-Briggs, the New York designer. Some have sitting areas, and others are graced with fireplaces, even whirlpool baths. The executive suites offer the most gracious living of any hotel in South Carolina, with four-poster king beds and all the comforts of the modern era, but the style of a more gracious century. You won't have to go far to eat well: The **Dining Room at Woodlands** (see chapter 7) is one of the grandest restaurants in the South.

125 Parsons Rd., Summerville, SC 29483. (C) **800/774-9999** or 843/875-2600. Fax 843/875-2603. www.woodlandsinn.com. 19 units. $250–$295 double; $305–$650 suite. **Amenities:** Restaurant; bar; outdoor pool; 2 clay tennis courts; spa; croquet; free bikes; business center; room service; massage; babysitting; laundry service; dry cleaning. *In room:* A/C, TV, hair dryer, safe.

# Where to Dine

Foodies from all over the Carolinas and as far away as Georgia flock to Charleston for some of the finest dining in the tri-state area. You get not only the refined cookery of the Low Country, but also an array of French and international specialties.

## 1 Charleston's Top Restaurants

### VERY EXPENSIVE

**Circa 1886 Restaurant** ✶✶ AMERICAN/FRENCH    Situated in the carriage house of the Wentworth Mansion (see chapter 6), this deluxe restaurant offers grand food and formal service. Begin by taking the invitation of the concierge for a view of Charleston from the cupola, where you can see all the bodies of water surrounding the city. Seating 50, two main rooms are beautifully set in the most idyllic place for a romantic dinner in Charleston. The chef prepares an updated version of Low Country cookery, giving it a light, contemporary touch but retaining the flavors of the Old South. Menus are rotated seasonally to take advantage of the best and freshest produce. For a first course, try the candied carrot soup with roasted garlic, or the spicy grilled shrimp over fried green tomatoes. Here the traditional gazpacho comes with celery instead of tomato and is flavored with carrot Tabasco oil. Featured main courses are prepared with consummate skill, especially the truffle oil-fried catfish, or the vanilla-glazed Berkshire pork chop. We're still smacking our lips over the strawberry shortcake soufflé hazelnut tart with lightly whipped cream and Orange Julius Sherbet.

Special attention is paid to the salad courses, as exemplified by a concoction of baby spinach, strawberries, wild mushrooms, and red onion, all flavored with a champagne-and-poppy seed vinaigrette.

Desserts, ordered at the beginning of the meal, include a unique "baked Carolina" with orange and raspberry sorbets, or pan-fried angel food cake with fresh berries and peach ice cream.

In the Wentworth Mansion, 149 Wentworth St. © **843/853-7828**. www.circa1886. com. Reservations recommended. Main courses $21–$34. AE, DC, DISC, MC, V. Mon–Sat 5:30–10pm.

**Peninsula Grill** ★★ CONTINENTAL/INTERNATIONAL
There's an old Southern saying about "country come to city." This
is one case where "city has come to country." The Peninsula Grill, in
the historic Planters Inn, has caused quite a stir in the gastronomic
world—not just in Charleston, but also around the country. Quaint
and quiet, the setting has a 19th-century charm unlike any other
restaurant in Charleston. The kitchen does a marvelous job of
bringing new cuisine to an old city without compromising the delicacies that have made dining in Charleston famous. The menu
changes frequently. You might start with a delicious lobster and corn
chowder, or butternut squash soup. Worthy of your palate are such
dishes as the roasted Cervena venison chops with roast garlic sweet
potato gratin, or the bourbon-grilled jumbo shrimp with Low
Country Hoppin' John and (a first for many) lobster-and-basil-
infused hush puppies. Even the *New York Times* and *Bon Appetit*
magazine have praised "the ultimate coconut cake," based on a
recipe from the chef's grandmother.

In the Planters Inn, 112 N. Market St. Ⓒ
 843/723-0700. www.peninsulagrill.com.
Reservations required. Main courses $28–$34. AE, DC, DISC, MC, V. Mon–Thurs
5:30–10pm; Fri–Sat 5:30–11pm.

**Robert's of Charleston** ★★★ AMERICAN/FRENCH   One of
the most unusual restaurants in Charleston, and one of the best and
most exclusive, this formal choice is a winner in cuisine, service, and
ambience. Chef/owner Robert Dickson brings a whole new dimension to dining in Charleston. His set menu, served in a long, narrow
room that evokes an intimate dinner party, is the town's finest.

Guests peruse the menu while listening to a pianist. The waiter will
explain each course on a menu that is seasonally adjusted. He'll also
give you a preview of each wine that you'll be served. Don't be surprised if the chef himself suddenly bursts through the door from the
kitchen in the back, singing *Oliver's* "Food, Glorious Food." Each
dish we've ever sampled here has been a delight in flavor and texture.
Start with tuna, shrimp, and calamari as an appetizer. The garnishes
served with the dishes—often ignored in most restaurants—are especially tasty here, including roasted red pepper or hot fried eggplant.
Tossed in a homemade vinaigrette, salads are zesty with wild mixed
greens and such vegetables as mushrooms and artichokes. For a
main course, dig into a beef tenderloin with a spinach gnocco and a
vegetable Caponata, or perhaps red snapper served with Beluga
lentils and asparagus. Desserts include the lemoncello olive oil cake
layered with mascarpone cheese.

# Historic Charleston Dining

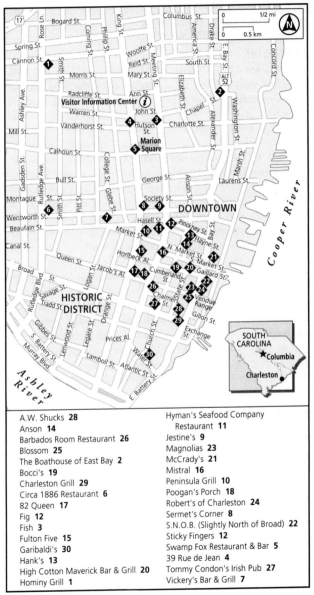

A.W. Shucks **28**
Anson **14**
Barbados Room Restaurant **26**
Blossom **25**
The Boathouse of East Bay **2**
Bocci's **19**
Charleston Grill **29**
Circa 1886 Restaurant **6**
82 Queen **17**
Fig **12**
Fish **3**
Fulton Five **15**
Garibaldi's **30**
Hank's **13**
High Cotton Maverick Bar & Grill **20**
Hominy Grill **1**

Hyman's Seafood Company
  Restaurant **11**
Jestine's **9**
Magnolias **23**
McCrady's **21**
Mistral **16**
Peninsula Grill **10**
Poogan's Porch **18**
Robert's of Charleston **24**
Sermet's Corner **8**
S.N.O.B. (Slightly North of Broad) **22**
Sticky Fingers **12**
Swamp Fox Restaurant & Bar **5**
39 Rue de Jean **4**
Tommy Condon's Irish Pub **27**
Vickery's Bar & Grill **7**

182 E. Bay St. ② 843/577-7565. www.robertsofcharleston.com. Reservations essential. 5-course fixed-price menu including wine and coffee $83 per person. AE, DC, DISC, MC, V. 1 seating Wed–Sat 7:30pm.

## EXPENSIVE

**Anson** 𝕾𝕾𝕾 LOW COUNTRY/MODERN AMERICAN  We think it's simply the best. Charlestonians know that they can spot the local society types here; newcomers recognize it as a hip, stylish venue with all the grace notes of a top-notch restaurant in New York or Chicago, but with reminders of Low Country charm. The setting is a century-old, brick-sided ice warehouse. The present owners have added New Orleans–style iron balconies, Corinthian pilasters salvaged from demolished colonial houses, and enough Victorian rococo for anyone's taste. A well-trained staff in long white aprons describes dishes that are inspired by traditions of the coastal Southeast. But this isn't exactly down-home cookery, as you'll see after sampling such appetizers as fried calamari with an apricot and shallot sauce, or cornmeal-dusted okra with chile oil and goat cheese. France meets the Deep South in one seafood selection: cashew-crusted grouper with Hoppin' John, green beans, and a champagne cream sauce. Our favorite is the crispy flounder, which rival chefs have tried to duplicate but haven't equaled. Some of the best meat selections include slow-roasted duck with duck confit potato cake and local peaches, or else a New York strip with Maytag blue cheese and an onion marmalade. A children's menu is available.

12 Anson St. ② 843/577-0551. www.ansonrestaurant.com. Reservations recommended. Main courses $18–$28. AE, DC, DISC, MC, V. Sun–Thurs 5–10pm; Fri–Sat 5–11pm.

**Charleston Grill** 𝕾𝕾𝕾 LOW COUNTRY/FRENCH  Chef Bob Waggoner, from the Wild Boar in Nashville, has a devoted local following. This is the most ostentatiously formal and pleasing restaurant in Charleston, with superb service, grand food, an impeccably trained staff, and one of the city's best selections of wine. His French cuisine draws rave reviews, earning the restaurant the Mobil Four-Star rating—the only restaurant in South Carolina to have such a distinction. The decor makes absolutely no concessions to Southern folksiness, and the marble-floored, mahogany-sheathed dining room is one of the city's most luxurious. Menu items change with the seasons, and you will be pleasantly surprised by how well Low Country and French cuisine meld. Absolutely delightful appetizers include oxtail ravioli, or else diver scallops with parsnip purée, lobster mushrooms and summer truffle broth. The chef's creativity is reflected in such main dish offerings as roasted veal tenderloin over truffle grits, or Atlantic salmon with German butter potatoes, wax beans, and Chervil butter. For dessert, nothing quite matches the "pistachio mousse martini" layered with bittersweet chocolate.

In the Charleston Place Hotel, 224 King St. ℂ 843/577-4522. www.charleston grill.com. Reservations recommended. Main courses $26–$39. AE, DISC, DC, MC, V. Sun–Thurs 6–10pm; Fri–Sat 6–11pm.

**Fig** ⭐⭐ SOUTHERN/INTERNATIONAL    Mustardy deviled eggs are served while you peruse the tempting menu that ranges from the best Portuguese fish soup in Charleston (complete with salt cod, squid, and chorizo) to roast suckling pig with a cabbage casserole and roasted beets. Charleston got lucky the day chef/owner Mike Lata hit town, coming down from Massachusetts via New Orleans and Atlanta. We like his dedication to locally grown vegetables and his respect for the best produce in any season. We've made an entire meal out of his vegetables alone, including a garlic-studded sautéed rapini or else butterbeans with prosciutto and basil butter. His hanger steak with caramelized shallots and an old-fashioned bordelaise sauce, plus a butterball potato purée, is a delight to the senses. The appetizers are also perfectly harmonious, including Swiss chard ravioli with walnuts and a white corn soup with applewood-smoked bacon and scallions.

232 Meeting St. ℂ 843/805-5900. Reservations required. Main courses $17–$23. AE, MC, V. Mon–Fri 11:30am–2:30pm, Mon–Thurs 6–11pm, Fri–Sat 6pm–1am.

**Fulton Five** NORTHERN ITALIAN    This off-the-beaten-path trattoria is a favorite of discerning locals. The decor is traditional European, and the menu reflects some of the best dishes of the northern Italian kitchen. Tucked away on a small street off King Street, it's an easy walk from the market district. Its antipasti are among the best in town, featuring such delights as roasted duck breast on a crisp risotto cake or a selection of roasted vegetables with prosciutto. The best *osso buco* (braised veal shank) in town is served here with saffron spinach, and a half rack of lamb is aromatically roasted and served with a bean purée, asparagus, and a minty pesto sauce. The chefs also produce an admirable whole seared fish daily, served with new potatoes, and feature a perfectly delightful caper-encrusted tuna with sun-dried tomatoes. Naturally, they pay careful attention to their pastas, as exemplified by *pappardelle* (wide noodles) with roasted rabbit.

5 Fulton St. ℂ 843/853-5555. Reservations recommended. Main courses $18–$29. AE, DC, MC, V. Mon–Thurs 5:30–11pm; Fri–Sat 5:30pm–midnight.

**High Cotton Maverick Bar & Grill** SOUTHERN/STEAK
Established in 1999, this blockbuster of a restaurant caters to an
increasingly devoted clientele of locals who prefer its two-fisted
drinks in an upscale macho decor, and a tasty cuisine that defines
the restaurant as a Southern-style steakhouse. It's also a good choice
for nightlife because of its busy and cozy bar. If you decide to stick
around for dinner, expect more than steaks. Dig into the buttermilk-fried oysters with arugula in a green goddess dressing, or the
shaved beef tenderloin carpaccio. Gourmets gravitate to the "Something Wild" section of the menu, featuring barbecue-spiced seared
flounder, or sliced medallions of venison au poivre. Most diners go
for one of the juicy, tender steaks, which are served with sauces ranging from bourbon to béarnaise. The chef's dessert specialties are
soufflés; the signature treat is a Charleston praline soufflé in chocolate sauce.

199 E. Bay St. ⓒ 843/724-3815. www.mavericksouthernkitchens.com. Reservations recommended. Main courses $19–$36. AE, DC, DISC, MC, V. Daily 5:30–10pm;
Sat 11:30am–2:30pm; Sun brunch 10am–2pm.

**McCrady's** ⭐⭐ AMERICAN/FRENCH    Charleston's oldest eating establishment, where none other than George Washington
dined, is one of the finest kitchens in the Low Country. Praising
both its wine list and well-chosen menu, *Esquire* named it one of the
best new restaurants in America. Entered down a mysterious-look-
ing "Jack the Ripper" alley, it looks like an elegant wine cellar, with
rough brick walls, exposed beams, and wide-plank floors. Cooking
times are unerringly accurate, and a certain charm and fragrance is
given to every dish. We still remember the Peekytoe crab and lobster salad. Ditto for the tartare of tuna with olives, red pepper, and
basil. A perfectly done sautéed halibut appears on your plate with
sides of spinach, and cauliflower purée. Slow-roasted Moulard duck
breast comes with chocolate balsamic jus, or else you might happily
settle for the herb-marinated rack of lamb. Desserts are expensive
but worth it, especially the warm chocolate lava cake with vanilla
bean ice cream with chocolate and caramel sauce.

2 Unity Alley. ⓒ 843/577-0025. www.mccradysrestaurant.com. Reservations required.
Main courses $25–$34. AE, MC, V. Sun–Thurs 5:30–10pm; Fri–Sat 5:30–11pm.

## MODERATE

**A. W. Shucks** ⭐ *Value* SEAFOOD    This hearty oyster bar is a
sprawling, salty tribute to the pleasures of shellfish and the fishermen who gather them. A short walk from the Public Market, set in

a solid, restored warehouse with rough timbers, the restaurant has a long bar where thousands of mollusks have been cracked open and consumed, as well as a dining room. The menu highlights oysters and clams on the half-shell, tasty seafood chowders, deviled crab, shrimp Creole, and succulent oysters prepared in at least half a dozen ways. Chicken and beef dishes are also listed on the menu, but they're nothing special. A wide selection of international beers is sold. Absolutely no one cares how you dress; just dig in.

70 State St. ℂ **843/723-1151.** www.a-w-shucks.com. Lunch $9–$12; main courses $12–$20. AE, DC, DISC, MC, V. Sun–Thurs 11am–10pm; Fri–Sat 11am–11pm.

**Barbados Room Restaurant** ★★★ SOUTHERN    Wonderful ingredients, bountiful servings, and the panache of the chefs make this one a winner. In the historic Mills House Hotel (see chapter 6), this restaurant enjoys a certain acclaim, including praise for serving the best Sunday brunch in Charleston. You'll feel like Miss Scarlett and Rhett Butler on a dining outing in the antebellum South. Few diners can resist Chef Gibson's jumbo crab cakes, and the hand-selected dry aged beef is the best in town. Ordering shrimp and grits will make you a local. We delight in the Low Country black-bean soup and the ginger-encrusted tuna steak.

The Mills House might turn out to be your best dining and drinking venue in town, as it also offers live entertainment. We always gravitate for an after-dinner drink to its popular rendezvous spot, the Fountain Courtyard. You can also enjoy cocktails in the First Shot Lounge, named for the first shot fired during the Civil War.

In the Mills House Hotel, 115 Meeting St. ℂ **843/577-2400.** Reservations recommended. Main courses $18–$28; Sun buffet brunch $18. AE, DISC, MC, V. Daily 7am–9pm.

**Blossom** ★★ MEDITERRANEAN/AMERICAN    Near Waterfront Park, in a contemporary-looking space, this cafe is a showcase for Chef Randy Williams. He takes the freshest locally caught seafood and combines it with the best regional produce from the fertile fields of South Carolina to create a cuisine that has, in some cases, strong Italian overtones. Instead of buying prepackaged stuff, they make their pastas on-site. Their house bakery also turns out rich desserts and aromatic breads. Appetizers show a certain flair, especially buttermilk-fried calamari with a mango and ginger laced chutney or the fried oysters with creamy goat cheese grits and a jalapeño lime honey mustard.

Pizzas from a wood-burning oven are among the best in Charleston—try one topped with oak roasted chicken. You can easily fill up on the handmade pastas and risottos, or else be tempted by the engaging main courses. The chef's specialties include one of our favorite dishes, cane sugar-encrusted salmon. Other delights include thyme and lemon stuffed trout with grape tomatoes, haricot verts, artichoke hearts, roasted garlic, and lemon olive oil. It's hard to find a better warm peach Johnnycake in Charleston than the one here.

171 E. Bay St. © **843/722-9200**. www.magnolias-blossom-cypress.com. Reservations recommended. Lunch $9–$29; main courses $12–$24; Sun brunch $6–$13. AE, DISC, MC, V. Mon–Thurs 11:30am–10pm; Fri–Sat 11:30am–midnight; Sun 11am–2:30pm and 4–10pm. Closed Jan 1 and Dec 25.

**The Boathouse on East Bay** SEAFOOD    Briny delights await you at this bustling restaurant at the corner of Chapel and East Bay. It is a curious blend of family friendliness and two-fisted machismo, appealing to a wide range of denizens from Charleston plus visitors who are just discovering the place. The setting is in a turn-of-the-20th-century warehouse where boats were once repaired. Massive antique timbers on the heavily trussed ceiling remain. On the northern perimeter of the historic core, the restaurant has a raw bar open daily from 4pm to midnight. Shellfish platters are the chef's specialty, including the "J Boat," which can be shared. On it are some of the city's best oysters, littleneck clams, smoked mussels, king crab legs, and fresh shrimp. Every night four different types of fish, ranging from mahimahi to black grouper, are grilled and served with a range of sauces, from mustard glaze to hoisin ginger.

Familiar Charleston specialties include spicy shrimp and grits, and crab cakes with green Tabasco sauce, the latter one of our favorites. For those who don't want fish, a selection of pasta, beef, and chicken dishes is also served. For dessert, opt for the strawberry cobbler or Key lime pie.

549 E. Bay St. © **843/577-7171**. www.boathouserestaurants.com. Reservations recommended. Main courses $20–$29. AE, DISC, MC, V. Sun–Thurs 5–10pm; Fri–Sat 5–11pm; Sun 11am–2pm.

**Bocci's** *Kids* ITALIAN    Lying just a short walk from the Old City Market and long a favorite of locals, this family dining room offers good value and good food at affordable prices. In fact, *USA Today* recently mentioned Bocci's as one of the leading Italian restaurants in the South. Many of our all-time Italian favorites appear on the menu, including a classic minestrone and tender fried calamari in a spicy marinara sauce. The homemade pastas are full of flavor and perfectly cooked, as evoked by the manicotti stuffed with spinach and three cheeses, or else pasta with sautéed chicken, mushrooms, and scallions in a delicate lemon and basil sauce. Seafood dishes we recently sampled include grilled yellowfin tuna, a savory seafood Alfredo with fresh shrimp and scallops, and a fresh oven-roasted Atlantic salmon topped with roasted garlic. There is a special menu for children.

158 Church St. ⓒ **843/720-2121**. Reservations recommended. Main courses $9.50–$19. AE, DC, DISC, MC, V. Sun–Thurs 4:30–10pm; Fri–Sat 4:30–11pm. Closed Thanksgiving.

**82 Queen** ⓡ LOW COUNTRY    In its way, this is probably the most unusual compendium of real estate in Charleston: three 18th- and 19th-century houses clustered around an ancient magnolia tree, with outdoor tables arranged in its shade. Menu items filled with flavor and flair include an award-winning version of she-crab soup laced with sherry. Some of the best Low Country meals in Charleston are served here, especially the Charleston bouillabaisse made with market-fresh seafood or the seasoned shrimp and crawfish jambalaya with tasso ham and red rice. Grilled dinners are also a specialty of the chef, especially the black-pepper New York strip with mashed red-skin potatoes and balsamic marinated portobello mushrooms.

82 Queen St. ⓒ **843/723-7591**. www.82queen.com. Reservations recommended for dinner. Main courses $20–$24. AE, DC, DISC, MC, V. Daily 11:30am–10:30pm.

**Fish** ⓡ SEAFOOD    With a name like fish, you know what to expect. Restaurant owners Charles and Celeste Patrick spearheaded the revitalization of North King Street when they restored and opened a restaurant in this 1830s former private home. Now visitors are flocking to an area once viewed as unsafe to enjoy some of the freshest and best seafood in the Low Country. The menu is seasonally adjusted. We recently dined on the scallop ceviche, whereas other members of our party opted for the seared foie gras with gerkins and champagne grapes. For a main course, perhaps "naked fish" is best—it's the fresh catch of the day and is prepared simply to bring out its natural flavor. Shrimp and grits with chorizo cream, peppers, and onion, is always a winning combination—as is the seared halibut in a cucumber yogurt sauce. An array of vegetable "sides" are among the city's best and freshest.

442 King St. ⓒ **843/722-3474**. www.fishrestaurant.net. Reservations recommended. Main courses $7–$11 lunch, $14–$23 dinner. AE, MC, V. Mon–Fri 11:30am–2pm and 5:30–10pm; Sat 5:30–10pm.

**Hank's** ⭐⭐ *(Kids)* SEAFOOD    In a converted turn-of-the-20th-century warehouse overlooking the Old City Market, this has been called the quintessential Low Country seafood restaurant and saloon. It's spacious and inviting, with a friendly staff that rushes about serving hot food against a backdrop of rich woods and regional artwork. Indeed, some of the finest Low Country dishes in Charleston are served here, especially the regional bouillabaisse and the she-crab soup. One of the widest selections of hot and cold appetizers in town is offered, ranging from a Charleston oyster stew to pan-fried crab cakes with a red-pepper basil sauce. Succulent oysters are served followed by any number of delectable seafood platters, including such delights as fried oysters, crab cakes, grouper filet, and crumb-fried shrimp, every dish accompanied by creamy Southern coleslaw. Most of the menu is geared toward seafood, although the chef can also whip you up a grilled chicken breast, perhaps with a mushroom ragout, or a 12-ounce New York strip with mashed potatoes laced with leeks and scallions. Many guests prepare to arrive early to enjoy the camaraderie of the friendly "Cheers"-type bar. The chefs also offer a kids' menu.

10 Hayne St. ℂ **843/723-3474.** Reservations recommended. Main courses $19–$24. AE, DISC, MC, V. Mon–Fri 5–10:30pm; Sat–Sun 5–11:30pm. Closed Jan 1.

**Magnolia's** *(Kids)* SOUTHERN    Magnolia's manages to elevate the regional, vernacular cuisine of the Deep South to a hip, postmodern art form that's suitable for big-city trendies, but is more likely to draw visiting families instead. The city's former Customs House has been revised into a sprawling network of interconnected spaces with heart-pine floors, faux-marble columns, and massive beams. Blackened catfish (how Southern can you get?) and the side dishes—including fried green tomatoes, cheese grits, and yellow corn salsa—make the platters whistle Dixie. Many diners fill up on soups and salads at lunch, ranging from a creamy tomato with lump crabmeat to a salmon BLT salad. The good-tasting "Down South" main dishes are the favorites, especially the pan seared mahimahi, or the buttermilk-fried chicken breast with cracked pepper biscuits, collard greens, and cream-style corn. A recently sampled dessert wins a prize: warm peach potpie with orange blossom syrup and white chocolate ice cream.

185 E. Bay St. ℂ **843/577-7771.** www.magnolias-blossom-cypress.com. Reservations recommended. Main courses $8–$20 lunch, $15–$25 dinner. AE, DC, MC, V. Mon–Thurs 11:30am–10pm; Fri–Sat 11:30am–10:45pm; Sun 11am–10pm.

**Mistral** FRENCH    In the center of the historic district, this is a quaint corner of Provence, offering live music 6 nights a week. The atmosphere is that of a European cafe or a little bistro hidden on Paris's Left Bank. It's a casual place, where fine products and good cooking emerge as you listen to some of Charleston's favorite Dixieland bands. Peter and Françoise Duffy, with their chef, David Thomasson, offer a good selection of classical French as well as time-tested recipes from Provence.

Onion soup, that eternal bistro favorite, is prepared very well here, as are the oysters in an almond crust with a garlic rémoulade. Look for such typical dishes as the house pâté of rabbit and pork, or else escargots in a wonderful garlic and herb butter. A local bouillabaisse has seasonal fresh fish and shellfish. Veal sweetbreads are a delight, coming in a brandy and mushroom cream sauce with puff pastry. Other old favorites include *coq au vin* (chicken in red wine) and roasted pork with apples and a Calvados cream sauce.

99 S. Market St. © 843/722-5708. Reservations recommended. Main courses $7–$20 lunch, $15–$20 dinner; brunch $8–$12. AE, DC, DISC, MC, V. Sun–Thurs 11am–11pm; Fri–Sat 11am–midnight. Closed Dec 25.

**S.N.O.B. (Slightly North of Broad)** ⓡ *Finds* SOUTHERN You'll find an exposed kitchen, a high ceiling crisscrossed with ventilation ducts, and vague references to the South of long ago—including a scattering of wrought iron—in this snazzily rehabbed warehouse. The place promotes itself as being Charleston's culinary maverick, priding itself on updated versions of the vittles that kept the South alive for 300 years but, frankly, the menu seems to be tame compared with the innovations being offered at many of its upscale, Southern-ethnic competitors. After you get past the hype, however, you might actually enjoy the place. Former diners include Timothy ("007") Dalton, Lee Majors, Sly Stallone, and superlawyer Alan Dershowitz. Main courses can be ordered in medium and large sizes—a fact appreciated by dieters. An array of freshly made salads, soups, sandwiches, and daily specials greet you at lunch. Dinners are more elaborate, including a classic red-bean soup, complete with tomato and jalapeño salsa, or an arugula salad with julienned apples and blue cheese. You can enjoy such main courses as jumbo lump crab cakes over a sauté of corn, okra, and roasted yellow squash, or else sautéed duck breast with a plum glaze. Together with sibling restaurants **Slightly up the Creek** and **Swamp Fox Restaurant & Bar,** the restaurant has launched a private-label wine, dubbed MSK (for "Maverick Southern Kitchen").

192 E. Bay St. ☏ **843/723-3424**. www.mavericksouthernkitchens.com. Reservations accepted only for parties of 5 or more at lunch, recommended for all at dinner. Main courses $9–$14 lunch, $17–$34 dinner. AE, DC, DISC, MC, V. Mon–Fri 11:30am–3pm and daily 5:30–11pm.

## Swamp Fox Restaurant & Bar ☽ AMERICAN

In the recently restored Francis Marion Hotel, which first opened its doors in 1924, this is a full-service restaurant, offering breakfast, lunch, and dinner to discerning palates. Many locals come here to celebrate special occasions, and the attentive staff offers excellent service. The carefully chosen dishes are made with market-fresh ingredients. Named for the Revolutionary War hero, General Francis Marion, the Swamp Fox celebrates a classic Southern cuisine that begins at breakfast with such dishes as grits and country ham. The lunch menu offers a wide array of soups, salads, sandwiches, and appetizers, including such Southern stalwarts as fried green tomatoes with Vidalia onion relish, and fried catfish tails with spicy roasted red pepper relish. The fried chicken is acclaimed by some locals as the best in town. The more elaborate dinner menu features such delights as a peach-glazed pork chop with collards and buttermilk-mashed potatoes, or pan-seared duck leg braised in brown gravy and served with greens over Hoppin' John. Among the luscious desserts are rich bourbon pecan pie and praline bread pudding.

In the Westin Francis Marion Hotel, 387 King St. ☏ **843/724-8888**. Reservations recommended. Main courses $4–$10 breakfast, $8–$13 lunch, $17–$20 dinner. AE, DISC, MC, V. Daily 6:30–11am, 11:30am–3pm, and 5:30–10:30pm.

## 39 Rue de Jean ☽ *Value* FRENCH/SUSHI

You'll think you've been transported back to the Left Bank at this new bistro, which pays homage (exceedingly well) to the classic brasserie cuisine of Paris. Justifiably popular for its inexpensive French cuisine, the restaurant comes complete with a traditional zinc bar, steak *frites,* and a great bottle of wine. Patio dining is an added attraction. The only incongruous note is the sudden culinary departure into Japanese sushi. All our favorite French appetizers are on the menu, including onion soup, truffle potato soup, and frisée lettuce with bacon lardons. Each day a special *plat du jour* is featured, and we always go for that, especially the Sunday rendition of a delectable bouillabaisse. It wouldn't be a Parisian bistro without escargots gratinée, steak *frites,* and foie gras, and the chefs do these time-honored dishes well. Special features are six preparations of mussels, and a whole fish *du jour* from the marketplace that morning.

39 John St. ✆ **843/722-8881.** www.39ruedejean.com. Reservations required. Main courses $7–$25 lunch, $14–$25 dinner. AE, DC, DISC, MC, V. Mon–Fri 11:30am–11pm; Sat–Sun 5:30pm–1am.

## INEXPENSIVE

**California Dreaming** ⓡ AMERICAN    Every table at this restaurant opens onto a waterfront view overlooking Charleston Harbor. The kitchen serves excellent prime rib, broiled steaks, seafood, and such stateside favorites as baby back ribs and burgers. Enjoy dishes that won the West, such as homemade chili, barbecue chicken nachos, and chicken wings marinated in hot peppers. Large shrimp are steamed to order; you simply peel and eat. Steaks are a specialty here, using choice aged beef—you get everything from a center-cut, 14-ounce New York strip to an 11-ounce sirloin marinated for 48 hours in fruit juices, fresh garlic, spices, and soy sauce. The chefs prepare seven different chicken dishes nightly, including one in marinara sauce. The pastry chef is known for his apple walnut cinnamon pie with French vanilla ice cream.

1 Ashley Pointe Dr. ✆ **843/766-1644.** Reservations recommended. Main courses $7–$24. AE, DC, DISC, MC, V. Sun–Thurs 11am–10pm; Fri–Sat 11am–11pm. Closed Thanksgiving and Dec 25.

**Garibaldi's** ITALIAN    Equally popular with both locals and visitors, this restaurant evokes the Mediterranean in its decor. A sibling of Anson's, the trattoria never rises to a status of grandeur but succeeds admirably in what it offers. You are well fed here, and the chefs prepare their dishes with the best produce found at the market. It's a clubby, warm, and inviting place.

The appetizers feature all the Italian favorites such as deep-fried artichoke hearts and stuffed mushrooms, followed by such classic soups as gazpacho or French onion. At least a dozen succulent and often creamy pastas are prepared nightly, ranging from fettuccine Alfredo to shrimp marinara. Nothing is bold or terribly creative, but oh, these dishes are good, especially the rigatoni with chicken, caramelized onions, shiitake mushrooms, and Marsala cream, or the *osso buco* (braised veal shank) with a creamy risotto, caramelized carrots, and fresh green beans.

49 S. Market St. ✆ **843/723-7153.** Reservations recommended. Main courses $9–$24. AE, MC, V. Sun–Thurs 5:30–10pm; Fri–Sat 5:30–11pm. Closed Thanksgiving Day and Dec 25.

**Hominy Grill** ⓡ ⓚⓘⓓⓢ LOW COUNTRY    Owned and operated by chef Robert Stehling, Hominy Grill features simply and beautifully prepared dishes inspired by the kitchens of the Low Country. Since its opening, it has gained a devoted following of families who come here to feast on such specialties as barbecue chicken sandwich, avocado and wehani rice salad and grilled vegetables, okra and shrimp beignets, and—a brunch favorite—smothered or poached eggs on homemade biscuits with mushroom gravy. At night, opt for one of the down-home specials such as grilled soft-shell crab with baked cheese grits and almond slaw, or else country-style pork ribs with red rice and pinto beans. For extra flavor, you can slather your chops with some blackstrap-molasses barbecue sauce. Stehling claims that he likes to introduce people to new grains in the place of pasta or potatoes; many of his dishes, including salads, are prepared with grains such as barley and cracked wheat. The menu is well balanced between old- and new-cookery styles. Dropping in for breakfast? Go for the buttermilk biscuits, the meaty bacon, and the home-style fried apples. There's even liver pudding on the menu. A lunch of shrimp gumbo with cornbread and salmon potato cakes is a temptation on a cold, rainy day, and the banana bread is worth writing home about.

207 Rutledge Ave. ✆ 843/937-0930. www.hominygrill.com. Main courses $5.25–$11 lunch, $8.50–$22 dinner; brunch from $10. AE, MC, V. Mon–Fri 7:30–11am and 11:30am–2:30pm; Mon–Thurs 5:30–9:30pm; Fri–Sat 5:30–10pm; Sun 9am–2:30pm.

### Hyman's Seafood Company Restaurant ⦾ SEAFOOD
Hyman's was established a century ago and honors old-fashioned traditions. The building sprawls over most of a city block in the heart of Charleston's business district. Inside are at least six dining rooms and a take-away deli loaded with salmon, lox, and smoked herring, all displayed in the style of the great kosher delis of New York City. One sit-down section is devoted to deli-style sandwiches, chicken soup, and salads; another to a delectably messy choice of fish, shellfish, lobsters, and oysters. We can ignore the endorsement of now-deceased Senator Strom Thurmond, but we take more seriously the praise of such big-time foodies as Barbra, Oprah, and Baryshnikov.

215 Meeting St. ✆ 843/723-6000. www.hymanseafood.com. Lunch $8–$25; seafood dinners and platters $9–$23. AE, DC, DISC, MC, V. Daily 11am–11pm.

### Jestine's SOUTHERN/SOUL FOOD
When the tourist board is asked "for a native place to eat," they most often send visitors here for some real Low Country flavors. This restaurant was named after

## (*Kids*)  Family-Friendly Restaurants

**Bocci's** (p. 76)    Good Italian fare at affordable prices and a special kids' menu mark this popular family spot.

**Hank's** (p. 78)    A friendly staff, plenty of elbowroom, and a special kids' menu make this a family favorite.

**Hominy Grill** (p. 81)    Locally loved, this grill has been a friendly, homelike family favorite since 1996. Fair prices, good food, and an inviting atmosphere lure visitors to sample an array of Southern specialties at breakfast, lunch, or dinner.

**Magnolia's** (p. 78)    Southern hospitality and charm keep this place buzzing day and night. Lunch is the best time for families and children. An array of soups, appetizers, salads, sandwiches, and pastas is available. But in-the-know local kids go easy on these items, saving room for homemade fare such as the warm cream-cheese brownie with white chocolate ice cream and chocolate sauce.

**Sticky Fingers** (p. 84)    Kids and adults alike enjoy the messy fun of eating the Memphis-style barbecue and barbecue ribs served here.

**Tommy Condon's Irish Pub** (p. 85)    A special menu for "little leprechauns" and spirited Irish singalongs make this a popular family spot, night and day.

the cook and housekeeper who reared the founder of the restaurant, Shera Lee Berlin. All of Jestine's recipes have been preserved to delight a new generation of diners who like to feast on such local favorites as country-fried steak, okra gumbo, fried chicken, shrimp Creole, fried oyster po' boys, country cream corn, black-eyed peas, and blueberry cobbler. There is a daily blue-plate special, and even a green-plate special for vegetarians. If you ever wondered what "red rice" is, ask for it here. The "table wine" is actually sugary tea in tumblers.

251 Meeting St. (*C*) **843/722-7224.** No reservations accepted. Main courses $7.95–$13. AE, DC, DISC, MC, V. Tues–Thurs 11am–9:30pm; Fri–Sat 11am–10pm; Sun 11am–9pm. Closed Dec 25 and Jewish holidays.

**Poogan's Porch** ⓡ *Finds* LOW COUNTRY    If you like jamba-laya, peanut butter pie, Carolina quail, crab cakes, and all those other down-home favorites, a table is waiting here for you in this restored 1891 house, where the decor is appropriately antiquey Victorian. The restaurant is named after a dog that used to stand on the porch greeting guests until he died in 1979. We remember him well. Some diners have reported hearing the tapping of Poogan's toenails across the porch as he greets guests (perhaps they'd had too much rotgut bourbon).

Everyone from politicians to visitors comes here for a good country "tuck in." Fresh local ingredients are used whenever possible to concoct a delightful repertory of dishes—Charleston sweet-potato pancakes, shrimp and grits, roasted sweet-corn chowder, pan-seared breast of duckling, sea scallops, and grilled pork tenderloin marinated for 24 hours. To go wild for your finishing touch to the meal, we suggest you dig into bread pudding with bourbon butter, a recipe that once appeared in a cookbook published by the Baptist Church until the pastor protested.

72 Queen St. ⓒ 843/577-2337. www.poogansporch.com. Reservations recommended for dinner. Main courses $7–$26; Sun brunch $7–$10. AE, MC, V. Daily 11am–3pm and 5–9:30pm; Sun brunch 9am–3pm.

**Sermet's Corner** ⓡ *Finds* MEDITERRANEAN/ITALIAN    With its large windows overlooking a bustling intersection, its good and modestly priced food, and its fun atmosphere, this discovery attracts a young crowd. Fresh, informal, and healthy, the cuisine contains any number of delightful dishes, including imaginative soups, appetizers, and salads. Try the cold cucumber with yogurt soup; or a portobello mushroom topped with sweet pepper, and lavender sauce. Or go for the savory shrimp, crawfish, and scallops with sun-dried tomatoes; grilled filet of beef, or the grilled seafood cakes in a Sambuca sauce. A special treat is parmesan basil encrusted salmon with sweet mashed potatoes. Most dishes are at the lower end of the price scale. Live jazz is heard on the mezzanine Tuesday to Saturday from 5pm to 2am.

276 King St. ⓒ 843/853-7775. Main courses $12–$17. AE, MC, V. Daily 11am–10pm.

**Sticky Fingers** ⓡ *Kids* AMERICAN/BARBECUE    The name says it all. This joint is locally famous for its Memphis-style barbecue, the kind that put those extra pounds on Elvis. The cooks actually use hickory to smoke their ribs. Good ol' boys come here and dig into the mountainous onion loaf or else hickory-smoked chicken wings. Naturally, even the salads served here come with meat. Nearly all diners follow with ribs that are prepared in the traditional slow-smoking process for extra flavor. The hickory-smoked chicken has real flavor, and it's served over dirty rice with cinnamon-baked apples. Lunch specials are featured, and a kids' menu draws the family trade.

235 Meeting St. ✆ 843/853-7427. Main courses $7–$16. AE, DC, DISC, MC, V. Daily 11am–10pm. Closed Dec 25.

**Tommy Condon's Irish Pub** *Kids* IRISH/LOW COUNTRY   Ireland is a long way from Charleston, but that country's spirit is evoked every night at this big, friendly place divided into four major sections, including a 100-seat covered deck. The interior pub with its hardwood bar is where you'll find us, downing a cold Irish beer. With its wainscoted walls, antique mirrors, and Irish memorabilia, it's just the place for the Irish singalongs staged here nightly. It's not so much a men's bar as a family bar, with a children's menu prepared for "little leprechauns."

Starters include crab dip, nachos, or else salads and sandwiches, including an excellent half-pound chargrilled burger. Fish and chips or shepherd's pie are the beloved favorites of Irish people, which might be followed by an Irish potato chowder from a 19th-century recipe. A delicious Low Country jambalaya appears nightly over Carolina white rice. For us, the best items on the menu are the Low Country seafood dishes, especially the local oysters and the Charleston crab cakes. A bread pudding was scrumptious with fat raisins and a warm caramelized sauce topped with vanilla-bean ice cream, although it might be more Irish to opt for Bailey's Irish Cream cheesecake.

160 Church St. ✆ 843/577-3818. Lunch $5–$11; main courses $7–$16. AE, DC, DISC, MC, V. Sun–Thurs 11am–10pm; Fri–Sat 11am–11pm. Closed Dec 25.

**Vickery's Bar & Grill** CUBAN/AMERICAN   When the restaurant owners recycled a former Goodyear Tire Store and made it into this inviting restaurant, they won an award for restoration. Its open patio and convenience have made it a favorite with shoppers along King Street. An unusual appetizer is the Southern-fried squid with a wasabi marmalade. The black-bean cake or barbecue ribs are more typical starters. A jumbo three-cheese ravioli is tossed with crawfish and tasso ham in a garlic Parmesan cream sauce, and the pecan-crusted snapper is slathered with a creamy bourbon and brown

---

*Tips*  **Where to Find Your Dining Choice**

For the location of restaurants outside the Historic Charleston district, refer to the map "Greater Charleston Accommodations, Dining & Attractions," in chapter 6.

---

sugar sauce. A local favorite, a Low Country sauté, means shrimp, crabmeat, and crawfish tails in bourbon butter served over creamy grits and topped with crispy fried oysters. Sandwiches and fat, juicy burgers are also featured.

15 Beaufrain St. ℭ 843/577-5300. Main courses $9–$23. AE, DISC, MC, V. Daily 11:30am–2am. Closed Thanksgiving and Dec 25.

## 2 Other Area Restaurants

### MOUNT PLEASANT

**EXPENSIVE**

**The Red Drum** 𝕣𝕣𝕣 AMERICAN/SOUTHWESTERN    Calling itself a gastropub, a sort of London version of the French brasserie, this restaurant draws visitors to Mount Pleasant. The chef and owner, Ben Berryhill, claims that food wasn't frozen in 1865, and he sees no reason for it to be so in the 21st century. Winner of numerous culinary awards, Berryhill believes in impeccably fresh ingredients. He maintains a constant search for the best produce South Carolina has to offer. The influence of the Southwest is applied to seafood such as wood-grilled salmon with a roasted red pepper purée and a sweet corn pudding in corn husks. The free-range chicken won us over when it was served with barbecued sweet potatoes and caramelized pumpkin seeds. You might also wisely opt for the roasted rack of lamb with a wild mushroom and potato crepe with a red currant pastille chile sauce. All the appetizers we've sampled have been full of flavor, especially the molasses-grilled quail with a cinnamon-roasted cornbread and applewood bacon or the rare yellowfin tuna with a spicy ginger vinaigrette.

803 Coleman Blvd. ℭ 843/849-0313. Reservations recommended. Main courses $16–$32. AE, MC, V. Mon–Fri 5–10pm, Sat 5pm–midnight.

**MODERATE**

**Locklears** SEAFOOD    In business for 2 decades, this restaurant has won a number of culinary prizes in competition, mainly for its oysters, chili, and she-crab soup. It is also the chief promoter in the area of heart-healthy dining. Only the freshest of ingredients, produce, and seafood are used in its repertoire of fine dishes. Partners Jack Anderson and Lance Howard lure you to their establishment with such appetizers as fried calamari with drawn butter or bacon-wrapped shrimp with a soy-and-ginger dipping sauce. A fried oyster salad is an unusual treat, and you can also order a seafood salad of the day. At lunch dig into one of their homemade sandwiches—even a crab burger is served, and it's delectable. Seafood plates, complete with fries and creamy cole slaw, take the prize here.

427 Coleman Ave. ⓒ 843/884-3346. Reservations recommended. Lunch $6–$10; main courses $6–$20. AE, DISC, MC, V. Daily 11:30am–1am. Closed Dec 25, Jan 1, and July 4th.

## INEXPENSIVE
### Gullah Cuisine Lowcountry Restaurant ⓡ *Finds* SOUTHERN
Do you think the vegetable okra is slimy and shun it? That culinary prejudice fades at this unpretentious little dive, today's tribute to the cuisine of the Gullah (as Low Country African-Americans are called). Here the okra pod is elevated to its rightful place in the pantheon of a great vegetable. Gullah cooking is evocative of Creole flavors, and the dirty rice served here delectably comes with fresh shrimp, chicken, and andouille sausage. The okra gumbo is a delight to us, as is the she-crab soup, some of the best served in Charleston. We love the "sides" (as they say in the South), especially that crisp, vividly green okra that not only thickens the gumbos but is served deep fried. Locals come from miles around to sample Charlotte Jenkins's southern fried chicken served with extra cheesy macaroni. Of course, you've got to like fried foods as well, at least for a day, especially the fried oysters that are succulent.

1717 U.S. 17. ⓒ 843/881-9076. Main courses $11–$20; Mon–Sat lunch buffet $8.75 with beverage; Sun brunch $13. MC, V. Mon–Sat 11am–9:30pm (buffet till 2:30pm); Sun 11am–3:30pm.

### J. Bistro ⓡ AMERICAN   Consistently voted best restaurant in Mount Pleasant by the local press, this popular dining venue features a decor that may be best described as a grown-up fun house. The owner/chef, James Burns, decorated his bistro with suspended panes of glass, metallic art, and what he calls "jolts" of color. Granite tabletops and large paintings round out the scene. The place is so popular you'll have to wait half an hour for a table. After 6:30pm, reservations aren't taken except for groups of seven or more.

The menu is relatively short but it's well chosen, good, and affordable—real stick-to-the-ribs kind of fare. The waitstaff brings around the menu tacked to a board. Tempting choices are drawn from land or sea. Look for the daily specials, which might include a perfectly prepared tuna steak with risotto. We like to start with the justly praised frisée salad with lentils, bacon, goat cheese, walnuts, and croutons, or else the lobster wontons. A house-cured salmon tartare with a sweet-potato side is a tasty treat. The sautéed grouper is one of their best dishes, though you may go more Southern and order the pan-roasted double-cut pork chop with roasted shallots and a bourbon glaze. The Sunday brunch is the best in Mount Pleasant. For dessert, go for their chocolate soufflé, the recipe of which has been published in the book *Great Chefs of the South*.

819 Coleman Blvd. ⓒ **843/971-7778.** Reservations recommended. Main courses $6–$25; brunch $15, children $8 (12 and under). AE, MC, V. Tues–Sun 5:30–10:30pm; Sun 10:30am–2:30pm. Closed Dec 25 and Jan 1.

## AWENDAW
### MODERATE

**See Wee** ⟨ *Finds* LOW COUNTRY   Did your doctor warn you about eating too many fried foods? Forget that admonition if you head here. The cooks make an art of Low Country frying, serving the best fried green tomatoes—dusted with corn flour—in the Charleston area. Its perfect accompaniment is a mild horseradish sauce. Cooks also fry okra, oysters, and yellow summer squash. And no one makes better fried pickles than the bubbas in the kitchen. Locals devour the freshest shrimp in the area with collard greens—but, of course. Nightly specials are written on a dry-erase board. You don't have to go fried all the way. Why not the grilled shrimp with a tomato basil cream sauce with lump crabmeat over pasta? It's just assumed that all diners like hush puppies. The waitress told us that "the cook is very proud of his chocolate pie." After sampling it, we know why. *The Post and Courier* claimed that this "arsenal of incredible cakes and pies will bring you to your knees with thanks and praise."

4808 Highway 17 N. ⓒ **843/928-3609.** Reservations not needed. Breakfast $6–$8; lunch $13–$14; main courses $19–$23. MC, V. Mon–Fri 9am–9pm; Sat 8am–9:30pm; Sun 11am–3pm.

## DANIEL ISLAND
### EXPENSIVE

**Sienna** ⟨⟨⟨ *Finds* ITALIAN   Chef Ken Vedrinski is one of the most remarkable in Charleston. You have to drive over to Daniel Island (once owned by the Guggenheims) to sample his wares, but it's worth the 5-mile trip from the center. Although Vedrinski might have been born into a Polish-American family, he learned the culinary secrets of his Italian grandmother. The mixing of Old World and New World is the motif in the restaurant, the design reflecting traditional Italian style through brick archways and the Wine Cave. Urban fabrics and designs such as the copper tile wall behind the bar make the place more contemporary. The dining room showcases bamboo flooring, a dropped ceiling, and an open-air kitchen. Sculptures and other artwork can be seen throughout. The chef likes flavors that "pop off the plate," as exemplified by the braised veal cheek-stuffed shells in a porcini broth, or the grilled rib-eye with an olive oil potato purée and smoked portobello mushrooms with a Barolo wine reduction. We returned again and again for the slow-cooked ranch pork in three preparations with a dried cherry barley risotto, and we fell in love with the aromatic moscato vinaigrette and could pour it over almost any main dish.

Want some real Low Country eating that will put hair on your chest? Opt for the pork and shellfish combo in the form of an intensely flavored guanciale composed of hog jowls and lightly cooked shrimp over hand-cut noodles. That's what we like about Dixie.

901 Island Park Dr. ✆ **843/881-8820.** Main courses $16–$28; tasting menu $46–$64 including wine; ultimate tasting menu $89 without wine. AE, MC, V. Mon–Sat 11:30am–2:30pm, 6–10pm.

## SUMMERVILLE
### VERY EXPENSIVE

**The Dining Room at Woodlands** ✦✦✦ LOW COUNTRY   To get a real feel for the grandeur of the South and for an exceptional dining experience, put on your Sunday best and head for this sumptuous retreat at the Woodlands Resort & Inn. How good is this place? A recent poll of *Condé Nast Traveler* readers rated Woodlands one of the top three restaurants in North America, plus it's the only restaurant in the state awarded AAA's coveted five diamonds. Executive chef Tarker King is widely regarded as the finest in South Carolina, and he is justly praised for taking full advantage of—and in the process helping sustain—locally grown produce and seafood. The location is in a 1906 Greek Revival home, where guests dine under 14-foot coffered ceilings, surrounded by French doors, antiques, and crystal chandeliers.

To truly sample the best of the cuisine here, we suggest you opt either for the chef's five-course tasting menu or, for an even more remarkable experience, his ultimate menu of seven to ten courses.

You will not only be served the best food in the entire greater Charleston area, but it's backed up by an award-winning wine list.

The day begins early here, when breakfast features such delights as lump crab hash with roasted peppers and poached eggs or buttermilk pecan pancakes topped with fresh berries. If you go for one of the chef's special menus, you may find yourself enjoying the most tender beef in the world—Kobe—seared with foie gras; wild Maine black mussels steamed in sake and served with a black-bean sauce; or a free-form lasagna made with rock shrimp, scallops, and truffles. Desserts don't get much better than the passion fruit mousse or the almond tart with fresh berries and apricot coulis.

125 Parsons Rd. ⓒ **800/774-9999** or 843/875-2600. www.woodlandsinn.com. Reservations required. Breakfast $10–$15; lunch $7–$19; 4-course dinner $69; tasting menu $78; chef's table menu $175; ultimate menu $115; Sun brunch $38. AE, DISC, MC, V. Daily 7–10am, 11am–2pm, and 6–9pm; Sun brunch 11:30am–2pm.

# 8

# Exploring Charleston

**O**nce we've settled in, we always head for the **Battery** (officially, White Point Gardens) to get into the feel of this city. It's right on the end of the peninsula, facing the Cooper River and the harbor. It has a landscaped park, shaded by palmettos and live oaks, with walkways lined with old monuments and other war relics. The view toward the harbor goes out to Fort Sumter. We like to walk along the seawall on East Battery Street and Murray Boulevard and slowly absorb the Charleston ambience.

Before you go, contact the **Charleston Area Convention and Visitors Bureau (CACVB)** (© **800/774-0006** or 843/853-8000; www.charlestoncvb.com) for information on tours, attractions, and special events.

*Note:* You can visit six of the attractions listed in this section by buying a **Heritage Passport ticket** for $40 ($23 children). The ticket provides admission to Middleton Place, Drayton Hall, the Nathaniel Russell House, the Gibbes Museum, Aiken-Rhett House, and the Edmondston-Alston House. You can purchase a ticket at the **main CACVB branch,** 375 Meeting St. (open Mon–Fri 8:30am–5pm), or at the attractions themselves.

## 1 The Top Attractions
### A CONFEDERATE FORT & A SUBMARINE

**Fort Sumter National Monument** 𝒜𝒜𝒜   It was here on April 12, 1861, that Confederate forces launched a 34-hour bombardment of the fort. Union forces eventually surrendered, and the Rebels occupied federal ground that became a symbol of Southern resistance. This action, however, led to a declaration of war in Washington. Amazingly, Confederate troops held onto Sumter for nearly 4 years, although it was almost continually bombarded by the Yankees. When evacuation finally came, the fort was nothing but a heap of rubble.

Park rangers today are on hand to answer your questions, and you can explore gun emplacements and visit a small museum filled with artifacts related to the siege. A complete tour of the fort, conducted daily from 9am to 5pm, takes about 2 hours.

Though you can travel to the fort via your own boat, most people take the tour of the fort and harbor offered by **Fort Sumter Tours,** 360 Concord St., Suite 201 (🕾 **843/881-7337;** www.fortsumter tours.com). You can board at either of two locations: Liberty Square in downtown Charleston; or Mount Pleasant's Patriots Point, the site of the world's largest naval and maritime museum. Sailing times change every month or so, but from March to Labor Day there generally are three sailings per day from each location, beginning at 9:30 or 10:45am. Winter sailings are more curtailed. Call for details. Each departure point offers ample parking, and the boats that carry you to Fort Sumter are sightseeing yachts built for the purpose; they're clean, safe, and equipped with modern conveniences.

In Charleston Harbor. 🕾 **843/883-3123.** www.nps.gov/fosu; www.spiritline cruises.com. Admission to fort free; boat trip $14 adults, $13 seniors, $8 children 6–11, free for children 5 and under.

**_H.L. Hunley_ Confederate Submarine** 🐾🐾🐾   One of the greatest and most sought-after artifacts in the history of naval warfare can now be viewed by the public. The Confederate submarine _H.L. Hunley,_ a hand-cranked vessel fashioned of locomotive boilers, sank the Union blockade vessel USS _Housatonic_ on February 17, 1864. The sinking of the Union ship launched the age of submarine warfare. The submarine and its nine-member crew mysteriously vanished off Sullivan's Island shortly after completing its historic mission. The vessel was finally located in 1995, sparking headlines across the world. The submarine was eventually raised and brought to the old Charleston Navy Base for preservation. The bones of its crew members were buried in a historic ceremony on April 17, 2004, at the Magnolia Cemetery. The sub, which rests in a tank of 50°F water, can only be visited weekends on 20-minute tours.

Warren Lasch Conservation Center, 1250 Supply St., Building 255, North Charleston. 🕾 **877/448-6539** or 843/744-2186. www.hunley.org. Admission $12, free for children 5 and under. Sat 10am–5pm; Sun noon–5pm.

## HISTORIC HOMES

**Aiken-Rhett House** 🐾🐾🐾   There is no better insight into antebellum life than that provided by the Aiken-Rhett House, built by merchant John Robinson in 1818 and greatly expanded by Governor and Mrs. William Aiken in the 1830s and 1850s. The property still looks as it did in 1858, 2 years before the outbreak of the Civil War. From Europe the governor and his lady brought back crystal

# Charleston Sights

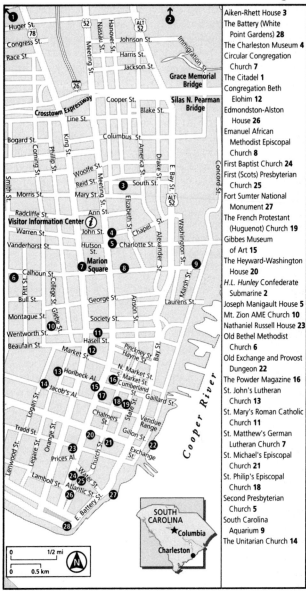

Aiken-Rhett House **3**
The Battery (White Point Gardens) **28**
The Charleston Museum **4**
Circular Congregation Church **7**
The Citadel **1**
Congregation Beth Elohim **12**
Edmondston-Alston House **26**
Emanuel African Methodist Episcopal Church **8**
First Baptist Church **24**
First (Scots) Presbyterian Church **25**
Fort Sumter National Monument **27**
The French Protestant (Huguenot) Church **19**
Gibbes Museum of Art **15**
The Heyward-Washington House **20**
*H.L. Hunley* Confederate Submarine **2**
Joseph Manigault House **5**
Mt. Zion AME Church **10**
Nathaniel Russell House **23**
Old Bethel Methodist Church **6**
Old Exchange and Provost Dungeon **22**
The Powder Magazine **16**
St. John's Lutheran Church **13**
St. Mary's Roman Catholic Church **11**
St. Matthew's German Lutheran Church **7**
St. Michael's Episcopal Church **21**
St. Philip's Episcopal Church **18**
Second Presbyterian Church **5**
South Carolina Aquarium **9**
The Unitarian Church **14**

and bronze chandeliers, classical sculpture and paintings, and antiques with which to furnish the elegant abode. Original outbuildings include the kitchens, slave quarters, stables, privies, and cattle sheds.

48 Elizabeth St. ℂ **843/723-1159**. Admission $10. Mon–Sat 10am–5pm; Sun 2–5pm.

### Edmondston-Alston House ⟅⟅⟅
On High Battery, an elegant section of Charleston, this house (built in 1825 by Charles Edmondston, a Charleston merchant and wharf owner) was one of the earliest constructed in the city in the late Federalist style. Edmondston sold it to Charles Alston, a Low Country rice planter, who modified it in Greek Revival style. The house has remained in the Alston family, which opens the first two floors to visitors. Inside are heirloom furnishings, silver, and paintings. It was here in 1861 that General Beauregard joined the Alston family to watch the bombardment of Fort Sumter. General Robert E. Lee once found refuge here when his hotel uptown caught on fire.

21 E. Battery St. ℂ **843/722-7171**. www.middletonplace.org. Admission $10. Guided tours Tues–Sat 10am–4:30pm; Sun 1:30–4:30pm; Mon 1–4:30pm.

### The Heyward-Washington House ⟅⟅⟅
In a district of Charleston called Cabbage Row, this 1772 house was built by Daniel Heyward, called the "Rice King." It was the setting for DuBose Heyward's *Porgy* and was also the home of Thomas Heyward, Jr., a signer of the Declaration of Independence. President George Washington bedded down here in 1791. Many of the fine period pieces in the house are the work of Thomas Elfe, one of America's most famous cabinetmakers. The 18th-century kitchen is the only historic kitchen in the city that is open to the public. It stands behind the main house, along with the servants' quarters and the garden.

87 Church St. ℂ **843/722-2996**. Admission $8 adults, $4 children 3–12; combination ticket to the Charleston Museum and Joseph Manigault House $21 adults, $4 children. Mon–Sat 10am–5pm; Sun 1–5pm. Tours leave every half hr. until 4:30pm.

### Joseph Manigault House ⟅
This 1803 Adamesque-style residence, a National Historic Landmark, was a wealthy rice planter's home. The house features a curving central staircase and an outstanding collection of Charlestonian, American, English, and French period furnishings. It's located diagonally across from the visitor center.

350 Meeting St. ℂ **843/723-2997**. Admission $8 adults, $4 children 3–12; combination ticket to the Heyward-Washington House and Charleston Museum $21 adults, $4 children. Mon–Sat 10am–5pm; Sun 1–5pm. Last tour at 4:30pm.

**Nathaniel Russell House** ⏣⏣⏣    One of America's finest examples of Federal architecture, this 1808 house was completed by Nathaniel Russell, one of Charleston's richest merchants. It is celebrated architecturally for its "free-flying" staircase, spiraling unsupported for three floors. The staircase's elliptical shape is repeated throughout the house. The interiors are ornate with period furnishings, especially the elegant music room with its golden harp and neoclassical-style sofa.

51 Meeting St. ⓒ **843/724-8481.** www.historiccharleston.org. Admission $10, free for children under 6. Guided tours Mon–Sat 10am–5pm; Sun and holidays 2–5pm. Last tour at 4:45pm.

## 2 Museums & Galleries

**The Charleston Museum** ⏣⏣    The Charleston Museum, founded in 1773, is the first and oldest museum in America. The collections preserve and interpret the social and natural history of Charleston and the South Carolina coastal region. The full-scale replica of the famed Confederate submarine *Hunley* standing outside the museum is one of the most-photographed subjects in the city. The museum also exhibits the largest silver collection in Charleston; early crafts; historic relics; and the "Discover Me" room, which has hands-on exhibits for children.

360 Meeting St. ⓒ **843/722-2996.** www.charlestonmuseum.org. Admission $10 adults, $4 children 3–12. Combination ticket to the Joseph Manigault House and Heyward-Washington House $21 adults, $4 children. Mon–Sat 9am–5pm; Sun 1–5pm.

**Gibbes Museum of Art** ⏣    Established in 1905 by the Carolina Art Association, the Gibbes Museum contains an intriguing collection of prints and drawings from the 18th century to the present. On display are landscapes, genre scenes, panoramic views of Charleston Harbor, and portraits of South Carolinians (see *Thomas Middleton* by Benjamin West, *Charles Izard Manigault* by Thomas Sully, or *John C. Calhoun* by Rembrandt Peale). The museum's collection of some 400 miniature portraits ranks as one of the most comprehensive in the country.

The Wallace Exhibit has 10 rooms, eight replicated from historic American buildings and two from classic French styles. Styles range from the plain dining room of a sea captain's house on Martha's Vineyard to the elegant drawing room of Charleston's historic Nathaniel Russell House (see "Historic Homes," above).

135 Meeting St. ⓒ **843/722-2706.** www.gibbesmuseum.org. Admission $7 adults, $6 seniors, students, and military, $4 children 6–18, free for children under 6.

Included in Passport Ticket (see earlier in this chapter). Tues–Sat 10am–5pm; Sun 1–5pm. Closed Mon and holidays.

## 3 More Attractions

**The Citadel** ⍟    The all-male (at that time) Citadel was established in 1842 as an arsenal and a refuge for whites in the event of a slave uprising. In 1922, it moved to its present location. Pat Conroy's novel *The Lords of Discipline* is based on his 4 years at the school. Since 1995, when the first woman notoriously enrolled, women now join the ranks with young men. The campus of this military college features buildings of Moorish design, with crenellated battlements and sentry towers. It is especially interesting to visit on Friday, when the college is in session and the public is invited to a precision-drill parade on the quadrangle at 3:45pm. For a history of the Citadel, stop at the **Citadel Memorial Archives Museum** (② 843/953-6846).

Moultrie St. and Elmwood Ave. ② 843/953-3294. www.citadel.edu. Free admission. Daily 24 hr. for drive-through visits; museum Sun–Fri 2–5pm, Sat noon–5pm. Closed religious, national, and school holidays.

**Old Exchange and Provost Dungeon** ⍟    This is a stop that many visitors overlook, but it's one of the most important colonial buildings in the United States because of its role as a prison during the American Revolution. In 1873, the building became City Hall. You'll find a large collection of antique chairs, supplied by the local Daughters of the American Revolution, each of whom brought a chair here from home in 1921.

122 E. Bay St. ② 843/727-2165. www.oldexchange.com. Admission $7 adults, $3.50 children 7–12. Daily 9am–5pm. Closed Thanksgiving and Dec 23–25.

**The Powder Magazine**    Used to store gunpowder in the defense of the city during the Revolutionary War, this is the oldest public building in South Carolina. It is the last of the buildings still standing from the heyday of the colonial governors of the state, called "Lord Proprietors." The "magazine" was constructed in 1713 to store the ammunition in the defense of Charles Town, which was the southernmost British settlement in the late 17th century. Charles Town was subjected to repeated attacks from Native Americans, pirates, and Spanish and French warships. Its 32-inch-thick brick walls were designed to withstand heavy bombardment. The tile roof was designed to implode on itself if there were any explosions within the building. Purchased by the National Society of Colonial Dames in 1899, the building is now a museum of early

Charleston history, displaying armor, costumes, antiques, and other memorabilia and artifacts of 18th-century Charleston.

79 Cumberland St. ✆ **843/722-9350**. Admission $2 adults, $1 children 6–12, free for children 5 and under. Thurs–Sun 10am–4pm.

**South Carolina Aquarium** ✿   Visitors can explore Southern aquatic life in an attraction filled with thousands of enchanting creatures and plants in amazing habitats, from five major regions of the Appalachian Watershed. Jutting out into the Charleston Harbor for 2,000 feet, the focal point at this attraction, which opened in 2000, is a 93,000-square-foot aquarium featuring a two-story Great Ocean Tank Exhibition. Contained within are more than 800 animals, including deadly sharks but also sea turtles and stingrays. Every afternoon at 4pm the aquarium offers a dolphin program, where bottlenose dolphins can be viewed from an open-air terrace. One of the most offbeat exhibits replicates a blackwater swamp, with atmospheric fog, a spongy floor, and twinkling lights. The newest attraction here is called Secrets of the Amazon, which features the diversity of this endangered region in sights, sounds, and adventure. You'll meet such creatures as a giant green anaconda, poison dart frogs, four-eyed fish, and flesh-devouring piranhas.

100 Aquarium Wharf. ✆ **843/720-1990**. www.seaquarium.org. Admission $15 adults, $13 seniors 62 and over and children 3–11, free for children under 2. April 1–Aug 15 Mon–Sat 9am–6pm, Sun noon–6pm; Aug 16–Mar 31 Mon–Sat 9am–5pm, Sun noon–5pm.

## 4 Historic Churches & Synagogues

Charleston offers the greatest collection of historic churches in the South. Some churches more or less keep regular visiting hours; others do not (see below for set hours, if available). Sometimes the doors will be closed, and you'll have to admire the church for its particular facade. If the doors are open, you're welcome to come inside. Of course, all persons are welcome to attend services.

**Circular Congregational Church**   Founded in 1681, this is one of the oldest churches in the South, its burial grounds dating back to 1695. In 1861 a fire destroyed the building. The fourth and present church to stand here dates from 1891. The structure you see today integrated the brick from earlier churches, one of which was leveled in an 1886 earthquake. Once called the Independent Church of Charles Towne, the church opened the first Sunday school in South Carolina.

150 Meeting St. ✆ **843/577-6400**. Free guided tours. Call ahead to confirm times.

**Congregation Beth Elohim**   This is the fourth-oldest synagogue in the United States and the oldest Reform synagogue in the world. A congregation was formed in 1749, and the synagogue was erected in 1794, although it was destroyed by fire in 1838. The present building was constructed in 1840 as one of the country's finest examples of Greek Revival architecture. Francis Salvador, a synagogue member, signed the Declaration of Independence. He became the first known Jew to die in the Revolutionary War.

90 Hasell St. ℭ **843/723-1090.** Free guided tours Mon–Fri 10am–noon (except during Jewish holidays), Sun noon–4pm.

**Emanuel African Methodist Episcopal Church**   Founded in 1791 by free blacks and slaves, this is the oldest church of its type in the South. With a sanctuary holding 2,500, it is the largest black congregation south of Baltimore. The original gas lanterns hanging date from its founding. In 1822 Denmark Vessey urged the congregation into an insurrection, although authorities learned of the rebellion, closing the church. In 1865 it was reopened and eventually rebuilt in 1891 into the present structure you can visit today.

110 Calhoun St. ℭ **843/722-2561.** Free admission. Mon–Thurs 9am–1pm and 2–4pm; Fri 9am–3pm.

**First Baptist Church**   Established in 1682, this was the first Baptist church to open in the South. In 1755 the pastor, Oliver Hart, founded the Charleston Baptist Association, the earliest organization for the education of Baptist ministers in the South. He fled from the British in 1780, never to return. Work on the present sanctuary was designed by Robert Mills, America's first native architect. The sanctuary has been prone to natural disasters, including a tornado in 1885, an earthquake in 1886, and Hurricane Hugo in 1989.

61 Church St. ℭ **843/722-3896.** Free tours Tues–Wed 10am–noon.

**First (Scots) Presbyterian Church**   This is the fifth-oldest church in Charleston, founded in 1731 by Caledonian immigrants who did not want to become members of the Anglican faith. The seal of Scotland in the windows over the main entrance can still be seen. The first congregation consisted of a dozen Scottish families who left the Independent Church of Charles Towne in 1731. Constructed in 1814, the design of the church was inspired by St. Mary's Cathedral in Baltimore, whose architect, Benjamin Latrobe, also

**Impressions**

*South Carolina is too small to be a sovereign nation and too large for an insane asylum.*
— Legislator James L. Petigru at the Secession Convention of 1861, urging South Carolina to stay in the Union

designed the U.S. Capitol. The walls of this massive brick church are 3 feet thick and covered with stucco, and twin towers rise above a pillared portico. The cemetery has more than 50 tombstones from the 16th century. The church bell that was donated to the Confederacy during the Civil War for cannons was recently replaced by an English bell made in 1814, the same time of the church's construction.

53 Meeting St. © 843/722-8882. Free admission. Open to the public but no set hours.

**The French Protestant (Huguenot) Church**    This is the only remaining independent Huguenot church in America, offering weekly church services in English but with an annual service in French conducted each spring. It was founded in 1681 by Huguenot refugees from Protestant persecutions in France. The first church built on this site in 1687 was destroyed in 1796 in an attempt to stop a fire. It was replaced in 1800, only to be dismantled in 1844 to make way for the present Gothic Revival building designed by Edward B. White. The church suffered heavy damage by shellfire during the Civil War and was nearly demolished in the earthquake of 1886. The original Tucker organ—one of the rarest in the country—is from 1845.

136 Church St. © 843/722-4385. Free admission. Call ahead for tour times.

**Mt. Zion AME Church**    Purchased in 1882, this was the first brick building owned by blacks in Charleston. It was purchased by members of the Emanuele AME Church when that sanctuary had become too crowded. The 54th and 55th Massachusetts Regiment worshipped here while stationed in Charleston. The church is known for offering the best choral music in Charleston, with six different choirs. Music ranges from classical to original and unarranged black spirituals, many from the 18th century.

5 Glebe St. © 843/722-8118. Free admission. Mon, Wed, and Fri 11:30am–1:30pm.

**Old Bethel Methodist Church**    This is the third-oldest church building surviving in Charleston. Founded and paid for by both white and black citizens, it was launched in 1797, with the finishing touches applied in 1807. By 1840 its black members seceded to form their own congregation. In 1852 the church was moved to the western part of its lot for the black population to use, and a new church was built on the original lot for the white worshippers. After that church was given to the black members in 1880, Old Bethel moved across the street to its present location, where it currently serves the black population, many of its members descendants of the 1880s congregation.

222 Calhoun St. ℂ 843/722-3470. Free admission. No set hours.

**Old St. Andrew's Parish Church** In the West Ashley area of Charleston, opening on Highway 61, this is the oldest surviving church in Charleston, having been founded and built in 1706. Part of the church was constructed from bricks used as ballast on ships arriving in the port of Charleston, and a number of historic tombs are found in the courtyard. In late March or early April—depending on flowers in bloom and the Easter holiday—the church sponsors its annual Tea Room and Gift Shop as a fundraiser, with waitresses dressed in period costumes serving such delicacies as magnolia pie. An on-site gift shop open daily (during the fundraiser) from 11:30am to 1:30pm sells cookbooks, jams, jellies, and crafts made by parish members.

2604 Ashley River Rd. ℂ 843/766-1541. Free admission. Mon–Fri 8am–2pm.

**St. John's Lutheran Church** Called "the Mother Church of Lutherans in South Carolina," this antique sanctuary celebrated its 250th anniversary in 1992. It was founded by German immigrants, but the congregation was actually established in 1742, with the first church begun in 1759. The edifice today is from 1817. Its church bell was melted down and given to the Confederacy for use as cannonballs in the Civil War. It wasn't until 1992 that these bells were replaced. After damage by Hurricane Hugo, the church spent $1 million in repairs and restoration. A prominent member of its congregation is former U.S. Sen. Ernest F. Hollings.

Corner of Clifford and Archdale sts. ℂ 843/723-2426. Free admission. Tours by appointment only.

**St. Mary's Roman Catholic Church** Established in 1789, this is the oldest Roman Catholic church in South Carolina and the mother church of the diocese for the state as well as North Carolina and Georgia. The original church was destroyed by fire in 1838 but was rebuilt in 1839, its ceiling hand-painted by Caesare Porte of

Rome. Many of the tombstones in the churchyard are in French, indicating the early French influence that prevailed at the church.

89 Hasell St. ☏ 843/722-7696. Free admission. No set hours.

**St. Matthew's German Lutheran Church**    Intended for German-speaking settlers, this was the second Lutheran congregation formed in the city in 1840. The building, erected in 1872 and rebuilt after a fire in 1965, is known for its 297-foot steeple. The steeple remains the tallest in the state. The stained-glass windows in the apse under the balcony are original to the building.

405 King St. ☏ 843/723-1611. Free admission. Mon–Fri 8:30am–4:30pm.

**St. Michael's Episcopal Church** ⍟    A National Historic Landmark, this is one of the most impressive of America's colonial churches, and its edifice remains the oldest church in Charleston. The architect is not known, but the church was constructed between 1752 and 1761. In some respects it evokes St. Martin-in-the-Fields, a London landmark by James Gibbs. Seen for miles around, its 186-foot steeple is a Charleston landmark, its clock bell towers imported in 1764. The steeple tower was used as a compass-positioning point for artillery targets during both the Revolutionary and Civil wars. Both George Washington and Robert E. Lee attended services here.

Meeting St. at Broad St. ☏ 843/723-0603. Free admission. Mon–Fri 9am–4:30pm; Sat 9am–noon. After the 10:30am Sun service there is an official 20-min. guided tour.

**St. Philip's Episcopal Church**    This impressive church is nicknamed the "Lighthouse Church," because a light was once put in its steeple to guide ships into the harbor. The present building dates from 1835 to 1838 and still houses the oldest congregation in South Carolina. During the Civil War, the church bells were donated to the Confederacy and were converted into cannonballs. Buried in the churchyard are such notables as John C. Calhoun, Edward Rutledge, Charles Pinckney, and DuBose Heyward.

146 Church St. ☏ 843/722-7734. Free admission. Mon–Fri 10am–noon and 2–4pm (call ahead to verify times).

**Second Presbyterian Church** ⍟    Built in 1809, this is the oldest Presbyterian church in Charleston, and it's been designated by the Presbyterian Church of the United States as Church Historical Site #1. When it was first constructed, it was so large and cavernous that the minister's voice couldn't be heard. Remodeling later solved that problem, when the floor was raised 3 feet and the ceiling lowered 16 feet.

Meeting St. at Charlotte St. ⓒ **843/723-9237.** Free admission. Call ahead if you plan to visit the church.

**The Unitarian Church** ⓐ   The oldest Unitarian church in the South, this is the second-oldest church in Charleston. Building began in 1774 but construction was halted when the Revolutionary War broke out. The site was used as a stable and as headquarters for the militia. It was restored and rededicated in 1787, and in 1852 it was remodeled and enlarged. Francis Lee designed the fan-vaulted ceiling, nave, and chancel, using the Chapel of Henry VII in West-minster Abbey in London for his inspiration. Designated a National Historic Landmark, the church is one of the country's most stellar examples of the Perpendicular Gothic Revival style, and was the first to incorporate this type of architecture.

4 Archdale St. ⓒ **843/723-4617.** Free admission. Call ahead to reserve a tour.

## 5 Parks & Gardens

See also the listing for Magnolia Plantation under "Nearby Planta-tions," below. Another park of great interest lies on the northern periphery of Charleston: **Palmetto Islands County Park** (see later in this chapter).

**Charles Towne Landing** ⓐⓐⓐ   This 663-acre park is located on the site of the first 1670 settlement. Underground exhibits show the colony's history, and the park features a re-creation of a small village. A brand-new visitors center/museum has been added with lots of interactive exhibits. You can rent a bike for $3 an hour. Because trade was such an important part of colonial life, a full-scale repro-duction of the 17th-century trading vessel *Adventure* is an excellent addition to the site. After touring the ship, you can step into the Set-tler's Life Area and view a 17th-century crop garden where rice, indigo, and cotton were grown. There's no flashy theme-park atmos-phere here: What you see as you walk under huge old oaks, past freshwater lagoons, and through the Animal Forest (with the same species that lived here in 1670) is what those early settlers saw.

1500 Old Towne Rd. (S.C. 171, between U.S. 17 and I-126). ⓒ **843/881-5516.** www.southcarolinaparks.com. Admission $5 adults, $3.25 seniors, $3 children 6–15, free for those with disabilities. Daily 9am–5pm. Closed Dec 24–25.

**Cypress Gardens** ⓐⓐ   This 163-acre swamp garden was used as a freshwater reserve for Dean Hall, a huge Cooper River rice plan-tation, and was given to the city in 1963. Today, the giant cypress trees draped with Spanish moss provide an unforgettable setting for flat-bottom boats that glide among their knobby roots. Footpaths in the garden wind through a profusion of azaleas, camellias, daffodils, and other colorful blooms. Visitors share the swamp with alligators, pileated woodpeckers, wood ducks, otters, barred owls, and other abundant species. The gardens are worth a visit at any time of year, but they're at their most colorful in March and April. Also on-site are a reptile center, aquarium, and aviary, plus a butterfly house.

U.S. 52, Moncks Corner. © 843/553-0515. www.cypressgardens.info. Admission $10 adults, $9 seniors, $5 children 6–12, free for children 5 and under. Daily 9am–5pm. Closed major holidays. Take U.S. 52 about 24 miles north of Charleston.

## 6 Nearby Plantations

**Drayton Hall** 🏵🏵    This is one of the oldest surviving plantations, built in 1738 and owned by the Drayton family until 1974. Framed by majestic live oaks, the Georgian-Palladian house is a property of the National Trust for Historic Preservation. Its hand-carved wood-work and plasterwork represent New World craftsmanship at its finest. Because such modern elements as electricity, plumbing, and central heating have never put in an appearance, the house is much as it was in its early years; in fact, it is displayed unfurnished.

Old Ashley River Rd. (S.C. 61). © 843/766-0188. www.draytonhall.org. Admission $14 adults, $8 children 12–18, $6 children 6–11, free for children 5 and under; included in Passport Ticket (see above). Mar–Oct daily 9:30am–4pm; Nov–Feb daily 9:30am–3pm. Tours on the hour. Closed Thanksgiving Day and Dec 25. Take U.S. 17 S. to S.C. 61; 9 miles northwest of Charleston.

**Magnolia Plantation** 🏵🏵🏵    Ten generations of the Drayton family have lived here continuously since the 1670s. They haven't had much luck keeping a roof over their heads; the first mansion burned just after the Revolution, and the second was set afire by General Sherman. But you can't call the replacement modern. A sim-ple, pre-Revolutionary house was barged down from Summerville and set on the basement foundations of its unfortunate predecessors.

The house has been filled with museum-quality Early American furniture, appraised to exceed $500,000 in value. An art gallery has been added to the house as well.

The flowery gardens of camellias and azaleas—among the most beautiful in America—reach their peak bloom in March and April but are colorful year-round. You can tour the house, the gardens (including an herb garden, horticultural maze, topiary garden, and biblical garden), a petting zoo, and a waterfowl refuge, or walk or bike through wildlife trails.

Other sights include an antebellum cabin that was restored and furnished, a plantation rice barge on display beside the Ashley River, and a Nature Train that carries guests on a 45-minute ride around the plantation's perimeter.

Low Country wildlife is visible in marsh, woodland, and swamp settings. The **Audubon Swamp Garden,** also on the grounds, is an independently operated 60-acre cypress swamp that offers a close look at other wildlife, such as egrets, alligators, wood ducks, otters, turtles, and herons.

3550 Ashley River Rd. (S.C. 61). © **800/367-3517** or 843/571-1266. www.magnolia plantation.com. Admission to garden and grounds $14 adults, $13 seniors, $8 children 6–12, free for children under 6. Tour of plantation house is an additional $7 for ages 6 and up; children under 6 not allowed to tour the house. Admission to Audubon Swamp Garden $7 adults, $6 seniors, $5 children 6–12, free for children under 6. Magnolia Plantation and Audubon Swamp Gardens summer daily 8am–5:30pm; winter daily 10am–5pm.

**Middleton Place** 🏵🏵🏵   This was the home of Henry Middleton, president of the First Continental Congress, whose son, Arthur, was a signer of the Declaration of Independence. Today, this National Historic Landmark includes America's oldest landscaped gardens, the Middleton Place House, and the Plantation Stableyards.

The gardens, begun in 1741, reflect the elegant symmetry of European gardens of that period. Ornamental lakes, terraces, and plantings of camellias, azaleas, magnolias, and crape myrtle accent the grand design.

The Middleton Place House itself was built in 1755, but in 1865, all but the south flank was ransacked and burned by Union troops. The house was restored in the 1870s as a family residence and today houses collections of fine silver, furniture, rare first editions by Catesby and Audubon, and portraits by Benjamin West and Thomas Sully. In the stableyards, craftspeople demonstrate life on a plantation of yesteryear. There are also horses, mules, hogs, cows, sheep, and goats.

A plantation lunch is served at the **Middleton Place Restaurant,** which is a replica of an original rice mill. *American Way* magazine cited this restaurant as one of the top 10 representing American cuisine at its best. Specialties include she-crab soup, Hoppin' John and ham biscuits, okra gumbo, Sea Island shrimp, and corn pudding. Service is daily from 11am to 3pm. Dinner is served daily 5 to 9pm, and is likely to include panned (pan-seared) quail with ham (a recipe from famed chef Edna Lewis, who was a consultant-in-residence here for years), sea scallops, or broiled oysters. For dinner reservations, call © **843/556-6020.**

4300 Ashley River Rd. (© **800/782-3608** or 843/556-6020. www.middletonplace. org. Admission to gardens and stableyards $25 adults, $5 children 7–15, free for children 6 and under. Tour of house additional $10 adults, $6 children 6–12. Gardens and stableyards daily 9am–5pm; house Mon 1:30–4:30pm, Tues–Sun 10am–4:30pm. Take U.S. 17 W. to S.C. 61 (Ashley River Rd.); 14 miles northwest of Charleston.

## 7 Especially for Kids

For more than 300 years, Charleston has been the home of pirates, patriots, and presidents. Your child can see firsthand the **Great Hall at the Old Exchange,** where President Washington danced; the **Provost Dungeons,** where South Carolina patriots spent their last days; and touch the last remaining structural evidence of the **Charleston Seawall.** Children will take special delight in **Charles Towne Landing** and **Middleton Place.** At **Fort Sumter,** they can see where the Civil War began. Children will also enjoy **Magnolia Plantation,** with its Audubon Swamp Garden.

Kids and Navy vets will also love the aircraft carrier **USS *Yorktown,*** at Patriots Point, 2 miles east of the Cooper River Bridge. Its World War II, Korean, and Vietnam exploits are documented in exhibits, and general naval history is illustrated through models of ships, planes, and weapons. You can wander through the bridge wheelhouse, flight and hangar decks, chapel, and sick bay, and view the film *The Fighting Lady,* which depicts life aboard the carrier. Also at Patriots Point are the World War II destroyer *Laffey;* the World War II submarine *Clamagore;* and the cutter *Ingham.* Patriots Point is open daily from 9am to 6pm April to October, until 5pm November to March. Admission is $14 for adults, $12 for seniors over 62 and military personnel in uniform, $7 for kids 6 to 11. Adjacent is the fine 18-hole public **Patriots Point Golf Course.** For further information, call (© **843/884-2727;** www.patriotspoint.org.

## 8 Organized Tours

**BY HORSE & CARRIAGE**   The **Old South Carriage,** 14 Anson St. ((© **843/723-9712;** www.oldsouthcarriagetours.com), offers narrated horse-drawn-carriage tours through the historic district daily from 9am to dusk. A 1-hour carriage tour goes for 2½ miles, covering 30 blocks of the historic district. The cost is $20 for adults, $14 for children 3 to 11.

**BY MULE TEAM**   **Palmetto Carriage Tours,** 40 N. Market St., at Guignard Street ((© **843/723-8145;** www.carriagetour.com), uses mule teams instead of the usual horse and carriage for its guided tours of Old Charleston. Tours originate at the Big Red Barn behind the Rainbow Market. The cost is $20 for adults and seniors, and $10 for children 4 to 11. Daily 9am to 5pm.

**BY BOAT** **Spiritline Cruises,** 360 Concord St., Suite 201 (✆ 800/ 789-3678; www.spiritlinecruises.com), offers a **Harbor and Fort Sumter Tour** by boat, departing daily from the City Marina and from the Patriots Point Maritime Museum. This is the only tour to stop at Fort Sumter, target of the opening shots of the Civil War. Rates are $14 for adults, $13 for seniors, $8 for children 6 to 11, free for children under 6. The operator also has an interesting **Charleston Harbor Tour,** with daily departures from Patriots Point. The 2-hour cruise passes the Battery, Charleston Port, Castle Pinckney, Drum Island, Fort Sumter, and the aircraft carrier *Yorktown,* and sails under the Cooper River Bridge and on to other sights. Prices are the same as those for Fort Sumter Tours.

**WALKING TOURS** One of the best offbeat walking tours of Charleston is the **Charleston Tea Party Walking Tour** (✆ 843/ 722-1779). It lasts 2 hours and costs $25 for adults or $10 for children 12 and under. Departing year-round Monday to Saturday at 9:30am and 2pm, tours originate at the Kings Courtyard Inn, 198 Kings St. The tour goes into a lot of nooks and crannies of Charleston, including secret courtyards and gardens. Finally, you get that promised tea. Reservations are required.

Tours of Charleston's 18th-century **architecture** in the original walled city begin at 10am and 2pm, and tours of 19th-century architecture along Meeting Street and the Battery begin at 2pm. Departures are from in front of the Meeting Street Inn, 173 Meeting St. Tours last 2 hours and are given every day but Tuesday and Sunday. The cost is $15 (free for children 12 and under). For reservations, call Charleston Lowcountry.com at ✆ **843/893-2327.**

## 9 Beaches & Outdoor Pursuits

**BEACHES** Three great beaches are within a 25-minute drive of the center of Charleston.

In the West Islands, **Folly Beach,** which had degenerated into a tawdry Coney Island–type amusement park, is making a comeback following a multimillion-dollar cleanup, but it remains the least-pristine beach in the area. The best bathroom amenities are located here, however. At the western end of the island is the **Folly Beach**

**County Park,** with bathrooms, parking, and shelter from the rain. To get here, take U.S. 17 East to S.C. 171 South to Folly Beach.

In the East Cooper area, both the **Isle of Palms** and **Sullivan's Island** offer miles of public beaches, mostly bordered by beachfront homes. Windsurfing and jet-skiing are popular here. Take U.S. 17 East to S.C. 703 (Ben Sawyer Blvd.). S.C. 703 continues through Sullivan's Island to the Isle of Palms.

**Kiawah Island** has the area's most pristine beach—far preferable to Folly Beach, to our tastes—and draws a more upmarket crowd. The best beachfront is at **Beachwalker County Park,** on the southern end of the island. Get there before noon on weekends; the limited parking is usually gone by then. Canoe rentals are available for use on the Kiawah River, and the park offers not only a boardwalk but also bathrooms, showers, and a changing area. Take U.S. 17 East to S.C. 171 South (Folly Beach Rd.), turn right onto S.C. 700 Southwest (Maybank Hwy.) to Bohicket Road, which turns into Betsy Kerrigan Parkway. Where Betsy Kerrigan Parkway dead-ends, turn left on Kiawah Parkway, which takes you to the island.

For details on the major resorts on Kiawah Island and the Isle of Palms, see chapter 11.

**BIKING**   Charleston is basically flat and relatively free of traffic, except on its main arteries at rush hour. Therefore, biking is a popular local pastime and reasonably safe. Many of the city parks have biking trails. Your best bet for rentals is **Mike's Bikes,** 808 Folly Rd. (© 843/795-3322), which rents bikes for $5 to $8 per hour or $20 for a full day. A credit-card imprint is required as a deposit.

**BOATING**   A true Charlestonian is as much at home on the sea as on land. Sailing local waters is a popular family pastime. One of the best places for rentals is **Isle of Palms Marina,** Isle of Palms (© 843/886-0209), where 18-foot boats, big enough for seven people, rent for around $240 for 4 hours, plus fuel. A larger boat, big enough for 10, goes for about $375 to $450 for 4 hours, plus fuel.

**DIVING**   Several outfitters provide rentals and ocean charters, as well as instruction for neophytes. At **Atlantic Coast Diving,** 426 W. Coleman Blvd., Mt. Pleasant (© 843/884-1500), you can rent both diving and snorkeling equipment. Diving equipment costs $40 per day. It's open Monday to Saturday from 10am to 6pm.

**FISHING**   Freshwater fishing charters are available year-round along the Low Country's numerous creeks and inlets. The waterways are filled with flounder, trout, spot-tail, and channel bass.

Some of the best striped-bass fishing available in America can be found at nearby Lake Moultrie.

Offshore-fishing charters for reef fishing (where you'll find fish such as cobia, black sea bass, and king mackerel) and for the Gulf Stream (where you fish for sailfish, marlin, wahoo, dolphin, and tuna) are also available. Both types of charters can be arranged at the previously recommended **Isle of Palms Marina,** Isle of Palms (© 843/886-0209). A fishing craft holding up to ten people rents for $525 to $575 for a full day, including everything but food and drink. Reservations must be made 24 hours in advance.

**Folly Beach Fishing Pier** at Folly Beach is a wood pier, 25 feet wide, that extends 1,045 feet into the Atlantic Ocean. Facilities include restrooms, a tackle shop, and a restaurant. It's accessible to people with disabilities.

**GOLF**   Charleston is said to be the home of golf in America. Charlestonians have been playing the game since the 1700s, when the first golf clubs arrived from Scotland. With 17 public and private courses in the city, there's a golf game waiting for every buff.

**Wild Dunes Resort,** Isle of Palms (© 888/778-1876 or 843/886-6000; www.wilddunes.com), offers two championship golf courses designed by Tom Fazio. **The Links** ✹✹✹ is a 6,722-yard, par-72 layout that takes the player through marshlands, over or into huge sand dunes, through a wooded alley, and into a pair of ocean-front finishing holes once called "the greatest east of Pebble Beach, California." The course opened in 1980 and has been ranked among the 100 greatest courses in the United States by *Golf Digest* and among the top 100 in the world by *Golf Magazine. Golf Digest* has also ranked the Links as the 13th-greatest resort course in America. **The Harbor Course** offers 6,402 yards of Low Country marsh and Intracoastal Waterway views. This par-70 layout is considered to be target golf, challenging players with 2 holes that play from one island to another across Morgan Creek. Greens fees at these courses can range from $79 to $155, depending on the season. Clubs can be rented at either course for $25 for 18 holes, and professional instruction costs $85 for a 1-hour session. Both courses are open daily from 7am to 6pm year-round.

Your best bet, if you'd like to play at any of the other Charleston-area golf courses, is to contact **Charleston Golf, Inc.** (© 800/774-4444; www.charlestongolfguide.com; Mon–Fri 8:30am–5pm). The company represents 20 golf courses, offering packages that range from $100 to $150 per person March to August. Off-season packages range from $75 to $110 per person. Prices include greens fees on one course, a hotel room based on double occupancy, and taxes. Travel pros here will customize your vacation with golf-course selections and tee times; they can also arrange rental cars and airfares. Reservations must be made 1 week in advance.

**HIKING**    The most interesting hiking trails begin around Buck Hall in **Francis Marion National Forest** (© **843/887-3257**), located some 40 miles north of the center of Charleston via U.S. 52. The site consists of 250,000 acres of swamps, with towering oaks and pines. Also in the national forest, **Buck Hall Recreation,** reached by U.S. 17/701 North from Charleston, has 15 camping sites ($15–$20 per night), plus a boat ramp and fishing. Other hiking trails are at **Edisto Beach State Park,** State Cabin Road, on Edisto Island (© **843/869-2156**).

**HORSEBACK RIDING**    One of the best riding stables in South Carolina is found at **M&M Farms,** 1859 Hoover Rd., Huger (© **843/336-5700**). These outfitters offer daily trail rides in the Francis Marion National Forest for $25; rides last 1 hour and depart daily at 10am, noon, 2pm, and 4pm. The stables are only a 20-minute drive from Charleston. Call for directions.

**TENNIS**    Charlestonians have been playing tennis since the early 1800s. Two miles west of Charleston on U.S. 17, the **Charleston Tennis Center,** 19 Farmfield Ave. (© **843/724-7402**), is your best bet, with 15 well-maintained outdoor courts lighted for night play. The cost is only $5 per person per hour of court time. The center is open Monday to Thursday from 8:30am to 9pm, on Friday from 8:30am to 7pm, on Saturday from 9am to 3pm, and on Sunday from 10am to 6pm.

## 10 A Side Trip to Mount Pleasant

Directly north of Charleston, and linked by a bridge, Mount Pleasant is where colonial locals first began retreating in summer from the city heat around the dawn of the 18th century. Since that time the community has grown and grown, containing hotels, restaurants, and strip malls. Many of the most popular of Charleston seafood restaurants are found here. To reach them and also to see the shrimp-boat fleet, turn right off U.S. 17 just beyond the bridge onto S.C. 703.

**Boone Hall Plantation**    This unique plantation is approached by a famous **Avenue of Oaks** ♠♠♠, huge old moss-draped trees planted in 1743 by Capt. Thomas Boone. Outbuildings include the circular smokehouse and slave cabins constructed of bricks made on the plantation. A large grove of pecan trees lies behind the house. Note that Boone Hall is not an original structure but a replica; diehard history purists may be disappointed in the house, which is elegantly furnished and open to the public, but the grounds are definitely worth seeing. While here, you can also visit the **Palmetto Islands County Park** (see below).

1235 Long Point Rd. (U.S. 17/701). ⓒ **843/884-4371.** www.boonehallplantation. com. Admission $15 adults, $13 seniors 55 and over, $7 children 6–12. Apr to Labor Day Mon–Sat 8:30am–6pm, Sun 1–5pm; day after Labor Day to Mar Mon–Sat 9am–5pm, Sun 1–4pm. Take U.S. 17/701 9 miles north of Charleston.

**Charles Pinckney National Historic Site**    Lying 6 miles from Charleston, this is the latest remnant of the once-famous Snee Farm, the country estate of one of the most famous names in South Carolina history, Charles Pinckney (1754–1824). One of the principal framers of the U.S. Constitution, Pinckney was both a statesman and a Revolutionary War officer. The main house contains a visitor center where information about this national historic site is provided. The 1828 building is a rare, well-preserved example of a once-common Low Country cottage. On-site exhibitions include archaeological discoveries, plus interpretations of African-American contributions during the colonial era.

1254 Long Point Rd. ⓒ **843/881-5516.** Free admission. Daily 9am–5pm (until 6pm Memorial Day to Labor Day). Closed Jan 1, Thanksgiving, and Dec 25. Hwy 17 N., left on Long Point Rd., ½ mile on left.

**Palmetto Islands County Park** *Kids*    At the site of Boone Hall Plantation (see above), this is a 983-acre park in a tropical setting. Designed for family fun, it features a playground, picnic sites with grills, nature trails, and the Splash Island Waterpark. You can also rent bikes and pedal boats for summer pleasures. Recreational opportunities abound, including crabbing and fishing from floating docks along tidal creeks and lagoons.

444 Needlerush Pkwy. ⓒ **843/884-0832.** www.ccprc.com. Admission $1. May–Aug daily 9am–7pm; Nov–Feb daily 10am–5pm; Mar–Apr and Sept–Oct daily 9am–6pm. Off Long Point Rd. (U.S. 17/701) 9 miles north of Charleston.

# 9

# Charleston Shopping

**K**ing Street is lined with many special shops and boutiques. The **Shops at Charleston Place,** 130 Market St., is an upscale complex of top-designer clothing shops (Gucci, Jaeger, Ralph Lauren, and so on), and the lively **State Street Market,** just down from the Old City Market, is another cluster of shops and restaurants.

## 1 Top Shops from A to Z

### ANTIQUES

**George C. Birlant and Co.** ☆   If you're in the market for 18th- and 19th-century English antique furnishings, this is the right place. This Charleston staple prides itself on its Charleston Battery Bench, which is seen (and sat upon) throughout the Battery. The heavy iron sides are cast from the original 1880 mold, and the slats are authentic South Carolina cypress. It's as close to the original as you can get. Open Monday to Saturday 9am to 5:30pm. 191 King St. ℭ 843/722-3842.

**King Street Antique Mall** ☆☆   This is the largest shop and the only antiques mall within the center of the historic district. The mall showcases the wares of some 9,000 dealers (8,000 of whom are indoors, with the other vendors occupying courtyard and garden space). It seems as if every attic in Charleston was emptied to fill this mall, which features fine antiques, collectibles, furnishings, china, silver, estate jewelry, and more. Open Monday to Saturday 10am to 6pm and Sunday noon to 5pm. 495 King St. ℭ 843/723-2211.

**Livingston Antiques**   For a quarter of a century, discriminating antiques hunters have patronized the showroom of this dealer. Both authentic antiques and fool-the-eye reproductions are sold. If you're interested, the staff will direct you to the shop's 30,000-square-foot warehouse on West Ashley. Monday to Saturday 10am to 5pm. 163 King St. ℭ 843/723-9697.

**Roumillat's Antique Mall & Auction** ☆☆   The Roumillats are one of the oldest families in Charleston selling antiques, having been in business since 1779. Two centuries later they established

Roumillat's Auction House, where regular public auctions of local estate wares are still staged on the first and third Saturdays of each month at 10am. In addition to their auctions, the Roumillats offer a 15,000-square-foot antiques mall and auction house featuring a little bit of everything, but specializing in American, French, and English furnishings dating from the early 19th century to pre–World War II. Open Monday to Saturday 10am to 6pm, Sunday 1 to 5pm. 2241 Savannah Hwy. (Hwy. 17 S.). ℂ **843/766-8899.**

## ART

**Audubon Gallery**   In the historic district near Horlbeck Abbey, this is the official gallery for the Southeastern Wildlife Exposition held in Charleston every February. For serious "birdies" who flock here, the store offers high-quality Audubon prints along with both original paintings and reproductions of such birds as the ruffed grouse or the white-headed eagle. It also sells hand-carved decoys and other wildlife work. Bronze sculptures and antique prints can be purchased here. Open Monday to Saturday 10am to 5:30pm. 177 King St. ℂ **843/853-1100.**

**East Bay Galleries** ⟨⟩   In the Mt. Pleasant area, this gallery is the South Carolina showcase for the work of some 400 artists. In business for some 2 decades, the shop sells paintings and is a leading exhibitor of art glass, jewelry, pottery, contemporary wood and metal art, textile art, wrought iron, mirrors, wind chimes, and eclectic one-of-a-kind pieces. The store also offers the largest selection of handcrafted fountains in the Southeast. Open Monday to Friday 10am to 6pm, Saturday 10am to 5pm, and Sunday noon to 5pm. 721 Coleman Blvd., Mt. Pleasant. ℂ **843/216-8010.**

**Lowcountry Artists**   In a former book bindery, this gallery is operated by eight local artists, who work in oil, watercolor, drawings, collage, woodcuts, and other media. Open Monday to Saturday 10am to 5pm, Sunday noon to 5pm. 148 E. Bay St. ℂ **843/577-9295.**

**Museum Shop**   This on-site museum store is the only agency in town authorized to sell reproductions of the famous etchings of Elizabeth O'Neill Verner, who was at the vanguard of the artistic movement of the 1920s and '30s known as the "Charleston Renaissance." Many visitors fall in love with her cityscapes and her delicate pastels of Charleston at the Gibbes Museum, then end their visit at this shop with a purchase of one or more of the Verner reproductions. Open Tuesday to Saturday 10am to 5pm, Sunday 1 to 5pm. 135 Meeting St. ℂ **843/722-2706.**

**Waterfront Gallery**   Facing Waterfront Park, this gallery is the premier choice for the work of South Carolina artists. The works of 21 local artists are presented. For sale are pieces ranging from sculpture to oils. Hours are Monday to Thursday 11am to 6pm, Friday to Saturday 11am to 10pm, Sunday noon to 5pm. 215 E. Bay St. (across from Custom House). ℂ 843/722-1155.

**Wells Gallery**   Works by artists from the Low Country and all over the Southeast are on display at this Charleston gallery. Specializing in Low Country landscapes, the gallery also offers works by artists from all over the U.S. Prices range from $600 to $12,000. Hours are Monday to Saturday 10am to 5pm. 103 Broad St. ℂ 843/853-3233.

## BOOKS

**Boomer's Books & Collectibles**   Near John Street in the city center, this huge store buys, sells, and trades books, offering some 50,000 previously owned titles, most sold at half-price. The store also sells popular reading material, and has a collection of rare books, along with collectibles, Low Country memorabilia, and gifts. Open Monday to Saturday 10am to 6pm, Sunday 2 to 6pm. 420 King St. ℂ 843/722-2666.

**Historic Charleston Foundation Shop & Bookstore**   In the historic district near Chalmers Street, this shop stocks books on the preservation and restoration of buildings. Its strong suit is a collection of coffee-table books, whose topics range from creating Southern gardens to selecting house colors popular during the reign of Queen Victoria. The shop also has a fine selection of gift items such as miniatures, reproductions in brass and china, textiles, and handicrafts. Open Monday to Saturday 10am to 5pm. 108 Meeting St. ℂ 843/724-8484.

**Preservation Society of Charleston Bookstore**   Near Queen Street in the historic district, this shop features a collection of books about Charleston and the Low Country. The outlet also sells art books, Southern literature, and even early recordings of Low Country lore told in the Gullah dialect. Local handicrafts, art prints, and the acclaimed architectural drawings of Jim Polzois are featured among the merchandise. Open Monday to Saturday 10am to 5pm. 147 King St. ℂ 843/722-4630.

## CARPETS

**Khoury Oriental Rugs**   This outlet features the best collection of hand-knotted Asian carpets in town. You'll find your "magic carpet"

## The Basket Ladies of the Low Country

Greatly diminished, but not lost, is the art of **sweetgrass basketry,** a living symbol of the antebellum plantation heyday in the Low Country. A tradition for 3 centuries, the art of basket weaving was brought to the Low Country when slaves were shipped here from the western coast of Africa, bringing their ancient basket-weaving skills with them. The skill had been passed down to them by their own mothers for generation after generation.

Originally, male slaves wove baskets used in agriculture, including the harvesting of rice. The women slaves wove a more functional but also decorative basket for the home, and these were used for food storage, sewing material, and the like. Sometimes if a plantation master took a liking to one of the more artfully executed baskets, he'd pass it along to a friend as a gift or else sell it for profit.

Low Country coil basketry remains one of the oldest crafts of African origin in the United States. To form the basket, pine needles, bulrush, and fiber strips from palmetto trees are used for binding. A basket can take anywhere from 12 hours to several months to make, depending on the design. Those that are true works of art command high prices and are often secured for exhibition in museums, including the Smithsonian. But you can easily obtain a fine basket for $40 and up.

The sweetgrass itself is a perennial, warm-season grass growing in the coastal dunes from North Carolina to Texas. Unfortunately, coastal development has greatly harmed the raw material used to produce these baskets, and sweetgrass becomes rarer and rarer. The Historic Charleston Foundation, hoping to save the industry, is sponsoring a test project on James Island to cultivate the native grass as a crop.

Today, the number of families engaged in sweetgrass baskets is estimated at around 300, a significant decline in the basket-making community. Most of the basket makers are from Mount Pleasant, north of Charleston. To purchase a sweetgrass basket for yourself, you can visit the Old City Market or else drive north on U.S. 17, where you'll see basket vendors in makeshift wooden stalls hawking their centuries-old wares along the roadside.

else reproductions). Rugs from China or India are also sold. In addition to these carpets, there is a tasteful selection of hand-painted Indian furniture and handcrafted Indonesian teakwood furniture. Open Monday to Saturday 9:30am to 5pm. 71 Wentworth St. $\mathcal{C}$ 843/720-7370.

## CIVIL WAR ARTIFACTS

**CSA Galleries**   In North Charleston, these galleries at the intersection of Montague Avenue and I-26 (exit 213) make up the largest Civil War and art gallery shop in the South. Its main specialty is Civil War prints, and it offers a full framing department. It is also an art gallery and peddles gifts and collectibles, clothing, glassware, videos, books, music boxes, and gourmet foods. In front of the building is Wilton House, a specialty gift shop selling everything from lamps to chess sets, including hand-painted glassware. Open Monday to Saturday 10am to 7pm. 2409A Mall Dr., Charles Towne Square, North Charleston. $\mathcal{C}$ 843/747-7554.

**Sumter Military Antiques & Museum**   Relics from the "War of Northern Aggression" are sold here. You'll find a collection of authentic artifacts that range from firearms and bullets to Confederate uniforms and artillery shells. There are some interesting prints, along with a collection of books on the Civil War. By appointment only. 341 King St. $\mathcal{C}$ 843/577-7766.

## CRAFTS & GIFTS

**Charleston Crafts** 🎨🎨   This is a permanent showcase for Low Country craft artists who work in a variety of media, including metal, glass, paper, clay, wood, and fiber. Handmade jewelry is also sold, along with basketry, leather, traditional crafts, and even homemade soaps. Open Monday to Saturday 10am to 5:30pm. 87 Hasell St. $\mathcal{C}$ 843/723-2938.

**Clown's Bazaar**   Store owner Deanna Wagoner's heart is as big as her smile. Her store is indeed one of a kind—the city's only tax-exempt, self-help crafts organization. Originally, it was in Katmandu, Nepal, founded to help Third World families help themselves. Economic and political circumstances forced the store's relocation to Charleston, but the objective of helping Third World families hasn't changed. The store features handmade carvings, silks, brasses, and pewter from exotic locales such as Africa, Nepal, India, Bangladesh, and the Philippines, as well as wooden toys and books, including some in Gullah, a nearly lost language that is still spoken

## Where All Visitors Go to Shop

The area around Market Hall, just south of the old residential suburb of Ansonborough, may never be what it was in its mid-19th-century prime when the Charleston Hotel stood here. One of America's grandest hotels, it attracted everyone from Jenny Lind to William Thackeray, from Daniel Webster to Queen Victoria.

Market Hall and the surrounding Charleston city market are still going strong today on land willed by the wealthy Pinckney family to be used as a market. The main building from 1841 is a bastardized version of the Grecian Doric temple of "Wingless Victory" in the city of Athens, Greece. It represented the finest achievement of Edward B. White, a leading architect and engineer of the mid-1800s. Made for the Confederacy in 1861, the cannon in the upper portico was the first manufactured in America.

Today the Old City Market sprawls across four buildings stretching from Meeting Street to East Bay Street. Hundreds of vendors hawk their wares within these precincts. For some reason, the market has a reputation as a flea market, although it is anything but that. High-quality merchandise is sold here, its most famous product being sweetgrass baskets. You can also purchase paintings, rugs, dolls, afghans, quality jewelry, local candies and cookies, even tapestries and rice and beans if you desire.

After falling into disrepair over the decades and suffering at the hands of Hurricane Hugo, the market bounced back in 2002 after a 4-year, $3.6-million restoration. It's the most festive place to shop in South Carolina, and it's open daily from 9am to 6pm.

in some areas of the city. Oh, and if you're looking for clown dolls, Deanna has those, too. Open Monday to Saturday 11am to 6pm, Sunday 10am to 5pm. 56 Broad St. ℂ **843/723-9769.**

**Indigo** Across from Waterfront Park, this store sells an eclectic variety of items ranging from folk to funk. It's all here: antique luggage, Mexican folk art, Brazilian textiles, Shaker boxes, wooden animals, luxury pillows, table linen, lamps, clocks, rugs, door knockers, lanterns, fountains, jewelry, mirrors, and wine accessories. Open Monday to Saturday 10am to 9pm, Sunday 10am to 7pm. 4 Vendue Range. ⓒ **843/723-2983.**

**People, Places & Quilts**    This full-service quilt shop also sells one-of-a-kind folk art from its premises near Elizabeth Street, off Marion Square. The store carries fabrics, books, patterns, kits, antique and new quilts, Sammy Gaillard Low Country scenes, and handcrafted wooden furniture. The store was chosen by *Better Homes & Gardens* as one of the 10 top quilt shops in North America. Open Monday to Saturday 10am to 5pm. 1 Henrietta St. ⓒ **843/937-9333.**

**The Silver Puffin**    Near Wentworth Street, this shop is unique in Charleston in that it seeks odd and interesting pieces from artists around the globe. You might find glass and jewelry from Finland or collectibles from Austria, maybe even a hand-carved wooden sculpture from Zimbabwe. The shop is strong on a charming selection of gifts for animal fanciers. Open Daily 10am to 6pm. 278 King St. ⓒ **888/ 723-7900** or 843/723-7900.

## DISHES & CRYSTAL

**Mikasa Factory Outlet Store**    You'll have to drive out of town to partake of these bargains, but at this factory outlet northwest of Charlestown in the town of Wando, you can pick up amazing bargains in dishes and crystal. These wares are sold alongside table accessories such as napkins and placemats. Many Mikasa items represent top quality and aren't rejects or "seconds." Sometimes only a damaged carton will cause an entire shipment to be rejected, which means the other crystal and dishes are top rate with no imperfections. The little town of Wando is the only Mikasa distribution center in America. Hours are Monday to Saturday 10am to 6pm, Sunday noon to 5pm. It's a 30-minute drive to Wando from the center of Charleston. 1980 Clements Ferry Rd. ⓒ **843/856-5064.** Take Highway 17 north to Highway 526 west, exiting at the Clements Ferry Road. Follow the signs from here.

## FASHION
### FOR CHILDREN

**82 Church Street**    In business for more than 6 decades, this outlet has traditionally dressed generations of Charleston children. Near Tradd Street in the historic district, the shop made a name for itself with its "Charleston Bonnet" for baby girls. The bonnet is puffed with a front-top bow and chin tie. The outlet also sells hand-smocked dresses, christening gowns, layette wear, boys' sunsuits, toys, and classic children's books, and a wide range of imported merchandise. Open Monday to Saturday 9:30am to 5:30pm. 1½ Broad St. © **800/377-1282** or 843/723-7511.

### FOR MEN

**Ben Silver**   One of the finer men's clothiers in Charleston, this is the best place to get yourself dressed like a member of the city's finest society. The store specializes in blazers and buttons; it has a collection of more than 600 blazer-button designs that are unique in the city. The store features house names and designs only, so don't go looking for Ralph Lauren here. Open Monday to Saturday 9am to 6pm. 149 King St. © **843/577-4556.**

### FOR WOMEN

**Nancy's**   On the main street, Nancy's specializes in clothing for the woman who wants to be both active and stylish. Complete outfits in linen, silk, and cotton are sold, along with such accessories as belts and jewelry. Nancy's aims for a "total look." Open Monday to Saturday 10am to 5:30pm. 342 King St. © **843/722-1272.**

## FOODSTUFFS & CANDIES

**Lucas Belgian Chocolate**   This is one of the truly fine chocolatiers in South Carolina, in business for more than 2 decades. In the historic district near Market Street, it sells imported Belgian chocolates, chocolate truffles, "turtles," and "clusters," among other mouthwatering confections. The store, in fact, features just about anything made of chocolate you might be seeking. Your purchases, incidentally, are beautifully wrapped. Hours are Tuesday to Saturday 10am to 6pm, Sunday 12:30 to 5:30pm. 73 State St. © **843/722-0461.**

**Market Street Sweets**   Following the success of a parent store in Savannah, this outlet opened in the historic district next to the Old City Market. The store is most famous for its pralines, although it also makes "bear claws," chocolates, and other homemade candy. Samples of its fudge, pralines, and other goodies are given out all day, and you can also watch candy being made and even talk to the chefs. The shop ships sweets anywhere. Open daily from 9am to 10pm. 100 N. Market St. © **843/722-1397.**

## FURNISHINGS

**Historic Charleston Reproductions** 𝕮𝕮   It's rare that a store with so much to offer could be not-for-profit, but that's the case here.

All items are approved by the Historic Charleston Foundation, and all proceeds benefit the restoration of Charleston's historic projects.

Licensed-replica products range from furniture to jewelry. The pride of the store is its home-furnishings collection by Baker Furniture, an esteemed company based in Michigan. What makes this collection unusual is the fact that the pieces are authentic mahogany adaptations of Charleston antiques that can only be found here.

If one of Charleston's iron designs around town has caught your eye, there's a chance that you'll find a replica of it in the form of jewelry. A collection of china from Mottahedeh is also featured.

The store operates shops in several historic houses, and offers more than just basic souvenirs; see its Francis Edmunds Center Museum Shop at 108 Meeting St. (© **843/724-8484**). Open Monday to Saturday 10am to 5pm, Sunday 1 to 5pm. 105 Broad St. © **843/723-8292**.

## GARDENING

**Charleston Gardens**    Close to Meeting Street, this is no ordinary garden store. In a carefully restored Victorian building, it has a courtyard garden designed by Robert Marvin, one of South Carolina's and the nation's leading landscape architects. It features one of the most extensive collections in America of English and French garden wares, including furniture, statuary, ornaments, terra-cotta pots, tools, and fountains. Gardening books, paintings, and prints are also offered. The store will ship anywhere. Open Monday to Saturday 9am to 5pm. 654 King St. © **843/723-0252**.

## HANDBAGS

**Moo Roo Handbags**    This is the flagship store of chic Moo Roo handbags, each personally signed and dated by Charleston-based designer Mary Norton. Celebrities are often photographed carrying these luxurious accessories. The array of different materials used to make these handbags—everything from exotic skins and feathers to semi-precious stones and the most elegant of fabrics—initially made them famous. The handbags are created in a workshop over this store. Other merchandise carried here includes scarves, wraps, and jewelry. Open Monday to Saturday 10am to 6pm. 316 King St. © **843/724-1081**.

## JEWELRY

**Croghan's Jewel Box**    You'll find gift ideas for any situation, from baby showers to weddings. Estate jewelry and some contemporary pieces are featured. This store also sets diamonds for rings and pendants, and can even secure the diamond for you, with the price depending on the type of stone and grade that you choose. Monday to Friday 9:30am to 5:30pm, Saturday 10am to 5pm. 308 King St. ℂ 843/723-3594.

**Dazzles**    One-of-a-kind jewelry is sold here, along with the finest collection of handmade 14-karat-gold slide bracelets in town. Some of the jewelry is of heirloom quality. The staff will also help you create jewelry of your own design, including a choice of stones. Open Monday to Saturday 10am to 7pm, Sunday noon to 5pm. Charleston Place, 226 King St. ℂ 843/722-5951.

**Geiss & Sons Jewelers**    Jewelry here is custom designed by old world–trained craftspeople. This is a direct offshoot of a store opened by the Geiss family in Brazil in 1919. It's an official watch dealer for names such as Rolex, Bertolucci, and Raymond Weil. Repair jobs are given special attention. Monday to Friday 10am to 5pm. 116 E. Bay St. ℂ 843/577-4497.

**Joint Venture Estate Jewelers**    This is an unusual jewelry store in that its major focus is on jewelry placed here on consignment. The pieces come from some 2,000 consignors of estates, as well as select pieces from private individuals and dealers. *Tip:* Because it doesn't own the inventory, the store sells at prices much lower than those of a traditional jewelry store. Open Monday to Saturday 10am to 5:30pm. 185 King St. ℂ 800/722-6730 or 843/722-6730.

## JOGGLING BOARDS
**Old Charleston Joggling Board Co.**    Since the early 1830s, joggling boards have been a Charleston tradition. These boards are the creation of Mrs. Benjamin Kinloch Huger, a native who sought a mild form of exercise for her rheumatism. Mrs. Huger's Scottish cousins sent her a model of a joggling board, suggesting that she sit and gently bounce on the board. The fame of the device soon spread, and the board soon turned up in gardens, patios, and porches throughout the Charleston area. After World War II, joggling boards became rare because of the scarcity of timber and the high cost of labor, but the tradition was revived in 1970. The company also produces a joggle bench, a duplicate of the joggling board but only 10 feet long (as opposed to the original 16 ft.) and 20 inches from the ground. Monday to Friday 8am to 5pm. 652 King St. ℂ 843/723-4331.

## LINGERIE

**Bits of Lace**    This lingerie boutique is the best in town. It has all the romance and beauty associated with a Harlequin novel. You'll find every type of merchandise here from a "diamond tea" cashmere robe to Lise Charmel bras. The staff is justifiably proud of its lace slip collection, as well as its wide range of clothing items in silk, lace, or soft cotton. Bra fittings from 32A to 44H. Open Monday to Saturday 10am to 6pm. 302 King St. ✆ **800/842-3999** or 843/577-0999.

## PERFUME

**Scents of Charleston**    Favorite fragrances are found here, and prices (for the most part) are relatively reasonable. The shop evokes a perfumery in Europe. Scents creates its own exclusive brands, and also features classic and popular fragrances. Monday to Thursday 10am to 9pm, Friday and Saturday 10am to 10pm, Sunday 10am to 6pm. 92 N. Market St. ✆ **843/853-8837**.

## SHOES

**Bob Ellis**    This is the most famous shoe store in Charleston, lying at the corner of King and George streets. In business for half a century, Bob Ellis provides an extensive selection of high-fashion or high-quality durable shoes, even featuring hard-to-find sizes for both women and men. The store also sells a fashionable assortment of women's handbags. Open Monday to Saturday 9am to 6pm. 332 King St. ✆ **843/722-2515**.

## SMOKE SHOP

**The Smoking Lamp**    This is Charleston's oldest smoke shop, with the most complete array of tobacco products in the city. You'll find an assortment of pipes, tobacco, cigars, even walking canes and other paraphernalia. Open Monday to Wednesday 10am to 10pm, Thursday to Saturday 10am to 11pm, Sunday 11am to 8pm. 189 E. Bay St. ✆ **843/577-7339**.

## SPORTING GOODS

**Half Moon Outfitters**    Launched in 1993, this store is staffed by folks who take their outdoor pursuits seriously. Surfers, climbers, paddlers, windsurfers, and backpackers are waiting to serve you and advise. Open Monday to Saturday 10am to 7pm, Sunday noon to 6pm. 280 King St. ✆ **843/853-0990**.

# 10

# Charleston After Dark

Not surprisingly, Charleston offers more nighttime diversions than any other city in South Carolina. It has a rich cultural life and also features a number of bars for good times and often live music.

## 1 The Performing Arts

Charleston's major cultural venue is the **Dock Street Theatre,** 133 Church St. (© **843/965-4032;** www.charlestonstage.com), a 463-seat theater. The original was built in 1736 but burned down in the early 19th century, and the Planters Hotel (not related to the Planters Inn) was constructed around its ruins. In 1936, the theater was rebuilt in a new location. It's the home of the **Charleston Stage Company,** a local not-for-profit theater group whose season runs from mid-September to May. Dock Street hosts performances ranging from Shakespeare to *My Fair Lady.* It's most active during the Spoleto Festival USA in May and June. The box office (© **843/577-7183**) is open Monday to Friday 10am to 5pm, Saturday 10am to 5pm and a half-hour before curtain, and Sunday from 10am to 3pm.

The **Robert Ivey Ballet,** 1910 Savannah Hwy. (© **843/556-1343**), offers both classical and contemporary dance, as well as children's ballet programs. The group performs at various venues throughout the Charleston area, with general-admission prices of $20 for adults and $15 for children.

**Charleston Ballet Theatre,** 477 King St. (© **843/723-7334;** www.charlestonballet.com), is one of the South's best professional ballet companies. The season begins in late October and continues into April. Tickets are $22 to $40.

**Charleston Symphony Orchestra,** 14 George St. (© **843/723-7528;** www.charlestonsymphony.com), performs throughout the state, but its main venues are the Gaillard Auditorium and Charleston Southern University. The season runs from September to May.

## 2 The Club & Music Scene

**Blind Tiger Pub**   Near Bay Street, this pub occupies a historic location, a bar having operated here since 1803. The name comes from the days when Charlestonians opened up illegal "parlors of consumption" before the days of speakeasies—these parlors were known as "blind tigers." The legend was that admission fees were paid to see the mythical beast known as a Blind Tiger, with "complimentary" cocktails served. The tiger never showed up, of course, and the drinks weren't really free. Lawyers and businessmen in suits frequent the on-site Four Corners Café at lunch, but at night more casual attire is worn by the crowd, usually in the 30- to 40-year age range. Live jazz or other kinds of music is played in the evening. Out back is a walled deck with subdued lighting and fountains. Cafe hours are Monday to Saturday from noon to 3pm and 5 to 10pm. The bar is open Monday to Friday from 4pm to 2am, Saturday 1:30pm to 2am, and Sunday 2pm to 2am. 38 Broad St. © 843/577-0088.

**Cumberland's**   If your musical tastes run from Delta blues to rock to reggae, this is the place for you. The dominant age group at this bar depends on the act playing. You will find that the generation gap isn't strong here, with college students toasting glasses with midlifers. Greasy chicken wings and lots of suds make this place ever popular. Music is the common bond. Daily 11am to 2am. 301 King St. © 843/577-9469. Cover varies.

**Henry's**   One of the best places for jazz in Charleston, this club features a live band on Friday and Saturday. Otherwise, you get taped top-40 music for listening and dancing. If you're a single man or woman with a roving eye, this is one of the hottest pickup bars in town. It attracts a mainly over-30 crowd. Happy hour, with drink discounts and free appetizers, is Monday to Friday from 4 to 7pm. Hours are Monday to Saturday 4pm to 2am and Sunday noon to 2am. 54 N. Market St. © 843/723-4363.

**Music Farm** ★★   This club describes itself as "Charleston's premier music venue." It covers nearly every taste in music, from country to rock. You're as likely to hear funkster George Clinton as you are country legend George Jones. The club hosts local and regional bands, as well as national acts. Music is present anywhere from 2 to 6 nights a week from 8am to 2am. Call © 843/853-3276 for schedules and information. 32 Ann St. © 843/722-8904. Cover $10–$25.

**The Rodeo Room** This is one of the most popular bars in Charleston County. It is a full 360-degree bar, with a huge stage for live music and such extra features as seven pool tables and all kinds of video games. Live entertainment—the best in country music—is most often featured, along with big-screen sporting events. There's also a full kitchen should you get hungry. The average age of the clients is 20 to 30, but all ages are welcome. The location is in North Charleston off West Aviation Avenue in "The Plex," the old Aviation Cinemas Building off I-26 leaving Charleston. Open Friday 7pm to 2am and Saturday 8pm to 2am. 2390 W. Aviation Ave. ✆ 843/225-7539. Cover $5 Fri–Sat.

**Tommy Condon's Irish Pub** Located in a restored warehouse in the city market area, this Irish pub and family restaurant is full of Old Ireland memorabilia. The bartender turns out a leprechaun punch, a glass of real Irish ale, and most definitely Irish coffee. The menu offers Irish food, along with Low Country specials such as shrimp and grits or jambalaya. Happy hour, with reduced drink prices, is Monday to Friday from 5 to 7pm. Live Irish entertainment is presented Wednesday to Sunday from 8:30pm until closing. Pub hours are Sunday to Thursday 11am to 10pm, Friday and Saturday 11am to 2am. 160 Church St. ✆ 843/577-3818.

**The Trio Club** This high-energy, live-music venue lies in the historic district near Meeting Street. If smoke gets in your eyes, you can flee to the outdoor patio for some fresh air. Featured are Latin, blues, folk, jazz, and rock performances, usually enjoyed by a crowd in its 20s and 30s. Open Thursday to Saturday from 8pm to 2am. 139 Calhoun St. ✆ 843/965-5333. Cover varies from $10–$25.

## 3 The Bar Scene

**The Brick** Set in what was built in the 19th century as a warehouse, this neighborhood bar is lined with handmade bricks and capped with heavy timbers. It receives a wide medley of drinkers, everyone from college students to local dockyard workers, as well as a scattering of travelers from out of town. Appetizers and burgers are the only food served, but at least a dozen beers are on tap. Live music begins at 9:30pm Wednesday to Saturday. The tavern is open daily 5pm to 2am. 213 E. Bay St. ✆ 843/720-7788.

**Charlie's Little Bar** Near Unity Alley, this bar lies above the restaurant Saracen. With its vaguely Moorish architecture, it is an inviting oasis with comfortable, big leather couches. Drawing patrons in their 30s and 40s, it's a cigar-and-martini kind of place. The dress is casual to stylish. Open daily from 8pm to 2am. 141 E. Bay St. © 843/723-6242.

**Club Habana**   With the ambience of a private club, this second-floor house from 1870 is where the Ernest Hemingway of today would head if he were in Charleston. Relax in one of three Gilded Age salons, each evocative of the Reconstruction era of the Old South. The house specializes in exotic cigars and martinis, and serves appetizers, desserts, fruit and cheese plates, and even some miniature beef Wellingtons. While filming *The Patriot,* Mel Gibson made Habana his second home in the city. You pass through a well-stocked tobacco store downstairs to reach the club. Open Sunday to Thursday 4:30pm to midnight, Friday and Saturday 4:30pm to 2am. 177 Meeting St. © 843/853-5900.

**First Shot Bar** ⊕   Our preferred watering hole is this old standby, where we've seen such visiting celebs as Gerald Ford and Elizabeth Taylor (not together, of course) over the years. The bar is one of the most elegant in Charleston, a comfortable and smooth venue for a drink. If you get hungry, the kitchen will whip you up some shrimp and grits. Open daily 4 to 10:30pm. In the Mills House Hotel, 115 Meeting St. © 843/577-2400.

**The Griffon**   Much Scotch and beer is consumed at this popular Irish pub. A full array of home-cooked specials from the old country is served as well, including such pub-grub favorites as steak pies, bangers and mash (English sausage and mashed potatoes), and the inevitable fish and chips. Open daily 11am to 2am; happy hour is Monday to Friday from 4 to 7pm. 18 Vendue Range. © 843/723-1700. Cover varies.

**Peninsula Grill Bar** ⊕⊕   In the swanky Planters Inn and attached to a deluxe restaurant, this upscale champagne bar has received national acclaim. It is a lavish setting for drinking, with velvet-paneled walls, oil paintings, and antique lamps, all of which create a 1930s supper-club ambience. The crowd tends to be middle-aged, and dress is business casual to stylish. You can order champagne by the glass and such delights as fresh oysters, lobster, and crab. The bar is open daily 4pm to 1am, and the restaurant is open Sunday to Thursday 5:30 to 10pm and Friday and Saturday 5:30 to 11pm. 112 Market St. © 843/723-0700.

**Roof Top at the Vendue Inn** If you like your drinks with a view, there is none more panoramic than the rooftop of this previously recommended inn. As you down your cocktails, you can take in a sweeping vista of Charleston that includes Waterfront Park, the Cooper River Bridges, and embattled Fort Sumter. Patronize this up-market bar for your "sundowner" (watching the sun set). From Sunday to Wednesday you can listen to live music, including jazz, reggae, and bluegrass. There's never a cover charge. Hours are daily 11:30am to 11pm. 19 Vendue Range. ℰ **843/845-7900.**

**Vickery's Bar & Grill** This is one of the most popular gathering places in Charleston for the younger crowd, especially students. It's also a good dining choice, with an international menu that includes jerk chicken and gazpacho. But the real secrets of the place's success are its 16-ounce frosted mugs of beer for $2.50 and the convivial atmosphere. Open daily 11:30am to 1am. 15 Beaufain St. ℰ **843/577-5300.**

## 4 Microbreweries

For some, an evening in a microbrewery is the way to go in Charleston. Our favorite is **Southend Brewery & Smokehouse,** 161 E. Bay St. (ℰ **843/853-4677**), which specializes in wood-fired pizzas and barbecue—washed down with a variety of original microbrews. Open Sunday to Thursday 11:30am to midnight, Friday and Saturday 11:30am to 2am.

## 5 Gay & Lesbian Bars

**Déjà Vu II** Some people say this is the coziest and warmest "ladies' bar" in the Southeast. The owners have transformed what used to be a supper club into a cozy enclave with two bars, weekend live entertainment (usually by "all-girl bands"), and a clientele that's almost exclusively gay and 75% lesbian. The ambience is unpretentious and charming, and definitely does not exclude sympathetic patrons of any ilk. This is a late-night spot, but hours vary; call ahead. 4634 Prulley Ave. N. Charleston. ℰ **843/554-5959;** www.dejavuii.com. Cover varies.

**Pantheon** This is the newest and hottest gay venue in town. Located in the historic district, near Meeting Street, it used to be known as Avalon's and was patronized by virtually every gay man in all parts of South Carolina. It is basically a bar with a dance floor, and entertainment is provided by DJs spinning tunes. On Friday

and Sunday nights that retro form of entertainment, female imper-
sonation, is presented. Open Friday to Sunday from 10pm until
2am. 28 Ann St. ℃ **843/577-2582.** Cover varies.

**Patrick's Pub & Grill**    If you like your men in leather, chances are
you'll find Mr. Right here. A gay pub and grill right outside
Charleston, this is a late-night venue for some of the hottest men in
Charleston. Levis take second place to leather. Open 6pm to 2am
daily. 1377 Ashley River Rd. (Hwy. 61). ℃ **843/571-3435.**

## 6 Late-Night Bites

**Kaminsky's Most Excellent Café**    Following a night of jazz or
blues, this is a good spot to rest your feet and order the power boost
you need to make it through the rest of the evening. The handsome
bar offers a wide selection of wines and is ideal for people-watching.
The desserts are sinful, especially the Italian cream cake and mountain chocolate cake. Open daily noon to 2am. 78 N. Market St. ℃ **843/
853-8270.**

# 11

# Nearby Islands

For their summer fun, the people of Charleston head southeast to a series of islands in the Atlantic Ocean. The more popular of these are the **Isle of Palms, Kiawah Island,** and **Sullivan's Island.** In July and August, these breeze-swept islands are the place to be.

Some of the islands now contain upscale resorts, and all have long sandy beaches. This chapter is for sun worshippers, surf fishermen, boaters, and beachcombers in general. It's for those who like to go hiking along nature trails such as those found on Edisto Island. White-tailed deer and bobcats live in the maritime forests. The endangered small tern and loggerhead turtles still nest and lay their eggs on some of these islands.

There are no tourist information offices on these islands except at Kiawah. For information before you go, contact the **Charleston Area Convention and Visitors Bureau,** 375 Meeting St. (© **800/774-0006** or 843/853-8000; www.charlestoncvb.com).

## 1 The Isle of Palms

10 miles N of Charleston

A residential community bordered by the Atlantic Ocean and lying 10 miles north of Charleston, this island of salt marshes and wildlife has been turned into a vacation retreat, albeit one that is more downscale than Kiawah Island (later in this chapter). The attractions of Charleston are close at hand, but the Isle of Palms is also self-contained, with shops, dining, accommodations, and two championship golf courses.

Charlestonians have been flocking to the Isle of Palms for holidays since 1898. The first hotel opened here in 1911. Seven miles of wide, white sandy beach are the island's main attraction, and sailing and windsurfing are popular. The more adventurous go crabbing and shrimping in the creeks.

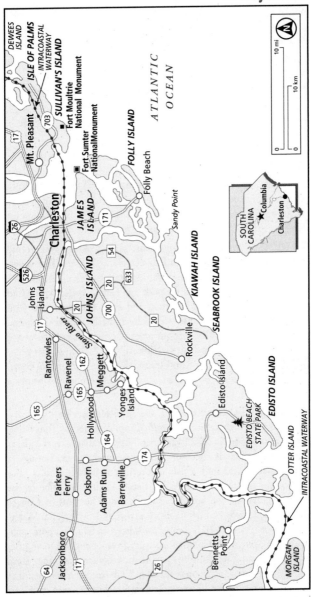

**GETTING THERE**    From Charleston, take U.S. 17 north to S.C. 517, then S.C. 703 to Isle of Palms. I-26 intersects with I-526 heading directly to the island via the Isle of Palms Connector (S.C. 517).

## OUTDOOR PURSUITS

**BEACHES**    The beach is often the center of activity on the Isle of Palms. You can enjoy the waves by renting a bodyboard from a nearby lifeguard stand, or play a friendly game of beach volleyball. Beachcombing for shells can net you treasures like sand dollars, whelks, and angel wings.

**BOATING**    A true Charlestonian is as much at home on the sea as on land. Sailing local waters is a popular family pastime. One of the best places for rentals is **Isle of Palms Marina** (© 843/886-0209), where 18-foot boats, big enough for seven people, rent for around $240 for 4 hours, plus fuel. A larger pontoon boat, big enough for 10, goes for $375 to $450 for 4 hours, plus fuel.

**FISHING**    Freshwater fishing charters are available year-round along the Low Country's numerous creeks and inlets. The waterways are filled with flounder, trout, spot-tail, and channel bass.

Offshore-fishing charters for both reef fishing (where you'll find fish such as cobia, black sea bass, and king mackerel) and Gulf Stream fishing (where you fish for sailfish, marlin, wahoo, dolphin, and tuna) are also available. Both types of charters can be arranged at **Isle of Palms Marina** (© 843/886-0209). A fishing craft holding up to ten people rents for around $525 to $575 for 6 hours, including everything but food and drink. Reservations must be made 1 week in advance.

**GOLF**    **Wild Dunes Resort** (© 843/886-6000; www.wilddunes. com) offers two championship golf courses designed by Tom Fazio. **The Links** 𝕬𝕬𝕬 is a 6,722-yard, par-72 layout that takes the player through marshlands, over or into huge sand dunes, through a wooded alley, and into a pair of oceanfront finishing holes once called "the greatest east of Pebble Beach, California." The course ranks among the top courses in the world. **The Harbor Course** offers 6,402 yards of Low Country marsh and Intracoastal Waterway views. This par-70 layout is considered to be target golf, challenging players with two holes that play from one island to another across Morgan Creek. Greens fees at these courses can range from $79 to $155, depending on the season. Clubs can be rented at either course for $25 for 18 holes, and professional instruction costs $85 for a 1-hour session. Both courses are open daily from 7am to 6pm year-round.

## WHERE TO STAY

**Wild Dunes Resort** 🌴🌴    A bit livelier than the Kiawah Island Golf Resort, its major competitor, this complex is set on landscaped ground on the north shore. The 1,600-acre resort has not only two widely acclaimed golf courses, but an array of other outdoor attractions. Many families settle in here for a long stay, almost never venturing into Charleston. Guests are housed in condos and a series of cottages and villas. Many accommodations have only one bedroom, but others have as many as six. Villas and cottages are built along the shore, close to golf and tennis. Furnishings are tasteful and resortlike, with kitchens, washers and dryers, and spacious bathrooms with dressing areas. Some of the best units have screened-in balconies.

**Edgar's Restaurant** serves standard American cuisine and regional specialties. The hotel also maintains a lounge, which stays open until 2am.

5757 Palm Blvd., Charleston, SC 29451. ✆ **888/778-1876** or 843/886-6000. Fax 843/886-2916. www.wilddunes.com. 500 units. $135–$320 double/suite; $255–$1,300 villa or cottage. Golf packages available. AE, DC, DISC, MC, V. Free parking. **Amenities:** 2 restaurants; bar; 4 outdoor pools; 2 18-hole golf courses; 18 tennis courts; fitness center; Jacuzzi; sauna; limited room service; massage; babysitting; laundry service; dry cleaning; nonsmoking rooms; rooms for those w/limited mobility. *In room:* A/C, TV, dataport, kitchen (in some), minibar, coffeemaker, hair dryer, iron, safe, washer/dryer (in some).

## WHERE TO DINE

**The Boathouse** 🌴 SEAFOOD    Seafood fresh from the fishing boats is deliciously prepared at this popular restaurant at the Breach Inlet Bridge. Expect abundant portions and the best raw bar selections in the area. If you don't like seafood (what are you doing here?), you'll find big, juicy steaks, homemade pastas, and in-house smoked chops. The list of appetizers is the best on island—old favorites such as fried green tomatoes with black-eyed pea vinaigrette and Roma tomato jam or else roasted corn and she-crab soup. The grilled fresh fish of the day comes with a number of sauces, ranging from pesto to tarragon butter, from soy-ginger butter to blackened seasoning. Breach Inlet littleneck clams come steamed in chardonnay, garlic, and fresh herbs over linguine.

101 Palm Blvd. ✆ **843/886-8000**. Reservations recommended. Main courses $14–$34; brunch $8–$13. AE, MC, V. Sun–Thurs 5–10pm; Fri–Sat 5–11pm; Sun brunch 11am–2pm. Closed Jan 1, Thanksgiving, and Dec 25.

## 2 Sullivan's Island

15 miles S of Charleston

Lying between the Isle of Palms to its east and historic Fort Sumter to its west, Sullivan's Island is the site of Fort Moultrie, dating back to the Revolutionary War, being the oldest fortification around Charleston. The island is steeped in history. On June 28, 1776, the Battle of Sullivan's Island became the first Patriot victory in the Revolutionary War. The fort also saw some of the earliest action of the Civil War. Even in World War II, its sea-facing bunkers and battlements were used by U.S. forces to spot German submarines.

Today this quiet residential community east of Charleston is visited mainly for its sandy beaches. Along with the Isle of Palms, Sullivan's Island has for years been one of the favored retreats of Charleston families. Large houses constructed on stilts line the dunes.

Sullivan's Island has more or less bounced back from the massive devastation caused by Hurricane Hugo in 1987. Still, beach erosion can be an issue, especially at high tide when the silvery, hard-packed sands run a bit thin.

**GETTING THERE**   From Charleston, take U.S. 17 N to S.C. 703.

## OUTDOOR PURSUITS

**BEACHES**   In the **East Cooper** area, Sullivan's Island offers miles of public sandy beaches, mostly bordered by beachfront homes. Windsurfing and jet-skiing are popular here.

## SEEING THE SIGHTS: ONE OF AMERICA'S OLDEST FORTS

**Fort Moultrie**   Only a palmetto-log fortification at the time of the American Revolution, the half-completed fort was attacked by a British fleet in 1776. Colonel William Moultrie's troops repelled the invasion in one of the first decisive American victories of the Revolution. The fort was subsequently enlarged into a five-sided structure with earth-and-timber walls 17 feet high. The British didn't do it in, but an 1804 hurricane ripped it apart. By the War of 1812, it was back and ready for action. Osceola, the fabled leader of the Seminoles in Florida, was incarcerated at the fort and eventually died here. During the 1830s, Edgar Allen Poe served as a soldier at the fort. He set his famous short story "The Gold Bug" on Sullivan's Island. The fort also played roles in the Civil War, the Mexican War, the Spanish-American War, and even in the two World Wars, but by 1947, it had retired from action.

1214 Middle St., on Sullivan's Island. (C) **843/883-3123.** www.nps.gov/fomo. Admission $3 adults, $1 seniors over 62, $5 family, free for children under 17. Federal Recreation Passports honored. Daily 9am–5pm. Closed Christmas Day and New Year's Day. Take S.C. 703 from Mt. Pleasant to Sullivan's Island.

## WHERE TO STAY

There are no hotels or multi-family housing units on the island. However, rental properties are available by calling either **Dunes Properties** at (C) **800/846-8301** or **Resort Quest** at (C) **800/344-5105.**

## WHERE TO DINE

**Atlanticville** ✿ ECLECTIC    Many residents of Charleston make the 10-minute drive from the city to dine here at night in a relaxed setting or to sit on the patio for their "sundowner." It's a romantic atmosphere—and the food's good, too.

The menu is the creation of Chef Phil Corr and his wife, Victoria Schippa Corr. Both are master chefs. Victoria, for example, is a master baker known for serving some of the finest desserts in the Low Country. The chefs range the world for their culinary inspiration, offering, for example, a Thai Tuesday, filled with specialties from Southeast Asia. The appetizers are the most imaginative in the area, including a slow-roasted duck mole burrito with a smoked apple salsa. They cook a lamb shank here so tender that the meat falls off the bone, and the deviled-crab-stuffed pork loin is sheer delight. The Sunday brunch is a well-attended event.

2063 Middle St. (C) **843/883-9452.** Brunch $6–$12; main courses $18–$25. AE, MC, V. Daily 5:30–10pm; Sun 10am–2pm. Closed Dec 24–25.

## 3 Kiawah Island

21 miles S of Charleston

This eco-sensitive private residential and resort community sprawls across 10,000 acres. Named for the Kiawah Indians who inhabited the islands in the 17th century, it today consists of two resort villages: East Beach and West Beach. The community fronts a lovely 10-mile stretch of Atlantic beach; magnolias, live oaks, pine forests, and acres of marsh characterize the island. Kiawah boasts many challenging golf courses, including one designed by Jack Nicklaus at Turtle Point that *Golf Digest* has rated among the top 10 courses in South Carolina. *Tennis* magazine rates Kiawah as one of the nation's top tennis resorts, with its 28 hard-surface or Har-Tru clay courts. Anglers are also attracted to the island, especially in spring and fall.

**GETTING THERE** From Charleston, take U.S. 17 E to S.C. 171 S (Folly Beach Rd.); turn right onto S.C. 700 SW (Maybank Hwy.) to Bohicket Road, which turns into Betsy Kerrigan Parkway. Where Betsy Kerrigan Parkway dead ends, turn left on Kiawah Parkway, which takes you to the island.

**VISITOR INFORMATION** The **Kiawah Island Visitors Center,** at 21 Beachwalker Dr. (© **843/768-9166**), is open Monday to Friday from 9am to 3pm.

## OUTDOOR PURSUITS

**BEACHES** **Kiawah Island** has the area's most pristine beach—far preferable to nearby Folly Beach, to our tastes—and draws a more up-market crowd. The best beachfront is at **Beachwalker County Park,** on the southern end of the island. Get there before noon on weekends; the limited parking is usually gone by then. Canoe rentals are available for use on the Kiawah River, and the park offers not only a boardwalk but also bathrooms, showers, and a changing area.

**GOLF** Designed by Jack Nicklaus, **Turtle Point Golf Course** (© **843/768-2121**) is an 18-hole, par-72, 7,054-yard course. From March to June and from September to December, Kiawah Island Resort guests pay $160 in greens fees and nonguests pay $205. Off season, guests of the resort pay $101 and nonguests pay $134.

The home of the 1991 Ryder Cup, the 1997 World Cup, the 2001 U.S. Warburg Cup, and the 2003 World Cup, **Ocean Point Golf Course** (© **843/768-2121**) was designed by Pete Dye. It is an 18-hole, par-72, 7,296-yard course, the finest in South Carolina—indeed, one of the top courses in America, and it was even featured in the movie *The Legend of Bagger Vance* in 2000. High season is March to June and September to December, when Kiawah Island Resort guests pay $265 in greens fees and nonguests pay $305. Call for off-season rates.

**TENNIS** One of the greatest tennis resorts in the South is found at the **Kiawah Island Tennis Resort** (© **843/768-2121**), with 28 hard-surface or Har-Tru clay courts. Kiawah Island Resort guests pay $24 per hour and nonguests $35. There are two tennis clubs here, including West Beach in the West Beach Village, as well as East Beach in East Beach Village. In summer, hours are daily 8am to 8pm, spring and fall daily 8am to 7pm, and winter daily 9am to 5pm.

## WHERE TO STAY

**The Sanctuary at Kiawah Island** ⭐⭐⭐    One of the greatest resorts in the Southeast opened in the summer of 2004. With its sweeping views of the Atlantic, this $125-million ultra-luxury resort and spa lies just south of Charleston. It is nestled among majestic live oak stands along the island's 10-mile beachfront. It was constructed in the grand tradition of a seaside mansion, offering guests preferred tee times at the island's five championship golf courses. The sprawling resort features some of the largest and most luxurious guest rooms in America, with 90% of the units opening onto the water. In addition, the resort offers two oceanfront restaurants, plus other dining choices. The entrance to the resort is lined with some 150 transplanted live oak trees.

12 Kiawah Beach Dr., Kiawah Island, SC 29455. ℂ **800/576-1570** or 843/768-2121. Fax 843/768-6099. www.kiawahresort.com. 255 units. $280–$600 double; from $900 suite. AE, DC, DISC, MC, V. **Amenities:** 5 restaurants; 4 bars; 3 pools (1 indoor); 5 18-hole golf courses; 28 tennis courts; fitness center; spa; sauna; 24-hr. room service; babysitting; laundry service; dry cleaning; nonsmoking rooms; rooms for those w/limited mobility. *In room:* A/C, TV, dataport, minibar, hair dryer, safe.

## WHERE TO DINE

**The Ocean Room** ⭐⭐⭐ ECLECTIC    One of the premier restaurants in Greater Charleston, this restaurant is as luxurious as the hotel in which it's nestled—The Sanctuary at Kiawah Island. As you enter through two grand gates made of wrought iron, framing the entrance, a mahogany-paneled bar with an equestrian decor appears. From your table, you can enjoy a panoramic ocean view. The chef, Chris Brandt, defines his cuisine as New American, focusing on the country's best produce, but the actual culinary influence is global. His most justifiably praised appetizer is a duck confit, the shredded meat combined with caramelized shallots and wild blueberries, served atop a crepe with a port reduction. The main courses are delectable, including the Ahi tuna from Hawaii paired with lavender-scented jasmine rice. There's always something new and exciting on the menu to tempt your palate.

12 Kiawah Beach Dr., Kiawah Island, SC 29455. ℂ **843/768-6253** or 843/768-6007 (Kiawah Island Resort Concierge). Reservations required. Main courses $32–$42. AE, DC, DISC, MC, V. Sun–Wed 6–10pm; Thurs–Sat 5:30–10pm.

## 4 Seabrook Island

21 miles S of Charleston

Seabrook Island as the "gated community" we know today originated in the 1970s, when a group of investors added electrical, water, and sewage lines to an isolated barrier island, connected it to the South Carolina mainland with a causeway, and hauled in construction teams for the erection of a wide array of generally upscale town houses, beach houses, and villas.

Today, the flat 2,200-acre island is dotted with carefully planned clusters of private homes, each with its own architectural style, but each corresponding to the demands imposed by the site and the island's role as a resort and retirement community. Seabrook's social centerpiece is a country club–inspired restaurant and bar, where many of the full-time residents catch up with the goings-on of their community. Other dining choices, in many price ranges, including some that are downright honky-tonk, lie on the South Carolina mainland, just across the causeway.

Entrance to the island is controlled by a security gate for the protection of guests and residents.

**GETTING THERE**   From Charleston, take U.S. 17 E to S.C. 171 S (Folly Beach Rd.), and turn right onto S.C. 700 SW (Maybank Hwy.) to Bohicket Road, which turns into Betsy Kerrigan Parkway. Turn right on Seabrook Island Road, then right on Persimmon Pond Court.

---

### Your Own Private Seabrook Condo

If this Seabrook lifestyle appeals to you, consider renting an apartment or house. Contact **Resort Quest,** one of the region's premier rental services, at 1001 Landfall Way, Seabrook Island, SC 29455 (℅ **800/247-5050** or 843/765-2300; www.seabrook.com). You can also book villas through **Seabrook Resort,** 1002 Landfall Way, Seabrook Island, SC 29455 (℅ **800/845-2233;** www.seabrook.com). Rates generally begin as low as $150 per day, going up to $450 or beyond. Credit cards (Amex, Discover, MasterCard, and Visa) are accepted.

## OUTDOOR PURSUITS

Once on the island, you'll find 3½ miles of unspoiled sandy beaches along with championship golf courses and other recreational activities. **Bohicket Marina** has 20 slips available for all sizes of boats, and rentals and charters for deep-sea fishing are also offered. The island's equestrian center is another recreational option.

**HORSEBACK RIDING**   Contact the **Seabrook Equestrian Center,** 1001 Landfall Way, Seabrook Island, SC 29455 (© **843/768-7541**). You should make reservations at least 1 week in advance of your trip (the center suggests even longer advance reservations around holidays). The equestrian center offers both trail rides and beach rides. Call for schedule and fees. The center also gives riding lessons and can be used by nonresort guests who make a reservation. Your pass will be available at the security gate at the entrance to the island.

# 12

# Hilton Head & Beaufort

Much more commercial than Charleston is Hilton Head Island, home of wealthy Northerners (mostly retired) and vacationers from all parts of the country. With myriad contemporary beachfront restaurants and rows of hotels, timeshare villas, and cottages, the island has recently sprouted boutiques and upscale shopping areas. Although the traffic is horrendous (there is only one main thoroughfare both on and off the island), development hasn't obliterated nature on Hilton Head, and you can find solitude at the north end of the beach.

On the positive side, the island has become socially and culturally oriented, playing host to presidents and world leaders and also supporting its own symphony orchestra and ballet company. **Sea Pines** on Hilton Head is one of the country's premier golf resorts, located on a 605-acre Wildlife Foundation preserve that's home to birds, squirrels, dolphins, and alligators. Hilton Head has 15 miles of bike paths and 5 miles of pristine beaches.

Also take time to stop in **Beaufort,** the inspiration for Pat Conroy's novel *The Prince of Tides* (among other bestsellers). The town is full of old-fashioned inns, rustic pubs, and tiny stores along a tailored waterfront park.

## 1 Hilton Head ★★★

100 miles S of Charleston

The largest sea island between New Jersey and Florida and one of America's great resort meccas, Hilton Head is surrounded by the Low Country, where much of the romance, beauty, and graciousness of the Old South survives. Broad white-sand beaches are warmed by the Gulf Stream and fringed with palm trees and rolling dunes. Palms mingle with live oaks, dogwood, and pines, and everything is draped in Spanish moss. Graceful sea oats, anchoring the beaches, wave in the wind. The subtropical climate makes all this beauty the ideal setting for golf and for some of the Southeast's finest saltwater fishing. Far more sophisticated and upscale than Myrtle Beach and the Grand Strand, Hilton Head's "plantations" (as most resort areas here call themselves) offer visitors something of the traditional leisurely lifestyle that's always held sway here.

Although it covers only 42 square miles (it's 12 miles long and 5 miles wide at its widest point), Hilton Head feels spacious, thanks to judicious planning from the beginning of its development in 1952. And that's a blessing, because about 2.3 million resort guests visit annually (the permanent population is about 35,000). The broad beaches on its ocean side, sea marshes on the sound, and natural wooded areas of live and water oak, pine, bay, and palmetto trees in between have all been carefully preserved amid commercial explosion. This lovely setting attracts artists, writers, musicians, theater groups, and craftspeople. The only city (of sorts) is Harbour Town, at Sea Pines Plantation, a Mediterranean-style cluster of shops and restaurants.

## ESSENTIALS

**GETTING THERE**    Many major airlines fly into Savannah, so it's easy to fly, rent a car, and drive to Hilton Head (about 65 miles north of Savannah). See chapter 4 for complete details on all the airlines flying into Savannah. If you're driving from other points south or north, just exit off I-95 to reach the island (Exit 28 off I-95 south, Exit 5 off I-95 north). U.S. 278 leads over the bridge to the island. It's 52 miles northeast of Savannah and located directly on the Intracoastal Waterway.

**VISITOR INFORMATION**    The **Island Visitors Information Center** is on U.S. 278 at S.C. 46 (© **843/785-4472;** www.enjoy hiltonhead.com), just before you cross over from the mainland. It offers a free *Where to Go* booklet, including a visitor map and guide. It's open Monday to Saturday from 9:30am to 5:30pm.

The **Hilton Head Visitors and Convention Bureau** (chamber of commerce), 1 Chamber Dr. (© **843/785-3673;** www.hiltonhead island.org), offers free maps of the area and will assist you in finding places of interest and outdoor activities. It will even make hotel reservations. It's open Monday to Friday 8:30am to 5:30pm.

**GETTING AROUND**    U.S. 278 is the divided highway that runs the length of the island.

The **Downtown Area Shuttle (DASH)** (© **843/724-7420**) is the quickest way to get around the main downtown area daily. The fare is $1.25, and you'll need exact change. A pass good for the whole day costs $4 and can be purchased on the bus.

# Hilton Head Island

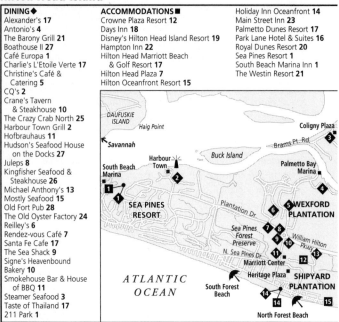

**DINING◆**
Alexander's **17**
Antonio's **4**
The Barony Grill **21**
Boathouse II **27**
Café Europa **1**
Charlie's L'Etoile Verte **17**
Christine's Café & Catering **5**
CQ's **2**
Crane's Tavern & Steakhouse **10**
The Crazy Crab North **25**
Harbour Town Grill **2**
Hofbrauhaus **11**
Hudson's Seafood House on the Docks **27**
Juleps **8**
Kingfisher Seafood & Steakhouse **26**
Michael Anthony's **13**
Mostly Seafood **15**
Old Fort Pub **28**
The Old Oyster Factory **24**
Reilley's **6**
Rendez-vous Café **7**
Santa Fe Cafe **17**
The Sea Shack **9**
Signe's Heavenbound Bakery **10**
Smokehouse Bar & House of BBQ **11**
Steamer Seafood **3**
Taste of Thailand **17**
211 Park **1**

**ACCOMMODATIONS■**
Crowne Plaza Resort **12**
Days Inn **18**
Disney's Hilton Head Island Resort **19**
Hampton Inn **22**
Hilton Head Marriott Beach & Golf Resort **17**
Hilton Head Plaza **7**
Hilton Oceanfront Resort **15**

Holiday Inn Oceanfront **14**
Main Street Inn **23**
Palmetto Dunes Resort **17**
Park Lane Hotel & Suites **16**
Royal Dunes Resort **20**
Sea Pines Resort **1**
South Beach Marina Inn **1**
The Westin Resort **21**

---

**Yellow Cab** (℗ **843/686-6666**) has flat two-passenger rates determined by zone, with an extra $2 charge for each additional person.

**SPECIAL EVENTS**   The earliest annual event is **Springfest,** a March festival featuring seafood, live music, stage shows, and tennis and golf tournaments. Outstanding PGA golfers also descend on the island in mid-April for the **MCI Heritage Tournament** at the Harbour Town Golf Links. To herald fall, the **Hilton Head Celebrity Golf Tournament** is held on Labor Day weekend at Palmetto Dunes and Sea Pines Plantation.

## BEACHES, GOLF, TENNIS & OTHER OUTDOOR PURSUITS

You can have an active vacation here any time of year; Hilton Head's subtropical climate ranges in temperature from the 50s in winter to the mid-80s in summer. And if you've had your fill of historic sights in Savannah or Charleston, don't worry—the attractions on Hilton Head mainly consist of nature preserves, beaches, and other places to play.

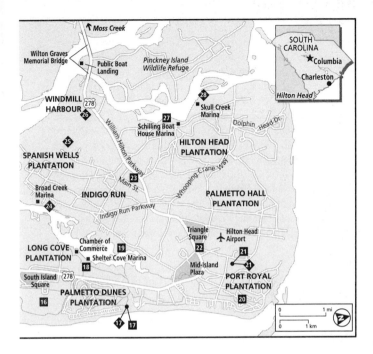

**Coastal Discovery Museum,** 100 William Hilton Pkwy. (© **843/ 689-6767;** www.coastaldiscovery.org), hosts 12 separate guided tours and cruises. Tours go along island beaches and salt marshes or stop at Native American sites and the ruins of old forts or long-gone plantations. Children can search for sharks' teeth with an identification chart. The nature, beach, and history tours generally cost $12 for adults and $7 for children. The dolphin and nature cruise costs $18 per adult, $12 per child; and a kayak trip costs $27 per person. Hours are Monday to Saturday 9am to 5pm, Sunday 10am to 3pm.

**BEACHES**    *Travel & Leisure* ranked Hilton Head's **beaches** ✸✸✸ among the most beautiful in the world; we concur. The sands are extremely firm, providing a sound surface for biking, hiking, jogging, and beach games. In summer, watch for the endangered loggerhead turtles that lumber ashore at night to bury their eggs.

All beaches on Hilton Head are public. Land bordering the beaches, however, is private property. Most beaches are safe, although there's sometimes an undertow at the northern end of the island.

Lifeguards are posted only at major beaches, and concessions are available to rent beach chairs, umbrellas, and watersports equipment.

There are a number of public access sites to popular beach areas. Our favorites are **Coligny Beach** at Coligny Circle at Pope Avenue and South Forest Beach Drive. This is the island's busiest strip of sands, with toilets, sand showers, a playground, and changing rooms. **Alder Lane,** entered along South Forest Beach Road at Alder Lane, offers parking and is less crowded. Toilets are also found here. Off the William Hilton Parkway, **Dreissen Beach Park** at Bradley Beach Road has toilets, sand showers, and plenty of parking as well as a playground and picnic tables. Of the beaches on the island's north side, we prefer **Folly Field Beach,** on Starfish Road, which has more limited parking but offers toilets and sand showers. The island also has a number of other less accessible and less desirable beaches.

Of the beaches on the island's north, we prefer Folly Field Beach because of the amenities available.

**BIKING**   Enjoy Hilton Head's 25 miles of bicycle paths. Bike paths even run parallel to U.S. 278. Beaches are firm enough to support wheels, and cyclists seem to delight in dodging the waves or racing the fast-swimming dolphins in the nearby water.

Most hotels and resorts rent bikes to guests. If yours doesn't, try **Hilton Head Bicycle Company,** off Sea Pines Circle at 112 Arrow Rd. (© **843/686-6888**). The cost is $28 per week. Call ahead for daily rates. Baskets, child carriers, locks, and headgear are supplied, and the inventory includes cruisers, BMXs, mountain bikes, and tandems. Hours are daily 9am to 6pm.

**CRUISES & TOURS**   To explore Hilton Head's waters, contact **Adventure Cruises, Inc.,** Shelter Cove Harbour, Suite G, Harbourside III (© **843/785-4558**). Outings include a 1¹⁄₂-hour dolphin-watch cruise, which costs adults $20 and children $10.

Another outfitter, **Drifter & Gypsy Excursions,** South Sea Pines Dr., South Beach Marina (© **843/363-2900**), takes its 65-foot *Gypsy,* holding 89 passengers, on dolphin watches, sightseeing cruises, and nature cruises. Call for more information to see what's happening at the time of your visit.

**FISHING**   No license is needed for saltwater fishing, although freshwater licenses are required for the island's lakes and ponds. The season for fishing offshore is April through October. Inland fishing is good between September and December. Crabbing is also popular; crabs are easy to catch in low water from docks, boats, or right off banks.

Off Hilton Head, you can go deep-sea fishing 𝔊 for amberjack, barracuda, shark, and king mackerel. Many rentals are available; we've recommended only those with the best track records. The previously recommended **Drifter & Gypsy Excursions,** South Sea Pines Drive, South Beach Marina (𝄞 **843/363-2900**), features a 50-passenger, 50-foot drifter vessel that offers 5-hour offshore and inshore fishing excursions. The 32-foot *Boomerang* fishing boat is available for private offshore and inshore custom fishing charters lasting up to 8 hours.

**Harbour Town Yacht Basin,** Harbour Town Marina (𝄞 **843/ 671-2704**), has four boats of various sizes and prices. *The Manatee,* a 40-foot vessel, can carry a group of six. The rates, set for six passengers, are $425 for 4 hours, $640 for 6 hours, and $850 for 8 hours. A charge of $13 per hour is added for each additional passenger.

*The Hero* and *The Echo* are 32-foot ships. Their rates for a group of six are $390 for 4 hours, $585 for 6 hours, and $780 for 8 hours. A smaller three-passenger inshore boat is priced at $325 for 4 hours, $490 for 6 hours, and $650 for 8 hours.

A cheaper way to go deep-sea fishing—only $47 per person—is aboard *The Drifter* (𝄞 **843/363-2900**), a party boat that departs from the South Beach Marina Village. Ocean-bottom fishing is possible at an artificial reef 12 miles offshore.

**GOLF**   With 24 challenging **golf courses** 𝔊𝔊𝔊 on the island and an additional 16 within a 30-minute drive, this is heaven for both professional and novice golfers. Some of golf's most celebrated architects—including George and Tom Fazio, Robert Trent Jones, Pete Dye, and Jack Nicklaus—have designed championship courses on the island. Wide, scenic fairways and rolling greens have earned Hilton Head the reputation of being the resort with the most courses on any number of the "World's Best" lists.

Many of Hilton Head's championship courses are open to the public, including the **George Fazio Course** 𝔊 at Palmetto Dunes Resort (𝄞 **843/785-1130**), an 18-hole, 6,534-yard, par-70 course that *Golf Digest* ranked in the top 50 of its "75 Best American Resort Courses." The course has been cited for its combined length and keen accuracy. The cost is $59 to $75 for 18 holes, and hours are daily from 6:30am to 6pm.

**Old South Golf Links** 𝔊𝔊𝔊, 50 Buckingham Plantation Dr., Bluffton (𝄞 **800/257-8997** or 843/785-5353), is an 18-hole, 6,772-yard, par-72 course, open daily from 7:30am to 7pm. It's recognized as one of the "Top 10 New Public Courses" by *Golf Digest,* which cites its panoramic views and setting ranging from an oak forest to tidal salt marshes. Greens fees range from $50 to $80. The course lies on Highway 278, 1 mile before the bridge leading to Hilton Head.

**Hilton Head National,** Highway 278 (© **843/842-5900**), is a Gary Player Signature Golf Course, including a full-service pro shop and a grill and driving range. It's a 27-hole, 6,779-yard, par-72 course with gorgeous scenery that evokes Scotland. Greens fees range from $55 to $79, and hours are daily 7am to 6pm.

**Island West Golf Club,** Highway 278 (© **843/689-6660**), was nominated in 1992 by *Golf Digest* as the best new course of the year. With its backdrop of oaks, elevated tees, and rolling fairways, it's a challenging but playable 18-hole, 6,803-yard, par-72 course. Greens fees range from $37 to $57, and hours are from 7am to 6pm daily.

**Robert Trent Jones Course** at the Palmetto Dunes Resort (© **843/785-1138**) is an 18-hole, 6,710-yard, par-72 oceanfront course. The greens fees are $89 to $105 for 18 holes, and hours are daily from 7am to 6pm.

**HORSEBACK RIDING** Riding through beautiful maritime forests and nature preserves is reason enough to visit Hilton Head. We like **Lawton Stables,** 190 Greenwood Dr., Sea Pines (© **843/671-2586**), offering rides for both adults and kids (kids 7 and under ride ponies) through the Sea Pines Forest Preserve. The cost is $50 per person for a ride that lasts somewhat longer than an hour. Riders must weigh less than 240 pounds. The stables are open Monday to Saturday 8:30am to 5:30pm. Reservations are necessary.

**JOGGING** Our favorite place for jogging is Harbour Town at Sea Pines. Go for a run through the town just as the sun is going down. Later, you can explore the marina and have a refreshing drink at one of the many outdoor cafes. In addition, the island offers lots of paved paths and trails that cut through scenic areas. Jogging along U.S. 278, the main artery, can be dangerous because of heavy traffic, however.

**KAYAK TOURS** **Cool Breeze Kayak Tours,** Pinckney Island Wildlife Refuge (© **877/286-5154**), operates guided tours in Broad Creek. The cost is $35 to $60 per person. Reservations are necessary but experience isn't.

**South Beach Marina Village** (© **843/671-2643**) allows you to tour Low Country waterways by kayak. A 2-hour Dolphin Nature Tour costs $40 (half-price for children under 12). The tour takes you through the salt-marsh creeks of the Calibogue Sound or Pinckney

Island Wildlife Refuge. The trip begins with instructions on how to control your boat.

**NATURE PRESERVES** The **Audubon-Newhall Preserve,** Palmetto Bay Road (📞 **843/689-2989**), is a 50-acre preserve on the south end of the island. Here, you can walk along marked trails to observe wildlife in its native habitat. Guided tours are available when plants are blooming. Except for public toilets, there are no amenities. The preserve is open from sunrise to sunset; admission is free.

The second-leading preserve is also on the south end of the island. **Sea Pines Forest Preserve** 🐾🐾, Sea Pines Plantation (📞 **843/363-4530**), is a 605-acre public wilderness with marked walking trails. Nearly all the birds and animals known to live on Hilton Head can be seen here. (Yes, there are alligators, but there are also less fearsome creatures, such as egrets, herons, osprey, and white-tailed deer.) All trails lead to public picnic areas in the center of the forest. The preserve is open from sunrise to sunset year-round. Maps and toilets are available.

**SAILING** *Pau Hana* and *Flying Circus,* Palmetto Bay Marina (📞 **843/686-2582**), are two charter sailboats on Hilton Head piloted by Capt. Jeanne Zailckas. You can pack a picnic lunch and bring your cooler aboard for a 2-hour trip—in the morning or afternoon, or at sunset. The cost is $30 for adults (12 and older) and $18 for children 11 and under. *Flying Circus* offers private 2-hour trips for up to six people costing $210. Both charters conduct dolphin watch tours. Call for daytime special rates for less than 6 people.

**H2 Sports,** Harbour Town Marina (📞 **843/671-4386**), offers jet-skiing, parasailing, eco-tours, and water-skiing. We especially recommend their eco-tours (or "enviro" as they are called). Passengers head out on Zodiac inflatable boats for close encounters with wildlife, including dolphin sightings and bird-watching. Rates are $26 to $34 for adults and $19 to $22 for kids 12 and under.

**SHOPPING** Hilton Head is browsing heaven, with more than 30 shopping centers spread around the island. Chief shopping sites include **Pinelawn Station** (Matthews Dr. and U.S. 278), with more than 30 shops and half a dozen restaurants; and **Coligny Plaza** (Coligny Circle), with more than 60 shops, food stands, and several good restaurants. We've found some of the best bargains in the South at **Factory Outlet Stores I and II** (📞 **843/837-4339**), on Highway 278 at the gateway to Hilton Head. The outlet has more than 45 factory stores, including Ralph Lauren, Brooks Brothers, and J. Crew. The hours of most shops are Monday to Saturday 10am to 9pm and Sunday 11am to 6pm.

**TENNIS** *Tennis* magazine ranked Hilton Head among its "50 Greatest U.S. Tennis Resorts." No other domestic destination can boast such a concentration of **tennis facilities** ⚡⚡⚡: more than 300 courts that are ideal for beginning, intermediate, and advanced players. The island has 19 tennis clubs, seven of which are open to the public. A wide variety of tennis clinics and daily lessons are available.

**Sea Pines Racquet Club** ⚡⚡⚡, Sea Pines Plantation (© **843/ 363-4495**), has been ranked by *Tennis* magazine as a top-50 resort and was selected by the *Robb Report* as the best tennis resort in the United States. The club has been the site of more nationally televised tennis events than any other location. Two hours of tennis are complimentary for guests of the hotel; otherwise, there's a $22-per-hour charge. The club has 23 clay courts (two are lighted for night play).

**Port Royal Racquet Club,** Port Royal Plantation (© **843/ 686-8803**), offers 10 clay and four hard courts, plus two natural-grass courts. Night games are possible on all courts. Charges range from $20 to $32 per hour, and reservations should be made a day in advance. Clinics are $20 per hour for adults and $15 for children.

**Hilton Head Island Beach and Tennis Resort,** 40 Folly Field Rd. (© **843/842-4402**), features 10 lighted hard courts, costing only $10 per hour (free to guests).

**Palmetto Dunes Tennis Center,** Palmetto Dunes Resort (© **843/ 785-1152**), has 23 clay and two hard courts (some lighted for night play). Hotel guests pay $23 per hour; otherwise, the charge is $28 per hour.

## WHERE TO STAY

Hilton Head has some of the finest hotel properties in the South, and prices are high—unless you book into one of the motels run by national chains. Most facilities offer discount rates from November to March, and golf and tennis packages are available.

The most comprehensive central reservations service on the island, **The Vacation Company,** P.O. Box 5312, Hilton Head Island, SC 29938 (© **800/845-7018** in the United States and Canada; www.hiltonheadcentral.com), can book you into private homes or villas on the island at no charge. It's open Monday to Saturday 9am to 5pm.

Another option is **Island Rentals and Real Estate** (© **800/845-6134** or 843/785-3813; P.O. Box 5915, Hilton Head Island, SC

29938). Contact them for up-to-date availability, rates, and bookings of private homes, villas, or condos. The toll-free number is in operation 24 hours, but office hours are Monday to Saturday 8:30am to 5:30pm.

By and large, the double rooms in the recommended hotels and inns below have private bathrooms with tub/shower combinations, unless otherwise noted.

## VERY EXPENSIVE

**Crowne Plaza Resort** 𝒢   Tucked away within the Shipyard Plantation, and designed as the centerpiece of that plantation's 800 acres, this five-story inn gives its major competitor, Westin Resort, stiff competition. It underwent a $10-million renovation in 1993 and today has the island's most dignified lobby: a mahogany-sheathed postmodern interpretation of Chippendale decor. The golf course associated with the place has been praised by the National Audubon Society for its respect for local wildlife. Guest rooms are nothing out of the ordinary, with simple furnishings, yet the sheer beauty of the landscaping, the attentive service, the omnipresent nautical theme, and the well-trained staff (dressed in nautically inspired uniforms) can go a long way toward making your stay memorable. On the premises are three restaurants. The most glamorous is **Portz,** off the establishment's main lobby. A good middle-bracket choice is **Brella's,** serving both lunch and dinner. Certain nights in the premier bar, **Signals,** feature line dancing and shag dancing.

130 Shipyard Dr., Shipyard Plantation, Hilton Head Island, SC 29928. © 800/334-1881 or 843/842-2400. Fax 843/785-8463. www.crowneplaza.com. 340 units. $142–$325 double; from $375 suite. AE, DC, DISC, MC, V. Free parking. **Amenities:** 3 restaurants; bar; 2 pools (1 indoor); fitness center; Jacuzzi; bikes; room service; laundry service; dry cleaning; nonsmoking rooms; rooms for those w/limited mobility. *In room:* A/C, TV, dataport, minibar, coffeemaker, hair dryer, iron, safe.

**Hilton Head Marriott Beach & Golf Resort** 𝒢𝒢   After a much-needed $23-million renovation, this aging property has emerged in its latest incarnation as a Marriott. Set on 2 acres of landscaped grounds and bordering the oceanfront, the hotel is surrounded by the much more massive acreage of Palmetto Dunes Plantation and is just 10 minutes from the Hilton Head airport. But the hotel's 10-story tower of rooms dominates everything around it.

Rooms open onto either ocean or island views. Some are smaller and less opulent than you might expect of such a well-rated hotel, but all are comfortably furnished, each coming with a tiled, midsize bathroom. Most rooms open onto small balconies overlooking the garden or the ocean. The hotel's program of sports and recreation is among the best on the island.

One Hotel Circle, Hilton Head Island, SC 29928. ℭ **800/228-9290** or 843/686-8400. Fax 843/686-8450. www.marriott.com. 512 units. $139–$319 double; $500–$700 suite. AE, DC, DISC, MC, V. Valet parking $15. **Amenities:** Restaurant; 2 bars; coffee shop; 1 indoor and 2 outdoor pools; 3 18-hole golf courses; 25 tennis courts nearby; health club; full spa; sauna; gift shop; hair salon; limited room service; babysitting; laundry service; dry cleaning; nonsmoking rooms; rooms for those w/limited mobility. *In room:* A/C, TV, dataport, wi-fi, minibar, coffeemaker, hair dryer, iron, safe, bathrobe.

**Main Street Inn** 🟊🟊🟊 *(Finds)*    Don't expect cozy Americana from this small, luxurious inn, as it's grander and more European in its motifs than its name would imply. Designed like a small-scale villa that you might expect to see in the South of France, it was built in 1996 in a format that combines design elements from both New Orleans and Charleston, including cast-iron balustrades and a formal semi-tropical garden where guests are encouraged to indulge in afternoon tea. Inside, you'll find artfully clipped topiary, French provincial furnishings, and accommodations that are more luxurious and more richly appointed than those of any other hotel in Hilton Head. Color schemes throughout make ample use of golds, mauves, and taupes; floors are crafted from slabs of either stone or heart pine; fabrics are richly textured; and plumbing and bathroom fixtures are aggressively upscale. Overall, despite a location that requires a drive to the nearest beach, the hotel provides a luxe alternative to the less personalized megahotels that lie nearby. AAA, incidentally, awarded it a much-coveted four-star rating. Breakfast and afternoon tea are served here.

2200 Main St., Hilton Head Island, SC 29926. ℭ **800/471-3001** or 843/681-3001. Fax 843/681-5541. www.mainstreetinn.com. 33 units. $159–$299 double. $35 surcharge for 3rd occupant of double room. Rates include breakfast. AE, DISC, MC, V. Free parking. **Amenities:** Breakfast room; outdoor pool; spa; massage; laundry service; dry cleaning; nonsmoking rooms; rooms for those w/limited mobility. *In room:* A/C, TV, dataport, minibar, coffeemaker, hair dryer, iron.

**The Westin Resort** 🟊🟊    Set near the isolated northern end of Hilton Head Island on 24 landscaped acres, this is the most opulent European-style hotel in town. Its Disneyesque design, including cupolas and postmodern ornamentation that looks vaguely Moorish, evokes fanciful Palm Beach hotels. If there's a drawback, it's the stiff formality. Adults accompanied by a gaggle of children and bathers in swimsuits will not necessarily feel comfortable in the reverently hushed corridors. The rooms, most of which have ocean views, are outfitted in Low Country plantation style, with touches of Asian art thrown in for additional glamour. The **Carolina Café** and the **Barony Grill** are the best places for food. Poolside dining is available, and there's also a seafood buffet restaurant.

Two Grasslawn Ave., Hilton Head Island, SC 29928. © **800/937-8461** or 843/681-4000. Fax 843/681-1087. www.westin.com. 412 units. $119–$199 double; $450–$1,900 suite. Children 17 and under stay free in parent's room; children 4 and under eat free. Special promotions offered. AE, DC, DISC, MC, V. **Amenities:** 3 restaurants; bar; 1 indoor and 2 outdoor pools; 3 18-hole golf courses; 16 tennis courts; health spa; Jacuzzi; room service; laundry service; dry cleaning; nonsmoking rooms; rooms for those w/limited mobility. *In room:* A/C, TV, dataport, minibar, coffeemaker, hair dryer, iron, safe.

## EXPENSIVE

**Disney's Hilton Head Island Resort** ☆☆    This family-conscious resort is on a 15-acre island that rises above Hilton Head's widest estuary, Broad Creek. When it opened in 1996, it was the only U.S.-based Disney resort outside Florida and California. About 20 woodsy-looking buildings are arranged into a compound. Expect lots of pine trees and fallen pine needles, garlands of Spanish moss, plenty of families with children, and an ambience that's several notches less intense than that of hotels in Disney theme parks. Part of the fun, if you like this sort of thing in concentrated doses, are the many summer-camp-style activities. Public areas have outdoorsy colors (forest green and cranberry), stuffed game fish, and varnished pine. References are made to Shadow the Dog (a fictitious golden retriever that is the resort's mascot) and Mathilda (a maternal figure who conducts cooking lessons for children as part of the resort's planned activities). All accommodations contain minikitchens, suitable for feeding sandwiches and macaroni to the kids but hardly the kind of thing that a gourmet chef would enjoy, as well as wooden furniture consistent with the resort's vacation-home-in-the-forest theme. For elaborate restaurants and bars, look elsewhere. **Tide Me Over** is a walk-up window serving Carolina cookery for breakfast and lunch. Those who don't cook their meals in-house can trek a short distance to the dozen or so eateries and bars in the nearby marina complex at Shelter Cove Harbour.

22 Harbourside Lane, Hilton Head Island, SC 29928. © **800/800-9800** or 843/341-4100. Fax 843/341-4130. www.dvc.disney.go.com. 123 units. $125–$280 studio; $160–$840 villa. AE, DC, DISC, MC, V. **Amenities:** 3 restaurants; bar; 3 outdoor pools; fitness center; health spa; babysitting; laundry service. *In room:* A/C, TV, dataport, kitchenette, coffeemaker, hair dryer, iron, safe.

**Hilton Oceanfront Resort** ☆    This award-winning property isn't the most imposing on the island. Many visitors, however, prefer the

Hilton because of its hideaway position: tucked at the end of the main road through Palmetto Dunes. The low-rise design features hallways that open to sea breezes at either end. The guest rooms are some of the largest on the island, and balconies angling out toward the beach allow sea views from all accommodations. **Mostly Seafood** is the resort's premier restaurant, although cafes and bars—and even a Pizza Hut on the grounds—serve less expensive fare.

23 Ocean Lane (P.O. Box 6165), Hilton Head Island, SC 29928. ℂ **800/845-8001** or 843/842-8000. Fax 843/341-8037. www.hiltonheadhilton.com. 324 units. $109–$179 double; $299–$627 suite. AE, DC, DISC, MC, V. Parking $6. **Amenities:** 3 restaurants; bar; 2 outdoor pools; fitness center; limited room service; laundry service; dry cleaning; coin-operated laundry; nonsmoking rooms; rooms for those w/limited mobility. *In room:* A/C, TV, dataport, kitchenette, coffeemaker, hair dryer, iron, safe.

**Royal Dunes Resort** ℱ    Comfortable and clean, but blandly standardized and somewhat anonymous, this is a compound of three-bedroom, three-bathroom apartments, occupancy of which has been aggressively marketed to independent investors as a time-share investment. Whenever the investors aren't in residence, the apartments become available for rentals on the open market. They occupy a quartet of four-story buildings located on the Port Royal Plantation. Each has a washer and dryer; a durable collection of wicker, rattan, and Southern colonial furniture; and tub/shower combinations. The compound's location is at the edge of a forested greenbelt, within a 10-minute walk from the beach.

8 Wimbledon Court, Hilton Head, SC 29928. ℂ **843/681-9718**. Fax 843/681-2003. www.royaldunes.com. 56 units. $175–$235 double. AE, MC, V. **Amenities:** 2 outdoor pools; children's wading pool; gym; bike rentals; barbecue area; sporting activities. *In room:* A/C, TV, full kitchen, iron, washer/dryer.

## MODERATE TO INEXPENSIVE

Hilton Head has a number of quality chain, motor, and budget hotels that offer good value and family-friendly atmosphere. Keep in mind that rates often go down even further in the off season. The **Holiday Inn Oceanfront** ℱ (1 S. Forest Beach Dr.; ℂ **888/465-4329** or 843/785-5126; fax 843/785-6678; www.holiday-inn.com; $179–$239 double) is the island's leading motor hotel, a five-story high-rise that opens onto a quiet stretch of beach on the southern side of the island, near Shipyard Plantation. In summer, planned children's activities are offered. Nonsmoking rooms and room for those with limited mobility are available. **Park Lane Hotel & Suites** (12 Park Lane, in Central Park; ℂ **877/247-3431** or 843/686-5700; fax 843/686-3952; $105–$165 suite) is set on the eastern edge of Hilton Head's main traffic artery, and both cost-conscious families and business travelers on extended stays appreciate the simple cooking facilities in each guest room.

**Hilton Head Plaza** (36 S. Forest Dr.; ✆ **800/535-3248** or 843/ 842-3100; $69–$139 double) is favored by families, especially during the peak holiday months of midsummer. **Days Inn** (9 Marina Side Dr.; ✆ **800/329-7466** or 843/842-4800; fax 843/842-5388; www.daysinn.com; $43–$169 double) provides easy access to the beach, golf, tennis, marinas, and shopping. Families save extra money by using one of the grills outside for a home-style barbecue. **Hampton Inn** (1 Dillon Rd.; ✆ **800/426-7866** or 843/681-7900; fax 843/681-4330; www.hampton-inn.com; $89–$129 double) is one of the most-sought-after motels on Hilton Head, especially by families and business travelers.

**South Beach Marina Inn** ❧ (232 S. Sea Pines Dr., in Sea Pines Resort; ✆ **800/367-3909** or 843/671-6498; www.southbeach village.com; $65–$179 one-bedroom apartment) is a charming clapboard-sided complex of marina-front buildings that meanders over a labyrinth of catwalks and stairways above a complex of shops, souvenir kiosks, and restaurants.

## VILLA RENTALS

**Palmetto Dunes Resort** ❧ *Kids*   This relaxed and informal enclave of privately owned villas is set within the sprawling 1,800-acre complex of Palmetto Dunes Plantation, 7 miles south of the bridge. Accommodations range all the way from one-bedroom condos, booked mostly by groups, to four-bedroom villas, each of the latter furnished in the owner's personal taste. This is the place for longer stays, ideal for families who want a home away from home when they're traveling. In fact, in 2003 it was ranked as the number-one family resort in the continental U.S. and Canada by *Travel & Leisure Family* and is still listed among the top ten. Villas are fully equipped and receive housekeeping service; they're located on the ocean, fairways, or lagoons. Each villa comes with a full kitchen, washer and dryer, living room and dining area, and balcony or patio.

Palmetto Dunes (P.O. Box 5606), Hilton Head Island, SC 29938. ✆ **800/845-6130** or 843/785-1161. Fax 843/686-2877. www.palmettodunes.com. 500 units. $750–$3,500 per week condo or villa. Golf and honeymoon packages available. 2-night minimum stay. 50% deposit for reservations. AE, DC, DISC, MC, V. Free parking. **Amenities:** 20 restaurants; 12 bars; 28 pools; 3 18-hole golf courses; 25 tennis courts; 200-slip marina; nonsmoking rooms; rooms for those w/limited mobility. *In room:* A/C, TV, dataport, kitchen (in some), safe (in some), washer/dryer (in some).

**The Sea Pines Resort** ✦✦✦　Since 1955, this has been one of the leading condo developments in America, sprawling across 5,500 acres at the southernmost tip of the island. Lodgings vary—everything from one- to four-bedroom villas to opulent private homes that are available when the owners are away. There is a minimum 1-week stay in the villas and town houses. The clientele here includes hordes of golfers, because Sea Pines is the home of the WorldCom Classic, a major stop on the PGA tour. If you're not a Sea Pines guest, you can eat, shop, or enjoy aspects of its nightlife. For full details on this varied resort/residential complex, write for a free "Sea Pines Vacation" brochure.

32 Greenwood Dr., Hilton Head Island, SC 29928. © **888/807-6873** or 843/785-3333. Fax 843/842-1475. www.seapines.com. 400–500 units. $170–$280 1-bedroom villa; $250–$350 2-bedroom villa; $280–$425 3-bedroom villa. (Rates are daily, based on 1-week stay.) AE, DC, DISC, MC, V. **Amenities:** 12 restaurants; 12 bars; 2 outdoor pools; 3 18-hole golf courses; 28 tennis courts; fitness center; health spa; watersports; horseback riding; massage; babysitting; nonsmoking rooms; rooms for those w/limited mobility. *In room:* A/C, TV, kitchen or kitchenette, washer/dryer.

## WHERE TO DINE
### EXPENSIVE

**The Barony Grill** ✦✦✦ INTERNATIONAL　The Barony, quick to promote itself as one of only two AAA four-star restaurants on Hilton Head Island, didn't shy away from installing decor that's a hybrid between a stage set in Old Vienna and a brick-lined, two-fisted steakhouse. The lighting is suitably dim; the drinks are appropriately stiff; and as you dine in your plushly upholstered alcove, you can stare at what might be the largest wrought-iron chandelier in the state. The place caters to a resort-going crowd of casual diners. Everything is well prepared and in copious portions, although the chef doesn't experiment or stray far from a limited selection of tried-and-true steak-and-lobster fare. Your meal might include New York strip steak, tenderloin of pork with purée of mangos, lobster thermidor, or fresh Atlantic swordfish with pistachios.

In the Westin Resort, 2 Grass Lawn Ave. © **843/681-4000.** Reservations recommended. Main courses $28–$37. AE, DC, DISC, MC, V. Wed–Sun 6–10pm.

**Michael Anthony's** ✦✦✦ ITALIAN　Nearly every food critic on the island has declared Michael Anthony's the best place to eat in Hilton Head. Chef Michael Cirafesi has created an exquisite menu blending traditional Italian flavors with regional low-country ingredients. Family owned and operated, the Fazzinis and Cirafesis are hands-on with every detail of the restaurant. Michael Anthony's also has a wine bar where you can enjoy your favorite beverage, dessert, or choose to have dinner—no reservations required. We started with the *antipasto della casa al Italiano,* an assortment of Italian meats, cheeses, and marinated vegetables. Our dining companion chose the local favorite *gnocchi di patate ai porcini,* homemade potato gnocchi with a sauce of porcini mushrooms with demi-glace and cream. The flavorful *involtini di vitello con spinachi, formaggio e salsiccia*—medallions of veal with spinach, cheese, and Italian sausage, sautéed with white wine—is a delectable specialty. Don't miss the chocolate soufflé cake, with a melted hot center of chocolate served with vanilla gelato.

37 New Orleans Rd. ℂ **843/785-6272.** Reservations required. Main courses $17–$30. AE, DC, DISC, MC, V. Mon–Sat 5:30–10pm.

## MODERATE

All of these so-called moderately priced restaurants have expensive shellfish dishes. However, if you order from the lower end of the price scale, enjoying mainly meat and poultry dishes, you'll find platters costing from $20 or less. Helpings for the most part are generous, so you'll rarely need to order appetizers, which will keep your overall cost in the more affordable price range.

**Alexander's** ℛ SEAFOOD/INTERNATIONAL   One of the most visible independent restaurants (in other words, not associated with a hotel) on Hilton Head lies in a gray-stained, wood-sided building just inside the main entrance into Palmetto Dunes. The decor includes Oriental carpets, big-windowed views over the salt marshes, wicker furniture, and an incongruous—some say startling—collection of vintage Harley Davidson motorcycles, none with more than 1,000 miles on them, dating from 1946, 1948, 1966, and 1993, respectively. Each is artfully displayed as a work of sculpture and as a catalyst to dialogue. Powerful flavors and a forthright approach to food are the rules of the kitchen. The chefs don't allow a lot of innovation on their menu—you've had all these dishes before—but fine ingredients are used, and each dish is prepared with discretion and restraint. Try the oysters Savannah or the bacon-wrapped shrimp, and most definitely have a bowl of Low Country seafood chowder. Guaranteed to set you salivating are the Salmon Oscar and the Blue Finn Crab Cakes. Steak, duck, rack of lamb, and pork—all in familiar versions—round out the menu.

76 Queen's Folly, Palmetto Dunes. ℂ **843/785-4999.** Reservations recommended. Main courses $19–$29. AE, DC, DISC, MC, V. Daily 5–10pm.

**Antonio's** ⊕ ITALIAN   Located at the Village at Wexford, this island favorite with its elegant decor and fine Italian cuisine continues its bold quest to duplicate the flavors of sunny Italy, and for the most part, succeeds admirably. Chef Mottram is a whiz at using recipes from all the provinces of Italy, although classic preparations of Italian seafood are clearly his favorite. Piano music adds to the ambience, as does a visit to the Wine Room where you can see Hilton Head's most comprehensive assemblage of Italian *vino*.

The antipasti selection is one of the island's best, including many classics such as mussels with chorizo sausage, wild mushrooms, grilled ciabatta, Peroni and lobster consommé; or crispy calamari with a honey chipotle aioli. The chef and his team prepare succulent pastas, including one based on such fruits of the sea as sautéed shrimp, scallops, and mussels flavored with a tomato and saffron broth. Veal saltimbocca appears delectably with crispy prosciutto and creamy roasted pancetta sage potatoes.

Village at Wexford, G-2. ⓒ **843/842-5505.** Reservations recommended. Main courses $16–$30. AE, DC, DISC, MC, V. Daily 5:30–10pm. Closed Dec 24.

**Boathouse II** (Kids) SEAFOOD   The nautical lodge decor and the view over salt marshes and Skull Creek form an appropriate venue for the serving of some fine seafood and affordable prices. From some tables you can see the Pinckney Island Wildlife Preserve and the adjacent marina. Walk under a canopy of giant oaks to enjoy a drink at the Market 13 outdoor bar. Live entertainment is offered, and it's a family-friendly place with a children's menu. Plenty of fresh seafood is prepared with that old Charleston flavor, including shrimp and stone-ground grits, Southern catfish with Carolina fixin's, and the chef's own Boathouse bouillabaisse. Some excellent crab cakes are another specialty. For meat fanciers, slow-roasted baby back ribs in a sour mash sauce, served with buttermilk "smashed" potatoes and collards, or filet mignon or prime rib seduce the palate.

397 Squire Pope Rd. ⓒ **843/681-3663.** Reservations not required. Brunch $8–$14; lunch $9–$13; main courses $17–$28. AE, DC, DISC, MC, V. Daily 11:30am–3pm and 5–9pm. Closed Dec 25.

**Café Europa** ⊕ CONTINENTAL/SEAFOOD   This fine European restaurant is at the base of the much-photographed Harbour Town Lighthouse, opening onto a panoramic view of Calibogue Sound and Daufuskie Island. In an informal, cheerful atmosphere, you can order fish that's poached, grilled, baked, or even fried. Baked Shrimp Daufuskie was inspired by local catches; it's stuffed with crab, green peppers, and onions. Grilled grouper is offered with a sauté of tomato, cucumber, dill, and white wine. Specialty dishes include chicken marsala and a baked shrimp Daufuskie. *Tournedos au poivre* is flambéed with brandy and simmered in a robust green-peppercorn sauce. The omelets, 14 in all, are perfectly prepared at breakfast (beginning at 10am) and are the island's finest. The bartender's Bloody Mary won an award as the island's best in a *Hilton Head News* contest.

Harbour Town, Sea Pines Plantation. © 843/671-3399. Reservations recommended for dinner. Lunch $8–$13; main courses $18–$28. AE, DC, MC, V. Daily 9am–2:30pm and 5:30–10pm.

**Charlie's L'Etoile Verte** 🍴🍴 INTERNATIONAL Outfitted like a tongue-in-cheek version of a Parisian bistro, our favorite restaurant on Hilton Head Island was also a favorite with former President Clinton during one of his island conferences. The atmosphere is unpretentious but elegant. The service is attentive, polite, and infused with an appealingly hip mixture of old- and new-world courtesy. Begin with roast portabellos and crab, and move on to tilapia sauté in a parmesan crust. End this rare dining experience with biscotti or a "sailor's trifle." The wine list is impressive.

8 New Orleans Rd. © 843/785-9277. Reservations required. Lunch $10–$15; main courses $23–$31. AE, DISC, MC, V. Tues–Sat 11:30am–2pm; Mon–Sat 6–9:30pm.

**Christine's Café & Catering** 🍴 AMERICAN Not only has Christine Bohn catered to the likes of John Mellencamp and Earth, Wind & Fire, she was also the recipient of the 2005 Small Business of the Year Award from the Hilton Head-Bluffton Chamber of Commerce—the first member of the hospitality industry to ever win the award. The main cafe now has a sister cafe in Coligny Plaza called Go Go Gourmet that features the same breakfast and lunch meals, but will serve prepared meals to go. Don't miss the homemade soups and bisques or the creative salads like Chipotle Shrimp or Fannie's Chicken Salad with hand-breaded chicken tenders, cheese, and tomatoes. Sandwiches are equally impressive with an old favorite like you've never tasted before—three kinds of cheeses, tomato, and bacon—for one of the best grilled cheese sandwiches we've ever eaten. Wraps, as well as meatloaf, fish and chips, and quiche are also delicious featured menu items.

24-F Palmetto Bay Rd. © 843/842-8830. Reservations not required. Main courses $4.50–$12. AE, DC, DISC, MC, V. Mon–Fri 10am–7pm; Sat 10am–3pm.

**CQ's** 🍴🍴 AMERICAN/LOW COUNTRY With a design based on a 19th-century rice barn, this Harbour Town restaurant is a successful conversion of an already existing property. The extensive wine list, some 400 vintages, is one of the best on the island. A tradition on Hilton Head since 1973, the restaurant will allow you to craft your own unique menu at *La Table du Vin,* with the assistance of a creative culinary team.

The well-thought-out menu of Low Country and American classics reflects the rich bounty of South Carolina—fresh seafood, beef, and game—and also shows a French influence. For a sampling of harmonious appetizers, try such delights as Brie *en croûte* with a raspberry purée and crisp apples, or a Maine lobster and Boursin cheesecake with a sherry butter cream, the latter one of our favorites.

Count yourself lucky if you arrive when game is on the menu. Our party recently took delight in the seared medallions of venison with roasted onion, shallots, leeks, and asparagus with a Madeira wine reduction adding that extra special flavor.

140-A Lighthouse Lane. ✆ **843/671-2779.** Reservations recommended. Main courses $19–$34. AE, DC, DISC, MC, V. Mar–May daily 5–10pm; June–Nov daily 5:30–10pm; Dec–Feb daily 5–9:30pm.

### Crane's Tavern & Steakhouse ⍟ STEAK/SEAFOOD The
original Crane's Steakhouse was launched in Philadelphia at the dawn of the 20th century and was one of the most popular taverns there until Prohibition. Always a family business, it was established by Hank Crane, who came over from Ireland, and passed the business down to generations of Crane sons, and now daughter, Beth Anne. Crane's is now a tradition on Hilton Head.

As Hilton Head restaurants rush to claim the best seafood, Crane's bases its simple, classic fare on prime beef. Each of the choicest cuts is prepared to your taste—can any trencherman cope with the whopper, 20 ounces? A 12-ounce prime rib was the best we could manage, and it was tender, well flavored, and quite succulent. Steaks get the focus, but the other offerings are good as well, including jumbo lump crab cakes or the stuffed chicken. The sweet potato ravioli was a delightful surprise in a molasses cream.

26 New Orleans Rd. ✆ **843/341-2333.** Reservations recommended. Main courses $17–$38. AE, DC, DISC, MC, V. Daily 5–10pm. Closed Thanksgiving and Dec 25.

### The Crazy Crab North 🄺🄸🄳🅂 SEAFOOD This is a branch of the
chain that's most likely to be patronized by locals. In a modern, low-slung building near the bridge that connects the island with the South Carolina mainland, it serves baked, broiled, or fried versions of stuffed flounder; seafood kabobs; oysters; the catch of the day; and any combination thereof. She-crab soup and New England–style

clam chowder are prepared fresh daily; children's menus are available; and desserts are a high point for chocoholics.

U.S. 278 at Jarvis Creek. ✆ 843/681-5021. Reservations not accepted. Lunch $7–$15; main courses $17–$35. AE, DC, DISC, MC, V. Daily 11:30am–10pm.

**Harbour Town Grill** ✿ *Finds* AMERICAN   For years, this woodsy-looking refuge of golfers and their guests was open only to members of the nearby golf club. Several years ago, however, it opened to the public at large, a fact that's still not widely publicized in Hilton Head, and which sometimes seems to catch some local residents by surprise. Looking something like a postmodern version of a French château, this small-scale affair has views over the 9th hole and room for only about 50 diners at a time. Inside, it's sporty-looking and relatively informal during the day, when most of the menu is devoted to thickly stuffed deli-style sandwiches and salads named in honor of golf stars. Dinners are more formal and more elaborate, with good-tasting dishes such as local shrimp sautéed with ginger, Vidalia onions, and collard greens; roasted rack of American lamb with white beans, spinach, and rosemary; and an array of thick-cut slabs of meat that include beef, lamb, veal, and chicken.

In the Harbour Town Golf Links Clubhouse, Sea Pines. ✆ 843/363-8380. Reservations recommended for dinner only. Lunch sandwiches and platters $9–$13; dinner main courses $24–$38. AE, DC, DISC, MC, V. Daily 7am–3pm, 5–10pm.

**Hudson's Seafood House on the Docks** SEAFOOD   Built as a seafood-processing factory in 1912, this restaurant still processes fish, clams, and oysters for local distribution, so you know that everything is fresh. If you're seated in the north dining room, you'll be eating in the original oyster factory. We strongly recommend the crab cakes, the steamed shrimp, and the especially appealing blackened catch of the day. Local oysters (seasonal) are also a specialty, breaded and deep-fried. Before and after dinner, stroll on the docks past shrimp boats, and enjoy the view of the mainland and nearby Parris Island. Sunsets here are panoramic. Lunch is served in the Oyster Bar.

1 Hudson Rd. ✆ 843/681-2772. Reservations not accepted. Main courses $8–$15 lunch, $15–$35 dinner. AE, DC, MC, V. Daily 11am–2:30pm and 5–10pm. Go to Skull Creek just off Square Pope Rd., signposted from U.S. 278.

**Juleps** ✿✿ AMERICAN/SOUTHERN   This is the Hilton Head restaurant where we'd take Jefferson Davis, former president of the Confederacy, should he miraculously appear and want dinner. It has that nostalgic atmosphere, with its beveled glass, French doors, glass-framed windows, cream and taupe colors—a walk into a time capsule. This is the friendly oasis maintained by Sam and Melissa Cochran—he a longtime islander and she a first-rate chef. Served in three dining areas, with a lively bar, are their original concoctions. Excellent ingredients go into such starters as barbecued duck breast over a corn pancake or Cajun-blackened oysters that are most savory. Here's your chance to try that Southern favorite, fried green tomatoes over creamy grits in a red pepper sauce seasoned with fresh scallions. Nothing is more typical of the Carolinas than a dish of quail with andouille sausage. Desserts are worth making room for, especially the berry shortcake full of strawberries, blackberries, and blueberries.

14 Greenwood Dr. ℂ 843/842-5857. Reservations recommended. Main courses $20–$26. AE, DC, DISC, MC, V. Mon–Sat 11:30am–2pm, 5:30–10pm. Closed July 4th and Dec 25.

**Kingfisher Seafood & Steakhouse** ℱ SEAFOOD/STEAK "Fresh fish—never frozen" is the motto of this popular restaurant at Shelter Cove, with a panoramic view of the harbor through large picture windows. All three of its dining rooms feature a water view, and there is live music nightly. You can request the fish catch of the day to be prepared several ways, including the standards such as grilled or blackened, but also herb encrusted or else Greek style with tomatoes, onions, mushrooms, spinach, artichokes, and feta cheese. Served crisp and cold, oysters come on the half shell. Each day different varieties are served. For pasta lovers, the chef makes a creative lasagna every day. Seafood selections range from a very respectable Scottish fish and chips to a more typical Charleston-style shrimp and grits in white gravy. Our recently sampled Ahi tuna came seared medium rare with a Ponzu sauce, wasabi mashed potatoes, and Asian slaw. The filet mignons offered here are tender and full of flavor and served with a creamy béarnaise sauce.

8 Harbour Lane. ℂ 843/785-4442. Reservations recommended. Main courses $15–$28. AE, DISC, MC, V. Daily 5–10pm. Closed Dec 24–25.

**Mostly Seafood** ℱℱ SEAFOOD/AMERICAN The most elegant and innovative restaurant in the Hilton resort, Mostly Seafood is noted for the way its chefs make imaginative dishes out of fresh seafood. Something about the decor—backlighting and glass-backed murals in designs of sea-green and blue—creates the illusion that you're floating in a boat. Menu items include fresh grouper, snapper, swordfish, flounder, salmon, trout, halibut, and pompano, prepared in any of seven ways. Dishes that consistently draw applause are corn-crusted filet of salmon with essence of hickory-smoked veal bacon and peach relish; and "fish in the bag," prepared with fresh grouper, scallops, and shrimp, laced with a dill-flavored cream sauce and baked in a brown paper bag.

In the Hilton Oceanfront Resort, Palmetto Dunes Plantation. ✆ **843/842-8000.** Reservations recommended. Main courses $19–$35. AE, DC, DISC, MC, V. Daily 5:30–10pm.

**Old Fort Pub** ✿✿ SOUTHERN   The setting doesn't get more romantic on Hilton Head. Surrounded by moss-draped live oak trees, the restaurant overlooks the Intracoastal Waterway on the banks of Skull Creek. We always like to come here with Hilton Head friends for sundowners, enjoying the view from the panoramic windows or the alfresco dining porch.

Recently named one of only two AAA four-star restaurants on Hilton Head, you receive a winning combination of Southern hospitality and award-winning Chef Josefiak's menus. Harmony and balance are achieved by such starters as a Vidalia onion short tart with goat cheese, arugula and pesto vinaigrette, or the barbeque pork empanada.

Sunday brunch here is among the best on the island, waking up your palate with such delights as white corn crepes with poached chicken, chanterelles, Boursin, asparagus, and sherry cream; or crab cakes with white poached eggs, spinach, asparagus, tomato salad, and Hollandaise sauce.

65 Skull Dr. ✆ **843/681-2386.** Reservations recommended. Brunch $9–$15; main courses $19–$34. AE, DC, DISC, MC, V. Daily 5–10pm; Sun 11am–2pm.

**The Old Oyster Factory** ✿ SEAFOOD/STEAK   Built on the site of one of Hilton Head's original oyster canneries, this landmark offers waterfront dining overlooking Broad Creek. The restaurant's post-and-beam decor has garnered several architectural awards. At sunset, every table enjoys a panoramic view as diners sip their "sundowners."

All the dishes here can be found on seafood menus from Maine to Hawaii. But that doesn't mean they're not good. The cuisine is truly palate-friendly, beginning with such appetizers as a tangy kettle of clams steamed in a lemon-butter sauce, or else a delectable crab cake sautéed and served in a chile-garlic tartar sauce. Will it be oysters Rockefeller (baked with spinach and béarnaise sauce) or oysters Savannah (shrimp, crabmeat, and smoked bacon)? Almond-crusted mahimahi is among the more tantalizing main courses, as are seafood pasta and broiled sea scallops. Non-seafood eaters can go for a chargrilled chicken breast.

101 Marsh Rd. ✆ **843/681-6040.** Reservations not accepted. Main courses $20–$26. AE, DC, DISC, MC, V. Daily 5–10pm (closing times can vary).

**Reilley's** IRISH/AMERICAN   A favorite with golfers, this is a good ol' boy place with an Irish pub atmosphere and Boston sports memorabilia on the walls. Opened in 1982, it's been going strong ever since. It offers a spacious dining area and a welcoming bar where you can order Harp, Bass, and, of course, Guinness on tap. Your hosts are Tom Reilley and Gary Duren, who very quickly get to know you. Located at the Sea Pines Circle, the pub draws its faithful clients along with constantly arriving drinkers "from anywhere." The menu is predictable with Blarney burgers including a hot one made with jalapeño peppers. Pastas are served, some with shrimp, and deli sandwiches range from a Dagwood to your own creation—choose either ham, turkey, corned beef, Genoa salami, or pastrami. Some of the biggest and best stuffed sandwiches are a daily feature, with everything from plump fried oysters in a hoagie to a meatloaf and cheddar concoction. The pub is also a place for children, and a special corner of the menu is reserved just for kids.

7-D Greenwood Dr. © **843/842-4414.** Reservations not required. Main courses $6–$28. AE, MC, V. Daily 11:30am–11pm; bar until 2am. Closed Dec 25.

**Rendez-Vous Café** ⨁ *Finds* FRENCH/PROVENÇAL   Some of the best French cuisine in eastern South Carolina is served here in this bistro, which offers a piano player on Wednesday and Thursday nights. Its decor transports you to the South of France. Inventive cookery with fresh flavors characterizes this popular dining spot. The list of hors d'oeuvres is the island's finest, ranging from many of the classics such as French onion soup gratinée or escargots bourguignon, but also taking in such delights as a French country pâté with duck mousse combo. The main courses are prepared with finesse, including crab cakes Mediterranean with ratatouille and polenta, or frogs' legs Provençal on a bed of couscous. Grouper is prepared Riviera style—that is, sautéed in olive oil with sweet red bell peppers. The chefs are diligent about maintaining high standards, and rely on market-fresh products. The good news: The dishes are nowhere as heavy or as laden with sauces as you might expect from a classic French restaurant serving food in the Escoffier tradition.

14 Greenwood Dr., Seapines Circle. © **843/785-5070.** Reservations recommended. Main courses $10–$17 lunch, $15–$30 dinner. MC, V. Mon–Fri 11:30am–2pm; Mon–Sat 5:30–9pm.

**Santa Fe Cafe** ⨁ MEXICAN   The best, most stylish Mexican restaurant on Hilton Head, the Santa Fe Cafe has rustic, Southwestern-inspired decor and cuisine that infuses traditional recipes with nouvelle flair. Menu items are often presented in colors as bright as the Painted Desert. Dishes might include tequila shrimp; herb-roasted chicken with jalapeño cornbread stuffing and mashed potatoes laced with red chiles; grilled tenderloin of pork with smoked habañero sauce and sweet-potato fries; and worthy burritos and chimichangas. The quesadilla is one of the most beautifully presented dishes of any restaurant in town.

700 Plantation Center. ℂ 843/785-3838. www.santafecafeofhiltonhead.com. Reservations recommended. Main courses $6.50–$8 lunch, $20–$30 dinner. AE, DISC, MC, V. Mon–Fri noon–2pm; daily 5–10pm.

**211 Park** AMERICAN/SOUTHERN/ITALIAN   In the Park Plaza Shopping Center, with a contemporary decor, this combined wine bar and bistro is a popular gathering place at night. Actual islanders posed for the mural used as a backdrop. Bill Cubbage, who long ago tired of hearing his name pronounced like a vegetable, opened this place in 1996, and has enjoyed a loyal following since.

Many of his dishes are adaptations of international recipes—for example, Bill's takeoff on traditional paella. Here it includes some of the same ingredients as in Spain, but it's served over grits. Shellfish is served in a black Thai sauce, and you might also watch for the specials announced nightly. Pizza comes with smoked salmon, feta cheese, dill, capers, and onions, or you might opt for one of the pasta dishes, the most ordered being a Jamaican-inspired "rasta pasta" with chicken, shrimp, andouille sausages, peppers, and a jerk cream sauce. The chef won our esteem with his cedar-planked salmon topped with whole-grain mustard and broiled to give the fish a slightly smoky flavor. The dish emerged with a sweet potato waffle and collards. (How Southern can you get?)

211 Park Plaza. ℂ 843/686-5212. Reservations recommended. Main courses $18–$28. AE, DC, DISC, MC, V. Mon–Sat 5:30–10pm. Closed Jan 1, Thanksgiving, Dec 25.

## INEXPENSIVE

**Hofbrauhaus** *Kids* GERMAN   A sanitized German beer hall, this family favorite serves locals and visitors such classics as grilled bratwurst and smoked Westphalian ham, along with Wiener Schnitzel and sauerbraten. One specialty we like is roast duckling with spaetzle, red cabbage, and orange sauce. Helpings are so big here that one main course is more than adequate for most appetites—there really is no need for appetizers. For example, a recent serving of a house specialty, prime strip of sirloin, turned out to be 14 ounces of aged beef, charbroiled and served with buttered whipped potatoes, fresh crisp garden vegetables, and a red-wine mushroom sauce. Note the stein and mug collection as you're deciding which of the large variety of German beers to order. A children's menu is available. Live music is offered on Tuesday, Wednesday, Thursday, and Friday nights.

In the Pope Ave. Mall. ⓒ **843/785-3663**. Reservations recommended. Early-bird dinner (5–6:30pm only) $14; main courses $17–$26. AE, MC, V. Daily 5–10pm.

**The Sea Shack** ⓡ *Value* SEAFOOD   Completely unpretentious, this seafood shack serves the freshest catch of the day in town and you can order it grilled, fried, or blackened. Stand at the counter and make your selection by reading the specialties on a board. Find a seat at one of the old tables, and your freshly ordered platter of seafood will be brought to you. We always like to begin with the fish soup as an appetizer. At lunch the fried oyster sandwich is a local favorite. At night we prefer the grilled grouper dinner. One of the chef's signature dishes is Caribbean jerk grouper, which you don't encounter too often. It's even been featured on *The Food Network*. Prices are affordable and the portions are most generous.

6 Pope Ave. ⓒ **843/785-2464**. Reservations not needed. Lunch main courses $5–$10; dinner main courses $10–$12. AE, MC, V. Mon–Sat 11am–3pm and 5–9pm.

**Signe's Heavenbound Bakery** ⓡⓡ BAKED GOODS   No one in this resort area turns out an array of delectable pastries and breads like Signe's. Featured on *The Food Network*, it has a menu that immediately starts your mouth watering: Hilton Head sourdough bread, along with specialty cakes such as pink lemonade cake, Key lime almond cake, pecan praline cream cake, carrot hazelnut cake, and forever Valentine (chocolate ganache over almond and chocolate layers with a raspberry filling). The bakery's butter pecan praline pound cake may be the best in South Carolina, and their old-fashioned cream cheesecake with a graham cracker crust is the stuff of dreams. In the cheery dining room, with its garden-inspired decor, you can enjoy breakfasts, perhaps with the signature blueberry French toast, or else fluffy frittatas. Lunches consist of hot and cold sandwiches made with bread freshly baked in the oven. Hob nobs are their latest version of the sub. Cold sandwiches feature the likes of beef and Swiss or else tuna salad.

93 Arrow Rd. ⓒ **843/785-9118**. Reservations not needed. Breakfast $6–$7.50; sandwiches $5–$8; cake slices from $2.50. AE, DC, DISC, MC, V. Mon–Fri 8am–4pm; Sat 9am–2pm.

**Smokehouse Bar & House of BBQ** *Kids* BARBECUE   This is Hilton Head's only authentic barbecue restaurant, serving fine, hickory-smoked meats in a casual Western atmosphere with a large outdoor deck attached to the restaurant. Takeout is also available.

It's an ideal family place with affordable prices. Both native islanders and visitors come here nightly, raving about the pulled pork, the sliced or pulled brisket, and the barbecued chicken. The joint has won awards for its barbecue and its chili, and the portions are man-sized. Beachgoers are welcome: Management only asks that you wear shoes. The menu is corny—salads are called rabbit food, appetizers "orderves." But once you get beyond that, the food is rather tasty. Their specialties are smokehouse ribs, either half or full rack. Other down-home favorites include a pork barbecue plate, barbecued chicken breast, and fried catfish.

102 Pope Ave. ℂ 843/842-4227. Reservations recommended. Main courses $6–$21. AE, MC, V. Daily 11:30am–10pm.

**Steamer Seafood** ℱ SEAFOOD/LOW COUNTRY   In Coligny Plaza, next to the Piggly Wiggly grocery store, lies this fun, affordably priced joint suitable for the whole family. It's a casual, very convivial tavern with Low Country specialties on the menu such as Charleston she-crab soup or shrimp gumbo to get you going. The fare is very familiar, and the portions are generous. Many old-time Southern coastal classics are offered, including Frogmore stew (large shrimp, smoked sausage, yellow onion, and red potatoes). You can ask the server to name the catch of the day, which is served grilled or blackened. The "rebel yell" rib-eye is a juicy, well-trimmed 14-ounce slab of beef blackened or char-grilled, as you desire it. The biggest seafood platters on the island are dished up here. After all that, dare you try the rich, creamy chocolate peanut butter pie or the fruit cobbler of the day?

29 Coligny Plaza. ℂ 843/785-2070. Reservations not required. Lunch $4.50–$7.95; main courses $6.95–$27. AE, MC, V. Daily 11:30am–10pm.

**Taste of Thailand** ℱ *Finds* THAI   Offering exotic flavors, this eatery does a bustling business among cost-conscious diners who appreciate the emphasis on exotic curries, lemon grass, and coconuts. Among scattered examples of Thai woodcarvings and handicrafts, you can enjoy a limited but choice menu offering beef, pork, chicken, shrimp, mussels, or tofu in a choice of different flavors. One of our favorite dishes is chicken with stir-fried vegetables, Thai basil, and oyster sauce. The hottest dish is the green curry, but equally delectable is the curry with roasted peanuts and red chiles flavored with cumin seeds. Thai spring rolls appear as an appetizer. A hot and sour soup is always on the menu, as is a spicy squid salad. Most dishes are at the low end of the price scale.

Plantation Center, 807 William Hilton Pkwy., Suite 1200. © **843/341-6500.** Reservations recommended. Main courses $14–$27. AE, DC, MC, V. Mon–Sat 5–11pm.

## HILTON HEAD AFTER DARK

Hilton Head doesn't have Myrtle Beach's nightlife, but enough is here, centered mainly in hotels and resorts. Casual dress (but not swimming attire) is acceptable in most clubs.

Cultural interest focuses on the **Arts Center of Coastal Carolina,** in the Self Family Arts Center, 14 Shelter Cove Lane (© **888/ 860-2787** or 843/842-2787; www.artscenter-hhi.org), which enjoys one of the best theatrical reputations in the Southeast. The Elizabeth Wallace Theater, a 350-seat, state-of-the-art theater, was added to the multiplex in 1996. The older Dunnagan's Alley Theater is located in a renovated warehouse. A wide range of musicals, contemporary comedies, and classic dramas is presented. Show times are 8pm Tuesday to Saturday, with a Sunday matinee at 2pm. Adult ticket prices range from $35 for a play to $45 for a musical. Children 16 and under are charged $18 to $23. The box office is open 10am to 5pm Monday to Friday, 10am to curtain time on performance days.

The island abounds in sports bars, far too many to document here. We recommend **Callahan Sports Bar & Grill,** 38 New Orleans Rd. (© **843/686-7665**); and **Casey's Sports Bar & Grill,** 37 New Orleans Rd. (© **843/785-2255**).

**Quarterdeck**   Our favorite waterfront lounge is the best place on the island to watch sunsets, but you can visit at any time during the afternoon and in the evening until 2am. Try to go early and grab one of the outdoor rocking chairs to prepare yourself for nature's light show. There's dancing every night to beach music and top-40 hits. Daily 11am to 2am. Harbour Town, Sea Pines Plantation. © **843/671-2222.**

**Remy's**   Got the munchies? At Remy's, you can devour buckets of oysters or shrimp, served with the inevitable fries. The setting is rustic and raffish, and live music is provided. Daily 11am to 4am. 28 Arrow Rd. © **843/842-3800.**

**The Salty Dog Cafe**   Locals used to keep this laid-back place near the beach to themselves, but now more and more visitors are showing up. Soft guitar music or Jimmy Buffett is often played. Dress is casual. Sit under one of the sycamores, enjoying your choice of food from an outdoor grill or buffet. Daily until 2am. South Beach Marina. © **843/671-2233.**

**Signals** In this upscale resort, you can enjoy live bands (often, 1940s golden oldies), along with R&B, blues, and jazz. The dance floor is generally crowded. Live bands perform Tuesday to Sunday evenings, and live jazz is presented on Monday nights. A Sunday jazz brunch is held from 11am to 1:30pm. 130 Shipyard Dr., in the Crowne Plaza Resort. ℂ 843/842-2400.

## 2 Beaufort ★★

70 miles S of Charleston

Beaufort (Low Country pronunciation *bew*-fort) is an old seaport with narrow streets shaded by huge live oaks and lined with 18th-century homes. The oldest house, the **Thomas Hepworth House** (at Port Republic and New sts.), was built in 1717. This was the second area in North America to be discovered by the Spanish (1520), the site of the first fort on the continent (1525), and the first attempted settlement (1562). Several forts have been excavated, dating from 1566 and 1577.

Beaufort has been used as a setting for several films, including *The Big Chill.* Scenes from the Paramount blockbuster *Forrest Gump,* starring Tom Hanks, and *The Prince of Tides* were also shot here.

### GETTING THERE

If you're traveling from the north, take I-95 to exit 33; then follow the signs to the center of Beaufort. If you are leaving directly from Charleston, take U.S. 17 S., then turn left on U.S. 21 and follow signs to Beaufort. From Hilton Head, go on U.S. 278 west, and after S.C. 170 N. joins U.S. 278, follow S.C. 170 into Beaufort.

### ORGANIZED TOURS

**Beaufort Chamber of Commerce,** 1106 Carteret St. (P.O. Box 910), Beaufort, SC 29901 (ℂ **800/638-3525** or 843/986-5400; www. beaufortsc.org), has information and self-guided tours of this historic town. It's open daily 9am to 5:30pm. If your plans are for early to mid-October, contact the **Historic Beaufort Foundation,** P.O. Box 11, Beaufort, SC 29901 (ℂ **843/379-3331;** www.historic-beaufort.org), for dates and details regarding its 3 days of antebellum house and garden tours.

A tour called **The Spirit of Old Beaufort,** 103 West St. extension (ℂ **843/525-0459;** www.thespiritofoldbeaufort.com), takes you on a journey through the old town, exploring local history, architecture, horticulture, and Low Country life. You'll see houses that are not accessible on other tours. Your host, clad in period costume, will guide you for 2 hours from Monday to Saturday at 10:30am and 2:30pm. The cost is $13 for adults, $8 for children 6 to 12. Tours depart from just behind the John Mark Verdier House Museum.

## SEEING THE SIGHTS

**John Mark Verdier House Museum,** 801 Bay St. (© 843/379-6335), is a restored 1802 house partially furnished to depict the life of a merchant planter during the period 1800 to 1825. It's one of the best examples of the Federal period and was once known as the Lafayette Building, because the Marquis de Lafayette is said to have spoken here in 1825. It's open Monday to Saturday from 11:30am to 3:30pm, charging $6 for adults, $3 for children; children under 6 are admitted free.

**St. Helena's Episcopal Church,** 507 New Castle St. (© 843/522-1712), traces its origin back to 1712. Visitors, admitted free Monday to Saturday from 10am to 4pm, can see its classic interior and visit the graveyard, where tombstones served as operating tables during the Civil War.

Beaufort is the home of the **U.S. Marine Corps Recruit Depot.** The visitor center (go to Building 283) is open daily from 6am to 6pm. You can take a driving tour or a bus tour (free) around the grounds, where you'll see an Iwo Jima monument; a monument to the Spanish settlement of Santa Elena (1521); and a memorial to Jean Ribaut, the Huguenot who founded Beaufort in 1562. Vehicle operators must possess a valid driver's license, vehicle registration, and proof of automobile insurance. You can expect tightened security.

## WHERE TO STAY
### EXPENSIVE

**The Beaufort Inn** 𝒦𝒦  Built in 1897, this is the most appealing hotel in Beaufort and the place where whatever movie star happens to be shooting a film in town is likely to stay. The woodwork and moldings inside are among the finest in Beaufort, and the circular, four-story staircase has been the subject of numerous photographs and architectural awards. The guest rooms, each decorated in brightly colored individual style, are conversation pieces. The inn also has a wine bar, a grill room, and a rose garden. Children 8 and older are welcome.

809 Port Republic St., Beaufort, SC 29902. © 843/521-9000. Fax 843/521-9500. www.beaufortinn.com. 21 units. $152–$235 double; $220–$295 suite. Rates include

# Beaufort

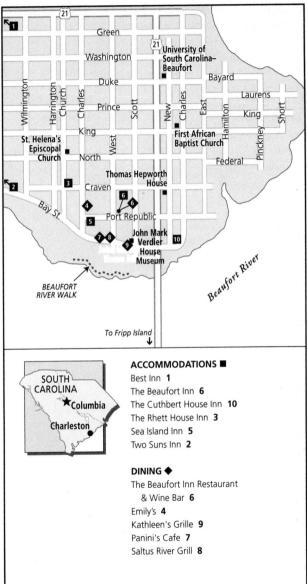

ACCOMMODATIONS ■
Best Inn **1**
The Beaufort Inn **6**
The Cuthbert House Inn **10**
The Rhett House Inn **3**
Sea Island Inn **5**
Two Suns Inn **2**

DINING ◆
The Beaufort Inn Restaurant
   & Wine Bar **6**
Emily's **4**
Kathleen's Grille **9**
Panini's Cafe **7**
Saltus River Grill **8**

full gourmet breakfast. AE, DISC, MC, V. No children under 8. **Amenities:** Restaurant; bar; limited room service; nonsmoking rooms. *In room:* A/C, TV, dataport, coffeemaker, hair dryer, iron.

**The Rhett House Inn** ⟨✦✦✦⟩   This inn is certainly very popular, at least with Hollywood film crews. Because it was a site for *Forrest Gump, The Prince of Tides,* and *The Big Chill,* chances are that you've seen it before. It's a Mobil and AAA four-star inn in a restored 1820 Greek Revival plantation-type home. Rooms are furnished with English and American antiques, and ornamented with Oriental rugs; eight contain whirlpools. The veranda makes an ideal place to sit and view the gardens. The inn is open year-round. Children 5 and older are welcome.

1009 Craven St., Beaufort, SC 29902. ⟨✆⟩ **888/480-9530** or 843/524-9030. Fax 843/524-1310. www.rhetthouseinn.com. 17 units. $195–$325 double. Rates include full breakfast, afternoon tea, and evening hors d'oeuvres. AE, DISC, MC, V. Free parking. No children under 5. **Amenities:** Breakfast room; lounge; nonsmoking rooms. *In room:* A/C, TV, dataport, wi-fi, minibar (in some), hair dryer, iron.

## MODERATE
**The Cuthbert House Inn** ⟨✦✦⟩   One of the grand old B&Bs of South Carolina, this showcase Southern home was built in 1790 in classic style. The inn was remodeled shortly after the Civil War to take on a more Victorian aura, but its present owner, Sharon Groves, has worked to modernize it without sacrificing its grace or antiquity. Graffiti carved by Union soldiers can still be seen on the fireplace mantel in the Eastlake Room. Guest rooms are elegantly furnished in Southern plantation style, and some have four-poster beds. All units come equipped with bathrooms containing tub/shower combinations; some bathrooms have old cast-iron soaking tubs. The inn is filled with large parlors and sitting rooms, and has spacious hallways and 12-foot ceilings characteristic of Greek Revival homes. At breakfast in the conservatory, you can order such delights as Georgia ice cream (cheese grits) and freshly made breads.

1203 Bay St., Beaufort, SC 29902. ⟨✆⟩ **800/327-9275** or 843/521-1315. Fax 843/521-1314. www.cuthberthouseinn.com. 7 units. $165–$225 double; $195–$265 suite. Rates include full breakfast and afternoon tea or refreshments. AE, DISC, MC, V. Free parking. **Amenities:** Breakfast room; lounge; bikes; nonsmoking rooms. *In room:* A/C, TV, dataport, fridge, hair dryer, iron.

**Two Suns Inn**   When this place was built in 1917, it was one of the grandest homes in its prosperous neighborhood, offering views of the coastal road and the tidal flatlands beyond. Every imaginable modern (at the time) convenience was added, including a baseboard vacuum-cleaning system, an electric call box, and steam heat. Later, when it became housing for unmarried teachers in the public schools, the place ran down. Now it's a cozy B&B. Part of the inn's appeal stems from its lack of pretension, as a glance at the homey bedrooms with simple furnishings and neatly kept bathrooms will show. Children 12 and older are welcome.

1705 Bay St., Beaufort, SC 29902. © **800/532-4244** or 843/522-1122. Fax 843/ 522-1122. www.twosunsinn.com. 5 units. $159–$181 double. Rates include full breakfast and afternoon cordials. AE, DISC, MC, V. Free parking. No children under 12. **Amenities:** Breakfast room; lounge; nonsmoking rooms; rooms for those w/limited mobility. *In room:* A/C, TV, dataport, hair dryer.

## INEXPENSIVE

**Best Inn** *Value*   You'll be happiest at this simple member of a local hotel chain if you know what it doesn't contain: There's no restaurant, no bar, and no pool. What you do get is a cost-effective hotel room outfitted in a bland contemporary style, with solid, well-maintained furnishings. Set 2 miles north of Beaufort's commercial core, it's a worthy choice for families with children or for business travelers who simply need a no-frills place to spend the night.

2448 Boundary St., Beaufort, SC 29903. © **843/524-3322.** Fax 843/524-7264. 51 units. $77–$85 double. Rates include continental breakfast. AE, DC, DISC, MC, V. *In room:* A/C, TV, iron.

**Sea Island Inn**   This is a basic two-story motel with reasonable rates for what you get. Few of the rooms have sea views; all contain well-kept bathrooms with tub/shower combinations. Although the rooms are nothing special, they're comfortable and clean.

1015 Bay St., Beaufort, SC 29902. © **800/528-7234** or 843/522-2090. Fax 843/ 521-4858. www.bestwestern.com. 43 units. $102–$165 double. Rates include continental breakfast. AE, DC, DISC, MC, V. **Amenities:** Breakfast room; lounge; outdoor pool; fitness center. *In room:* A/C, TV, hair dryer.

## WHERE TO DINE
### EXPENSIVE

**The Beaufort Inn Restaurant & Wine Bar** ✿ INTERNA-TIONAL   Stylish and urbane, and awash with colonial lowland references, this is the local choice for celebratory or business dinners, amid candlelit surroundings. Meat courses include chicken piccata with artichokes and sun-dried tomatoes, and an excellent grilled filet mignon with herbed Gorgonzola butter and shiitake mushrooms; vegetarian main courses include roasted-pepper-and-eggplant torte. On the menu is a variation on a dish whose invention has been claimed by a string of other restaurants in the South Carolina Low Country: crispy whole flounder with strawberry-watermelon chutney.

In the Beaufort Inn, 809 Port Republic St. ⓒ **843/521-9000.** Reservations recommended. Main courses $19–$30. AE, DISC, MC, V. Mon–Sat 6–10pm; Sun 11:30am–2pm and 6–10pm.

**Emily's** INTERNATIONAL   This is our favorite restaurant in Beaufort, a spot whose ambience and attitude put us in mind of Scandinavia. That's hardly surprising, because the bearded owner is an émigré from Sweden who feels comfortable in the South Carolina lowlands after years of life at sea. Some folks just go to the bar to sample tapas: miniature portions of tempura shrimp, fried scallops, stuffed peppers, and at least 50 other items. Menu items might include rich cream of mussel and shrimp soup; filet "black and white" (filets of beef and pork served with béarnaise sauce); duck with orange sauce; and a meltingly tender Wiener Schnitzel. Everything is served in stomach-stretching portions.

906 Port Republic St. ⓒ **843/522-1866.** Reservations recommended. Tapas $8-10; main courses $20–$27. AE, DISC, MC, V. Drinks and tapas Mon–Sat 4–10pm; main courses Mon–Sat 6–10pm.

## MODERATE
**Kathleen's Grille** ⓐ *(Finds)* SEAFOOD/SOUTHERN   This local eatery has plenty of Low Country atmosphere and is known for its fresh fish dinners. We'd go here for its Southern starters alone, including fried green tomatoes topped with a shrimp salsa, or the "classy" crab chowder. For lunch, try an offering from the "sandwich showcase," including soft-shell crab or fresh grouper. Salads, including a seafood pasta version, are made fresh daily. At night the restaurant serves some of the best fish platters in the area, including grilled shrimp and boiled oysters. For the meat lover, there is the inevitable rib-eye or pork chop, the latter coming with a sweet and spicy berry glaze. One section of the menu is reserved for "Kathleen's kids," but the offerings are so meager (fresh boxed cereals, a hot dog), your little ones may end up nutritionally deprived.

822 Bay St. ⓒ **843/524-2500.** Reservations recommended. Lunch $7–$9; main courses $15–$18. AE, DISC, MC, V. Mon–Fri 10am–1am; Sat–Sun 8am–1am.

**Panini's Cafe** AMERICAN   Known for its good food, this restaurant lies on Bay Street with a waterfront view from its terrace. The building was once a bank and later a movie theater, and what you see today has garnered several renovation awards for returning the building to its former grandeur. In this setting, experience lunch specialties like Mediterranean shrimp and grits with pancetta polenta and an olive tomato sauté, or the equally unique crab lasagna with marscarpone, spinach, artichoke, and tomato couli. Dinner main courses include a delicious grilled lobster and shrimp carbonara with applewood smoked bacon, peas, asparagus, and a light parmesan cream over capellini; or Spanish paella with shrimp, mussels, clams, red snapper, monkfish, chorizo saffron rice, tomatoes, onions, and garlic.

926 Bay St. ⓒ 843/522-8831. Reservations recommended. Lunch $9–$11; main courses $18–$23. AE, DC, DISC, MC, V. Daily 11am–10pm. Closed Thanksgiving and Dec 25.

### INEXPENSIVE
**Saltus River Grill** 𝍫𝍫𝍫 SEAFOOD    Saltus River Grill is a sister restaurant to the more casual Plums Restaurant in Beaufort, but that's where the similarities end. Elegant and sophisticated, Saltus River Grill looks out over the Intracoastal Waterway and provides spectacular scenery to match its equally spectacular menu. Named after shipbuilder John Saltus, the building where the restaurant resides was constructed in 1787. Chef Jim Spratling prepares his menu with the freshest ingredients available and produces tantalizing meat selections from the grill, as well as having an oyster bar and a full-menu sushi bar. Start with the steamed pork dumplings as appetizer and follow with main dishes of cornmeal seared jumbo sea scallops with sweet potato-bacon hash, warm pickled onions, and balsamic-fig molasses. If you crave fine beef, then order the grilled barrel-cut filet of beef with chèvre-scalloped potatoes, shiitake mushroom and onion confit, and a natural demi-glace.

904 1/2 Bay St. ⓒ 843/379-3474. Reservations required. Main courses $18–$29. AE, DISC, MC, V. Daily 4–10pm, Sun brunch 10:30am–3pm.

# Index

See also Accommodations and Restaurant indexes below.

## RESTAURANTS

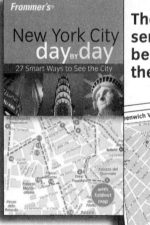

# FROMMER'S® COMPLETE TRAVEL GUIDES

# FROMMER'S® DAY BY DAY GUIDES

# PAULINE FROMMER'S GUIDES! SEE MORE. SPEND LESS.

# FROMMER'S® PORTABLE GUIDES

## FROMMER'S® CRUISE GUIDES

Alaska Cruises & Ports of Call | Cruises & Ports of Call | European Cruises & Ports of Call

## FROMMER'S® NATIONAL PARK GUIDES

Algonquin Provincial Park
Banff & Jasper
Grand Canyon

National Parks of the American West
Rocky Mountain
Yellowstone & Grand Teton

Yosemite and Sequoia & Kings
    Canyon
Zion & Bryce Canyon

## FROMMER'S® MEMORABLE WALKS

London
New York

Paris
Rome

San Francisco

## FROMMER'S® WITH KIDS GUIDES

Chicago
Hawaii
Las Vegas
London

National Parks
New York City
San Francisco

Toronto
Walt Disney World® & Orlando
Washington, D.C.

## SUZY GERSHMAN'S BORN TO SHOP GUIDES

France
Hong Kong, Shanghai & Beijing
Italy

London
New York

Paris
San Francisco

## FROMMER'S® IRREVERENT GUIDES

Amsterdam
Boston
Chicago
Las Vegas

London
Los Angeles
Manhattan
Paris

Rome
San Francisco
Walt Disney World®
Washington, D.C.

## FROMMER'S® BEST-LOVED DRIVING TOURS

Austria
Britain
California
France

Germany
Ireland
Italy
New England

Northern Italy
Scotland
Spain
Tuscany & Umbria

## THE UNOFFICIAL GUIDES®

Adventure Travel in Alaska
Beyond Disney
California with Kids
Central Italy
Chicago
Cruises
Disneyland®
England
Florida
Florida with Kids

Hawaii
Ireland
Las Vegas
London
Maui
Mexico's Best Beach Resorts
Mini Mickey
New Orleans
New York City

Paris
San Francisco
South Florida including Miami &
    the Keys
Walt Disney World®
Walt Disney World® for
    Grown-ups
Walt Disney World® with Kids
Washington, D.C.

## SPECIAL-INTEREST TITLES

Athens Past & Present
Best Places to Raise Your Family
Cities Ranked & Rated
500 Places to Take Your Kids Before They Grow Up
Frommer's Best Day Trips from London
Frommer's Best RV & Tent Campgrounds
    in the U.S.A.

Frommer's Exploring America by RV
Frommer's NYC Free & Dirt Cheap
Frommer's Road Atlas Europe
Frommer's Road Atlas Ireland
Great Escapes From NYC Without Wheels
Retirement Places Rated

## FROMMER'S® PHRASEFINDER DICTIONARY GUIDES

French | Italian | Spanish

# THE NEW TRAVELOCITY GUARANTEE

## EVERYTHING YOU BOOK WILL BE RIGHT, OR WE'LL WORK WITH OUR TRAVEL PARTNERS TO MAKE IT RIGHT, RIGHT AWAY.

*To drive home the point,
we're going to use the word "right" in every single sentence.*

Let's get right to it. Right to the meat! Only Travelocity guarantees everything about your booking will be right, or we'll work with our travel partners to make it right, right away. Right on!

*Here's a picture taken smack dab right in the middle of Antigua, where the guarantee also covers you.*

*The guarantee covers all but one of the items pictured to the right.*

For example, what if the ocean view you booked actually looks out at a downright ugly parking lot? You'd be right to call – we're there for you. And no one in their right mind would be pleased to learn the rental car place has closed and left them stranded. Call Travelocity and we'll help get you back on the right track.

Now, you may be thinking, "Yeah, right, I'm so sure." That's OK; you have the right to remain skeptical. That is until we mention help is always right around the corner. Call us right off the bat, knowing that our customer service reps are there for you 24/7. Righting wrongs. Left and right.

Now if you're guessing there are some things we can't control, like the weather, well you're right. But we can help you with most things – to get all the details in righting,* visit **travelocity.com/guarantee**.

*Sorry, spelling things right is one of the few things not covered under the guarantee.

*I'd give my right arm for a guarantee like this, although I'm glad I don't have to.*

**travelocity**
*You'll never roam alone.*

**IF YOU BOOK IT, IT SHOULD BE THERE.**

Only Travelocity guarantees it will be, or we'll work with our travel partners to make it right, right away. So if you're missing a balcony or anything else you booked, just call us 24/7 1-888-TRAVELOCITY

travelocity
You'll never roam alo